The
Fashionable
Mind

The Fashionable Mind

Reflections on Fashion

1970–1982

by

Kennedy Fraser

NONPAREIL
BOOKS

David R. Godine · Publisher · Boston

This is a NONPAREIL BOOK first published in 1985
by DAVID R. GODINE, PUBLISHER, INC.
306 Dartmouth Street, Boston, Massachusetts 02116

This book was first published in slightly different
form in 1981 by Alfred A. Knopf, Inc., New York.

Library of Congress Cataloging in Publication Data
Fraser, Kennedy.
The fashionable mind.
(A Nonpareil book; 36)
Articles from the author's column in the New
Yorker. Originally published: 1st ed. New York:
Knopf, 1981.
1. Fashion—History—20th century—Addresses,
essays, lectures. 2. Fashion—United States—
History—20th century—Addresses, essays, lectures.
I. Title. II. Series.
GT596.F73   1984   391'.009'047   84–10207
ISBN 0–87923–543–8 (soft: alk. paper)

All essays in this book first appeared
in *The New Yorker*.

This book has been printed on acid-free paper and
bound in signatures. The paper will not yellow with
age, the binding will not deteriorate, and
the pages will not fall out.

Printed in the United States of America

To my mother,

with love

Contents

Contents

Contents

Foreword

By chance, I took over the "Feminine Fashions" column of *The New Yorker* at the very moment that feminine fashions ceased to count. Women's refusal to lengthen their hemlines in 1970 may not have been the grand gesture of feminist independence that some chose to claim, but it is a convenient watershed in the history of fashion. After that, there was no longer any unabashedly accepted, universal fashion authority, and no real point in reporting the latest word of fashion news each season. In becoming a fashion critic, I was like a diplomat arriving at a foreign posting on the day an earthquake strikes. I see this more clearly, of course, in hindsight and on rereading these essays. At the outset, I had no idea how intangible and unfamiliar my sort of fashion would turn out to be, how different from the fashions that had paraded so confidently and for close to half a century through the columns of my predecessor, Lois Long. Nor, I suspect, did my editor, William Shawn—who with his inimitable courage had given me the column when I was just out of university and new to this country from my native England—realize how unstraightforward fashion would prove for me. He simply gave me absolute and sometimes unnerving freedom to make of my subject whatever I would. Off I marched into what I came to see was a world of hints and tricks and dreams and metaphors —a place of confusing, sometimes falsified signposts where time, by running sideways or in big backward loops, contrived to stay just ahead of us all.

If the old rules and rhythms of fashions have long since gone, this is not to say that men and women are not, in this competitive and "visual" age, intensely interested in the way they look. Sociologists, psychologists, anthropologists, career counselors, and museums have all, in recent years, lent weight to the idea that dress is significant. Perversely enough, I regard with some suspicion the increased respect accorded to appearances, even though that respect has made it easier for me to give at least semi-serious thought to what everyone used to dismiss as an utterly frivolous theme. All in all, my feelings about dress are very mixed. I am capable of regarding clothes with curiosity or tenderness from time to time, but I have no interest in seeking out or wearing the latest thing. The capriciousness of fashion fascinates me, but it also alarms me, and I am gratified to see how many of my concerns in these pieces have stayed constant over the years. Inevitably, though, I have in some places denounced styles for which I had earlier expressed enthusiasm, just as I have contemptuously dismissed styles toward which, at least at this moment, I feel quite benign. For this book, I have chosen to leave my opinions frozen in their original time and have also, on occasion, left the business careers of some designers artificially stopped in mid-stream.

I have never really, in these eleven years, even come up with a definition of fashion that I might choose to stick with or that I would enjoy being called upon to defend. My pursuit of a definition through these pages has been a highly personal journey, full of fits and starts and contradictions, and probably a wild goose chase in the end. I have come at my subject from odd angles, hoping to catch it by surprise. Or I have been baffled by it all and kept silent for ages, having nothing particular to say. The only conclusion I reach at this point is that fashion isn't simply hems and feathered hats and that it's connected very, very closely with how we live.

Kennedy Fraser
New York, 1981

1970

Hail, Covered Knee!

The fashionable woman has long legs and aristocratic ankles but no knees. She has thin, veiled arms and fluttering hands but no elbows. Her chest is rather flat; so are her hips. She has a tiny waist and lots of ribs. She wears her skirt around the calf. She welcomes the return of the dress and is happy to find clothes that look new and that are not, perforce, some kind of trouser suit, pajama suit, or jumpsuit. She wants soft fabrics—light wool, jersey, crêpe, chiffon, and crêpe de Chine—in tranquil colors, such as brown, smoky blue, mauve, gray, and deep, dull pink. She likes beige and black but never chooses royal blue, or white, or red. She wants no linings and no stiffening. She takes fresh pleasure in the elegant detail of pleats and tucks and smocking. She wears few underclothes. She prizes practicality and comfort but does not fear experiment. Most of all, she wants to have fun. She is in genteel revolt against all clothes kinetic, psychedelic, geometric. She is wearied by cutouts, by zips that end in curtain rings, by vinyl, and by paramilitary buttons. She is tired of looking like an upside-down ice-cream cone with arms and legs. She rejected this uniform shape, and the above-knee length, some time ago, and she toys with mid-calf coats and maxicoats and trousers. She wraps herself in wayside blossoms, or dresses up in mock Schiaparelli and revels in a display of real or spurious decadence. She is unperturbed by occasional vulgarities and is never boring.

This woman could be any age. It is possible that there are

no fashions that age the wearer but simply more or less fashionable clothes. I saw a woman at a party who must have been a stylish girl in 1910. She would have looked no younger in a dress above her knees. With a mid-calf cocktail dress of black cut velvet—rediscovered or never relinquished—she wore the face of twinkling satisfaction that is a frequent accessory to very fashionable clothes. (A new face is probably a necessary adjunct to the longer lengths. Those who do not wish to change their makeup might sport a new expression—raised brows, perhaps, or drooping lids; with the peasant look, a smile could scarcely go amiss.)

It would indeed be startling if women were suddenly to add three feet to their skirts. In fact, those who have worn the miniskirt have long been exploring other trends. Tidy, chiseled shapes appropriate to the computer age, and the revolutionary designs of Cardin, Courrèges, and Quant, were intended for the young. Their mothers, finding that the stiff, bright triangles flatter a less-than-perfect figure, adopted them. The young shortened the designers' skirts and began to turn elsewhere. They rummaged in another generation's cast-off clothes, and sought out ruffles, shawls, and fringe. They took emancipation and the Space Age quite for granted, and preferred the costume of romance, and jokes, and drama.

Before embarking on this game of fashion, you might determine the ages that are ripe for sartorial parody. To blindly ape the fifties could lead to serious blunders. That decade is being closely studied by a coterie of specialists, and normal people should not meddle with Monroe evening gowns and Elvis waistcoats before the dust of innovation settles. Dior's New Look might also be a pitfall. Some of the prints and fabrics of the twenties and thirties are an inspiration to today's designers, but none of the cut, the padding, and the interfacing of the postwar years. Since the last time we saw calf-length skirts, fitted waists, and peplums, a new sense of the body has developed. A generation of women has grown up with bodies of significantly different shape. And over the past few years, with the mini, the midi, the maxi, and trousers, women have probably known, simultaneously, more radically different silhouettes than at any other time. With each look, they have learned additional ways of walking, sitting, and gesticulating. It is too late to return in earnest to the fashions of the fifties and too soon to mock them. To return to the straight, square skirts of the early sixties or to lengthen the A-line skirt of a year ago would be humorless regression. Those who come to the calf-length skirt unfettered by a memory of earlier versions are its most enthusiastic exponents.

Some women are not exactly fashionable but like to look nice and avoid dowdiness. For their benefit, in these puzzling times, store presidents and their advertising agencies have issued bulletins; these intend to soothe the customer and interest her in present stock. Among these public protestations of faith in the individuality and taste of women are tight-lipped reprimands to those who hesitate to buy or are unable to find what they know they want. The stores inform us that we can—indeed, should—wear the longer lengths for autumn but imply that we are sheep if we demand them now. Persistence by the converted will, however, be rewarded. The new lengths are at hand, and soon there will be enough of them to allow us to select with proper care. It is easy, at the beginning of a fad, to allow enthusiasm for the principle to dim our judgment of the example. Many purchasers of maxicoats fell victim to that snare. The streets are swarming still with gaffes.

A flood of verbiage about the necessity for new and correct "proportions" in longer lengths might seem like further propaganda. By chance, this dogmatism has some basis, and women and designers may profitably take note. Indiscriminate lengthening of hems might be disastrous. And do not be tempted to shake the mothballs from a dress you never got round to taking up. Five years ago, clothes were cut more loosely, sleeves were wider, and waists baggier. Besides, the dress you didn't shorten was probably a dress you didn't like, and it will not look better after several years of darkness. A return to the kind of clothes we wore then would fail to take account of the elegant light-heartedness that, even more than length, line, cut, and fabric, characterizes this year's fashion.

The Secret Power
of Dress

The number of people who feel passionately about their clothes is far greater than their appearance or their conversation might lead one to suppose. And a good many women who buy new clothes are afflicted by the delusion that they will thereby change their state of mind, the attitude of their companions, and their lives. If, in addition to the performance of these miracles, we ask also of our clothes that they be fashionable, we are obviously a little foolish. And yet a fashionable purchase will give the greatest pleasure. Since the yearning for adornment is rarely analyzed, we lack standards and are easily confused. In normal life, perhaps, we struggle for consistency, rationality, or independence. In fashion, we vacillate from week to week and are desperate for guidance. We may in theory reject good taste, and elegance may seem outmoded. And still we go on groping for these firefly generalities. The prospect of the longer lengths—which flusters men for different reasons—bewilders many women and makes them feel incompetent. We sense that we must soon adopt a whole new look, decide upon a length to suit our leg, and, somehow, pick out new accessories.

If people care about their clothes, they seldom talk of it. Although appearance is a public statement, the acquisition of its separate elements is a private, almost furtive matter. We gossip, or chat about a fashionable best-seller, but think our clothes too trivial for debate. Possibly they are purely visual or have no worthwhile intellectual content. We hardly notice the technical details of clothes and have only vague impressions of cut, cloth, and trimmings. Dressing and the choice of clothes is for most women an emotional, illogical business. We have all been made gloomy by the feeling that we are wrongly dressed, or elated by appreciation of our clothes. The woman who is admired finds it easier to look well-dressed, while the lonely girl may dress meticulously and still feel dowdy. Clothes have a life that is quite independent of their shape and color. Among changing landscapes, different faces, they can seem concrete, and a dress can give a reassuring sense of continuity in a variety of settings. But at other times clothes are simply puffs of sentiment, and their vitality will seep out overnight. "I haven't got a thing to wear" does not, of course, mean that we must resort to nakedness or seclusion; it means that our wardrobes contain nothing that might match our mood or offer a just reflection of our current lives.

Long before a dress gets shabby or goes out of fashion, its moment of glory is past. Much of our delight in clothes is in the future-perfect tense, and happy contemplation of them depends to an alarming extent on the possibility of possession. We catch sight of a dress in a shop window or drift past its picture in a fashion magazine, and find our thoughts returning to it for days, until it is examined, bought, or exorcised. Sometimes, in energetic periods of leisure, we look in lots of shops, pretending to compare prices and weigh decisions. The best things, however, are bought erratically. They are often spotted quite by chance, when we are really concentrating on the search for something else. There are millions of ways to shop. For this reason, shared expeditions—those, at least, with serious intent—are usually frustrating. The pleasure purchase can afford is very brief. The most rewarding moment in the process may come as we try on a garment for the second time. Having, between the first essay and this, tried others that are unmistakably inferior, we know that we are close to owning this one but can wallow once again in hesitation. The shopper is often panic-stricken as the dress is carried away to be wrapped, but likes to grip the handle of the box on its return. The dress worn three times becomes as friendly as a pair of slippers or else an embarrassment. However sparse our wardrobes, some things seem woebegone from the beginning and will droop, unworn, for years. The second time a dress is worn is most likely the best; the first is often fraught with doubt. Hats never lose their power to make me nervous. To buy and wear a hat is to accept a passionate relationship. I have taken pride in hats or loathed them; I have never worn a hat for which I felt affection.

If, for many women, the choice of clothes is an anxious, irrational affair, it is made doubly so by our craving to be fashionable. The vagaries of fashion are a denial of constant aesthetic standards, objective ideas of grace or flattery, and the fact that women's bodies remain much the same from one season to the next. The present hemline crisis exemplifies the divorce of fashion from most other spheres of civilized life. Once we accept that longer hemlines are a good idea, we begin to find short skirts repellent and the sight of knees distasteful. A few months ago, we thought in all sincerity that they were pleasing. It is fashion's business to manipulate our memories. Fashion is in ceaseless pursuit of things that are about to look familiar and in uneasy flight from things that have just become a bore. Pretending, frenziedly, to market enthusiasm for novelty, in fact it sells disgust for previous modes. A designer may produce clothes that would last year have been considered beautiful, and might be so again next year; this year they can look repetitive and sadly wrong. This spring, the king of the collections is Valentino, with his longer lengths, elegant line, and carefully thought-out accessories. Cardin and Ungaro, our gods of earlier years, now seem for the moment unfashionable. We once adored Courrèges's brilliant gaiety; virtually the same ideas now seem clashingly inopportune. Practicable, craftsmanlike, imaginative clothes are worthless if the designer's vision of his customers does not correspond to some impulse of their own. Women must have some concept, however inarticulate, of what they want before a couturier is free to dominate them. Lest this give the impression that women have too strong an influence on the fashions they will wear, let it be said that no amount of protest, at this point, will stem the tide of longer skirts. Designers are producing them in droves, and retailers are busily laying them in for autumn. The powerlessness of customers is dispiriting only to those who think that it is worth resisting fashion. I suspect that resistance is a waste of energy, since you can fight fashion only be being unfashionable. This course is open to all, but it appeals to too few for dissidence to be effective. No doubt short skirts will be in stock for years to come, and you can always take things up. But to buy short clothes will be to choose the tired, frayed ends of earlier styles. Fashion is an amorphous monster. It doesn't go away because we turn our backs on it, and no amount of pummeling on anybody's part will guarantee to lay it low. The designer may fail to capture the feeling in the air; the retailer, subject to like incalculables, may be too early or too late. And the customer is limited to what is available.

Pity the seeker after fashion. Now she has the feeling that she should forget the teen-age, bouncy look and aim for elegance again. But if elegance ever did exist, we have lost our ability to recognize it. A small band of lively, diligent ladies with large sums of money in the bank have probably always been elegant. Their ranks are yearly dwindling. Once, elegant women were so sure of taste that they could afford to flout it. In a recent interview, a Parisian fabric designer happily recalled his prewar print of giant orange lobsters, which was worn by the Duchess of Windsor. If elegance is back again, the accessibility of expensive-looking fabrics might seem to make things easy for us. But we no longer have the stamina to dress perfectly to the last button, and the kind of elegant imagination that could be practiced even in poverty, and that depended on the skillful knotting of a scarf, is lost to most of us. Be this as it may, "elegant" is a fashionable adjective once more, while "chic" is not, and the seventies are already being vaunted as the years of elegance.

Burrows' World
at Bendel's

Among the hawkers and the preachers in the market-place of longer lengths, fashion's roundabout goes spinning on. A boutique called Stephen Burrows' World has opened at Henri Bendel. Stephen Burrows is a young designer and his world a very fashionable place. The essence of fashion is still in the hands of the young, the thin, and the fickle. For them, dress is not an issue but a way of life. They watch each other with a stony eye and call today's innovator by his Christian name while looking over his shoulder for tomorrow's man. They are frantically enthusiastic or blissfully forgetful, but they never complain. The group knows no more dynamic moment than the launching of a young designer in a new boutique. At last he has the money to give substance to his visions, and he is not yet bogged down in the problems of filling orders and backing winners. The fashion of boutiques and young designers is desperately ephemeral. Too much success with original ideas can be as harmful as oblivion; those in pursuit of fashion will cast off anything that begins to seem widely popular. Where constant novelty is absent, they get the scent of failure, then make it certain by moving on. The clothes in a boutique should look fresh from the sketch block and the workroom. A favored shop gets heavy wear and tear, which causes suspect shabbiness; its appearance must change with its stock. The boutique presents a reasonable choice, laced with the authority of consistency. When timing and management are right, it should not be hard to convince the shopper that she has stumbled on her El Dorado of tasteful, flattering fad. Often she is encouraged to gratify her individuality as well. Several of the most typical of Burrows's designs—such as a black leather gaucho suit with nailhead trim—are made to order in Bendel's eighth-floor studio. And no two of his multicolored sweater-shirts, which fit as neatly as a coat of paint, will be exactly alike. Yet the real aim of fashionable purchase is not uniqueness but the appearance of belonging to a company of leaders. If you buy a Burrows outfit, you should look as though your rightful place were Burrows's world, and Bendel's.

Bendel's people are probably Burrows's people, too. Henri Bendel is really a department store for women, but its principles are those of the successful boutique and its concerns the exclusive, the transitory, and the young designer in his prime. Like the boutique, it stands midway in the fashion process between the artistic and the personal, and manufacture, promotion, and profit. Bendel was among the first stores to fill up with little shops, and they appear like mushrooms and vanish while you blink. New things are entirely absorbing. If you return and search plaintively for something that was once in a prominent place, you cannot claim to be a Bendel's person. Within the last few months, the Bendel boutique devoted to Sonia Rykiel has seemed less exciting, and anyway a second New York store now also sells her clothes. (To be fair, many of Bendel's clothes are imported, and sometimes apparent dullness ends with the arrival of a new shipment.) But the cache of Thea Porter's costumes from a lordly ragbag has been replaced on the second floor by a new John Kloss boutique, and Savvy—an array of shoes under thirty-five dollars, clothes under a hundred—has taken up the fourth. It appears that when things cease to make the shopping heart beat faster, they will not be treated sentimentally. Fashion's vigor is assured by constant pruning. Bendel's people—customers, salesgirls, and the men around both—resemble one another closely and can be quite intimidating. They are young, handsome, and traveled.

Their allegiance to the present is awe-inspiring. Only a fool or an eccentric would visit the store if she is fat, dowdily dressed, or accompanied by someone who will not pass for the right accessory, so it is not easy to start becoming a Bendel's person. A suspicious mind will wonder whether initiates always look so fashionable or whether they keep aside a special outfit for Bendel's expeditions. Their perfection can send you empty-handed onto Fifty-seventh Street, feeling dazed and overweight. (Skeletal salesgirls may be seen chatting with ethereal customers: "Of course you could wear a size 4. I do, and you can't weigh more than ninety pounds.") Every visitor does not live up to the ideal. There is a kind of Bendel's customer who is not a Bendel's person. She has small bones carefully peeled by diet but seems to think of herself as being "petite." She often has thick blond hair puffed back from her forehead and falling to her shoulders. She has a stiff little walk, Deneuve's expression of brainless and dependent vulnerability, and an air of wealth. (Bendel's way can cost you dear.) Real Bendel's people are tall enough to be models, and tend to lope. They step proudly in a glow of unconventionality and well-paid imagination. Neither their intellect nor their state of mind can be assessed, since their thought is completely fused in their zealously adorned and disciplined bodies. Clothes alone will never make you fashionable. Friends, thoughts, face, and life must match. Burrows's clothes are made for the fashionable lives and bodies of Bendel's people. He has his own system of sizing: 1 (normally 3 and 5), 2 (6 and 8), and 3 and 4, for the unmentionables above that. He uses leatherwork, patchwork, appliqué, and nailheads, to show alignment with youth and trend, but beyond this you must rely on faith in Bendel's instincts. While the official taste of the season is for the exotic (Indian fabrics, embroidered and printed panne velvets, Tartar and peasant costumes, Persian-carpet prints, snakeskin, butterflies, and snakeskin butterflies) or the ladylike (muted colors and more formal lengths), he offers sportive simplicity and brilliant colors. His favorite skirt length is mid-knee. The collection consists mainly of separates: skirts, sweaters, trousers, gauchos, and vests.

Stephen Burrows's world met recently on the third floor of Bendel's to watch and wear his rainbow clothes and launch the new boutique. A catwalk ran through the black, nail-studded shop, rushed through the home of Cachet coats, and turned its back at the gateway of Sonia Rykiel. The fashion press, in summer frocks and bras, and with an alien emanation of long hours and deadlines in an office full of women, watched the crowd assemble and began to feel that it had blundered on a very private party. People looking for the safety of a seat fell over the parallel rows of dressing-room lights laid down to mark a runway, so it came to look like faulty teeth. Smarter friends of Burrows and Bendel's milled about, graceful in the cramped conditions and fashionable—in spite of the heat of the day—in boots and jersey gauchos. Their glittering eyes and vagabond absorption in the moments they were living might baffle anyone trying to live by prediction and plans. Virtual strangers busied themselves with the noisy exchange of kisses for the benefit of total strangers looking on. A photographer hopped among them, adding to the bulging dossier of *Women's Wear Daily* evidence of the arrival of its "longuette." The Burrows intimates were dressed impeccably in Burrows clothes. (Others present had studied all this season's fashion words and photographs but fell short of the celestial. They looked smug about their hats and hem lengths but less than sure of the superiority of their lives. For all the fretful thought he may have given them, one young man's digger's hat, hip-length lemon T-shirt, worked-leather belt, and workmen's crushed-patent boots could not conceal his loose-limbed mind. His trousers were positively baggy. Perhaps, ill-fated lad, he bulged.) The new haircuts—short on top, and chewed and straggled to the shoulders—made several male and female heads look slim. A youth in black wore his hair close-cropped except for a fingerthick lock at the back, tied up with Indian beads. Many of the most impressive bodies sported trousers, and particularly the patchwork leather ones that Burrows used to make. It is always good, as you join in the feverish joy of his public success, to show that you have known all about the man for ages. A wide-eyed sylph shook the prancing fringes of her patchwork leather trousers at the gathering. Her chiffon blouse was brown and feather-printed. The brim of her Christopher Robin sunhat turned back to show her painted face and drooped to shield her nape from anything unpleasant. A wispy harlequin in thonged and parti-colored trousers trimmed with nailheads and a T-shirt splashed with circles of appliqué bowed and bobbed his wren's head in greeting. (Some time ago, Stephen Burrows shaved his head. It has now grown out a bit, and laggardly friends have trimmed theirs back to meet it. They wear neat mustaches, to distinguish them from skinheads.) At last, the strollers and their outfits were cleared from the runway by Geraldine Stutz, the brain behind Bendel's, who introduced the official fashion show with the uneasy poise of a permissive mother at a birthday party when the jellies start to fly. She wore one of the simplest dresses of the collection: knee-length black jersey with canary collar, hem, and dickey. When she stepped down, frivolity was king. A black model tripped by in the first outfit and a burst of rock. The clothes alone would have sustained the mood of delirious excitement: Astaire trousers, pleated at the waist, with a matching tunic in heavy jersey printed round with mauve and scarlet lightning. A mid-knee cardigan with patches of white knit at the waist; raglan shoulders of black jersey; orange and artificial grass–green in body and skirt; one yellow pocket, one scarlet; and, at the hem, a band of yellow jersey topped with rusty suede. A jersey jigsaw-puzzle dress, with yoke and sections curving into improbably gaudy neighbors. A footballer's dress, with upper arms, cuffs, and body in black; one cerise sleeve, one yellow; a six-inch band at the hem, lit with tennis-ball circles of suede; and a turtle's hood of scarlet edged with black. Over this, a harness of black cabretta leather, decorated with red and yellow, to circle the waist and shoulders and fasten in front with silver snaps and buckle. A black dress with leather eyes staring wildly from the bust. Knee-high purple soccer socks, leather chokers and tam-o'-shanters. Huge shoulder bags made from two skins of suede, their wobbly edges still uncut.

No costume closer in time than that of the court jester

seems to inspire Burrows, but the element of parody lacking in his clothes was supplied for the show by his models. Since the joyous display of Burrows's world had been in progress before they appeared, it seemed only fair that the models should put aside their wooden smiles and entertain their friends in the audience. (Facial expressions, rather than walk or bearing, usually differentiate the showroom model on the runway from a human being. Because a smile has sentimental associations for most of us, its use as a rapid piece of business is especially chilling. While flowing on toward the turn, the model seems to catch the eye of someone in the fourth row. She lingers with her mask of warmth turned sidewise long enough to give a new line to her body and her outfit. Before it has time to look contented, and after it has ceased to look spontaneous, she gets bored with her smile, rearranges the muscles of her mouth, and hurries on.) Burrows's models really grinned, and their play-acting was honest. Some of the white models wore their hair frizzed out to collar height. The style looked like a flattened Afro or a badly mixed home perm. When the hair was not fluffing out from the Burrows hat, it was parted in the middle and gripped on both sides by bobby pins. One of the black models had a shaven head; another wore her hair slicked back to a bun. They all wore glossy mulberry lips and nails. The spectators stamped their feet and stretched out their hands to the clothes and the girls, whose performance reduced Saint Laurent's current games with Carmen Miranda outfits to a modest giggle suppressed behind a lady's clean white glove. Uproarious fans reveled as the girls impersonated women, mocking and exaggerating every female pose: a maiden from the silent screen placed the back of her hand to her forehead and scanned a terrifying horizon; starlets from the fifties, a hand behind their neck, thrust out their bosoms and wiggled their bottoms, and added to the joke by showing that they hadn't much of either. They spread a blood-tipped hand across a hipbone and gazed longingly over a curled shoulder. Once, the music failed the rippling, posturing parade. A girl with a small, anxious face found herself padding sadly through a shocked and silent audience. After the machine was repaired, the cheers began again. They became a bloodcurdling roar as Burrows himself strode by, in nail-studded black leather and with a matching girl. Another firework hour was ended. The funny world of fashionable youth—where men carry handbags and women have no bosoms, where noon is night, white are black, and people are their clothes—exists because its populace is always passing through. Even Burrows's birds of paradise are not eternally immune to age, bulge, and boredom.

Painted Women

Women and makeup is a subject that abounds in inconsistencies. Few of us, if we are challenged, can give account of aims and motives, and we often look quite different from the way we think we do. A woman will "put on her face" before she leaves the house. This "face" represents many things to her. It is at once a mask to shrink behind and a way of flaunting herself and exaggerating life. It is something separate, to be assembled and donned at will, and yet it becomes as much her own as her flesh and bones. The real face is the most revealing part of us; the false face may be used to conceal age, ill-health, tiredness, or disconsolacy. Before she allows the world to judge her face, a woman is entitled to create it. Makeup begins by being a trick to play upon society, then becomes a trick we play upon ourselves. We set out to fool and falsify with the aid of pots and tubes of color, but we are reluctant to accept this as artifice. "Naturalness" is the effect most women who wear makeup seek, and "natural" the favorite word of all cosmetic companies. Many people seem to be frightened by the term "makeup." They think it smacks too much of vulgar, theatrical deceit. It is sometimes used, in a restricted sense, to describe the kind of matte covering foundation that is no longer fashionable. Fashion magazines deal with makeup in a section touchingly called "Beauty." Things were clearer when there were two kinds of women: women who wore paint, and decent women, who did not. For some years, women have been applying makeup with the intention of seeming to wear none. This year, the distinction between Nature and artifice, Beauty and her handmaids, is smudgier than ever.

Two vague tendencies may be detected. They sometimes contradict each other, and they often merge. In the first place, the face is to be treated as an extension of the body—not the same, tired old body but the lissome, affluent, and gleaming body that frequents the figure salons, disports itself frenetically along the bridleways of Central Park, and is immersed in scented unguents and invigorating rubs. The face to complement it is pared and healthy, lightly blushing, and looks good with a suntan. The wearer of this face is often quite concerned about looking young. The look is not entirely natural; in fact, the principle of the new transparent blushing gels—which look convincing—may be almost decadent. Contrivance and sophistication usurp the spontaneity of the ingenuous.

The marriage of face and body is reflected in the advertisements of cosmetic firms. Sex is no longer used to sell makeup—there is little suggestion that lipstick makes your lips more kissable—but is elevated, for the sale of products for the body and the bath, to something far more rare and dignified. Most cosmetic advertisers now appeal to narcissistic instincts. Beautiful women are untouchable, and are glimpsed as they muse upon the dewy innocence of their expression and the opulent perfection of their setting. The women of Revlon's Ultima range of goods are too subtly private to be subjected to the camera; they are sketched in sepia tints, lolling on their yachts or mounting marble stairs. Everything is muted. Makeup, it appears, belongs neither with real life nor with art but in a world of dream. The language of cosmetics is almost entirely euphemistic and incantatory. Complexions glow and blush, become tender and translucent; eyes peer out of smoky, opalescent shadows, and even mascara is guileless and natural. A favored description of fashionable makeup is that it is nothing, or looks like nothing. (This is a notion equally dear to lingerie manufacturers, and one firm advertises underwear as "translucent body makeup." The links between non-makeup and non-underwear are very close, and many new products are the facial equivalent of the body stocking.)

A second tendency is toward the face as face, as the focus of intelligence, experience, and feeling, and aims to exaggerate the part of you that is most alive. Fashions in clothes are drawing attention away from the legs and hair and toward the features. The face is treated as a canvas, to be painted with craft and boldness. This trend includes, among extreme exponents, the use of makeup as fantasy and costume and, more moderately, as a visible accessory. In this spirit, the girls in London paint their lids with Union Jacks or rainbows, or recreate the face Serge Lutens designed for Dior, without brows or false lashes but with bright question marks of rouge to curl from brow to cheekbone. The wildest examples of the costumed face are better suited to women who are young than to those who wish to appear to be so. To wear makeup noticeably or as a joke is to belong to a generation that is bored by prettiness. The two types of fashionable face are often jumbled up. A lipstick in deeper colors may be used, but it will be a transparent tinting rather than a coat, thus nodding to both Costume and Nature.

A way is surely to be found between the two. There is a limit to the amount of color we find acceptable, and if we err too far toward the natural, makeup becomes a waste of time. If, as seems probable, lips and nails are to become darker—toward scarlet and even mulberry—the eyes will look much softer. Eyeliner is beginning to look wrong, and the eye should not be ringed with lines. The new eye wears somewhat shiny shadow, which may be taken far toward the brow and around beneath the eye. If eyeliner disappears, false eyelashes will be in jeopardy, since a line is needed to hide the strip where the false lash is glued near the base of your own. I find a lengthening mascara quite enough, but some people are known to be addicted to false eyelashes. Thick dark lashes like furry caterpillars are too heavy for this season's eye. Brows should be fairly narrow; nails should be short; and lips may be glossy. Neither lips nor nails should be pale pink or pearly. It seems clear that foundations will be more revealing, and that cheek-bones, earlobes, chins, and foreheads may safely wear a pink and lightly polished blush.

To generalize about the fashionable face, however, is to presuppose a woman who is happy with her face. That makeup be fashionable is probably the least of all the things we ask of it. The illusion of perfectibility is a commodity and the cosmetics industry, in its own interest, asserts that fashions in makeup change just as frequently as those in clothes. It is doubtful whether many women change their style of makeup as often as they buy new clothes. Woman buy clothes and makeup for quite different reasons. Clothes are a social statement; makeup is closer to our secret hopes and fears. Many women wear makeup to conceal flaws whose hideousness they alone could ever recognize. They may consider their eyes small, their skin sallow, their lashes laughably thin. (Many are hoping to hide the advance of years. The value of makeup as the cloak of age is dubious. It is generally agreed that as you get older, you should wear less.) A woman's picture of her face is not invariably accurate, but she can be brutally rude about how it looks without makeup. Yet makeup becomes so closely associated with the face it adorns that any observation about it is liable to give offense. You may remove a smut from a woman's cheek, or a smear of lipstick from a man's, but it is perilous to tell a woman that her eyeliner is wobbly or that she has too much powder on her nose. She is likely to take this to mean that her eyes are too small or her nose is too big. The woman who replaces her lipstick at the end of a meal often does so with a desperation which suggests that her mouth itself has been obliterated by chewing and by conversation.

Women wear makeup for their own benefit. Unless something happens to it—an eyelash begins to peel, or the lipstick goes askew—or unless they see someone without it for the first time, women hardly give a thought to other women's makeup. Men are blind to all but great changes and excess. Yet in some strange way makeup persuades us to feel better and more confident. Irrationality and insecurity are the very stuff of makeup. We know that our makeup cannot look the same at the end of the day as it does in the morning, but we feel easier if we know that it was once there and once looked satisfactory. Women may feel naked without certain cosmetics—lipstick, or something on the eyes—but this worry is far from constant. The absence of makeup might disturb us at a party but not at a picnic. Since it muddles logic and touches so upon our sensibilities, we should at least make an effort to enjoy it. It is possible to get the whole job done in seconds, but this seems a little sad; it is worth one's while to indulge in our lonely games with paints and brushes. If we put on a face mechanically and do not dare experiment, we succumb entirely to ritual and folly. Makeup has no real purpose save that of adding drama to routine.

Recently, still feeling puzzled by the whole idea of makeup, I went to talk to people who should be counted on to have a clearer view. The high-up offices of Estée Lauder, Inc., testify to Mrs. Lauder's love of beauty, and to visit them is like looking at a face of perfect makeup. The arts of interior decoration and cosmetics merge particularly well in a reception room that is a study in blue eyeshadow, and in Mrs. Lauder's office, a place of powder shades and blushes. She bubbles with enthusiasm about the powdered shadows for her Gaucho Eye, her Fresh Air Makeup Base, and all her range of products called the Little Nothings. These nothings consist of eleven tones of Tender Makeup Base, twenty-three shades of lipstick—Tender Lip Tints—and a group of soft, reddish blush jellies known as Face and Cheek Tints. Several ladies of her staff were settled down on sofas of tea-rose watered silk and smiling upon each other's makeup. Mrs. Lauder made friendly little rushes at me with Tender products, and led me by the hand to a gilt-framed mirror—the kind whose liver spots betray distinguished age—to show me the blushes she had wrought.

Throughout these activities, she talked. "Of course there are fashions in makeup as in anything else. When I went to the Paris showings, I was looking not at lengths but at the faces beneath pulled-back hair. The new look of the face is ladylike but not casual. The face is the focus, and no longer the legs. It should have the young, bright, soft look. Face and Cheek Tint looks young and gives shine and glow. It makes you look as though you have been outdoors and love to be kissed. We are all trying to look young, and Face and Cheek Tint can be worn by the sixteen-year-old and the sixty-year-old. In fact, the older the person, the younger she will look when wearing Little Nothings. There is no age in makeup, and none in clothes."

Mrs. Lauder thinks that no fastidious, well-groomed woman would go without makeup. Making-up is no more mysterious to her than putting on one's shoes and stockings. "Makeup should not be the same in the evening as by day, and women should have a wardrobe of makeup—four or five lipsticks, four or five shadows, and two glows. We dress the face just as we dress the body. No one should take more than five minutes to put on her makeup in the morning. After lunch, replenish your lipstick and your Face and Cheek Tint."

A telephone coughed behind a bowl of flowers, and Mrs. Lauder tried to answer it but found that she was not connected to the caller. She wandered out to take the call elsewhere. Mrs. Ida Stewart, vice-president of merchandising, assured me that it takes Mrs. Lauder three minutes to apply her impeccable makeup. I admired Mrs. Stewart's eye makeup and asked about new ways with shadows. "The fashion for heavy liners and no mouth is quite gone. The halo eye, with shadow above and below it, pulls the eye down into the face. After all, there isn't all that much going on beneath the eye. The new eye is big and blurred, not just that little old eye, with its ball and pupil." This talk of eyes was accompanied by gestures, and Mrs. Stewart illustrated the use of the index and middle fingers for initial application and smoothing of eyeshadow, and the fourth —still clean—to take up the surplus from the lid and stroke it on below the eye. When Mrs. Lauder returned, Mrs. Stewart asked her to lower her eyes so that I could see her masterly blending of shadows. By some miracle Estée Lauder's eyelids matched her hair.

All this seemed reasonable, but I wondered whether a man might have a more detached view of women's wiles, and I took the elevator ten flights up to Revlon. From here, the Park and the roof of the Pierre are even more tenderly muted. Revlon's advertising is often prefaced by playfully authoritative statements about women, life, and fashion, which are signed by its chairman and give the impression that Charles Revson is the philosopher-king of the cosmetics world. He is also, obviously, an artist. As he pondered the subject of women and their makeup, he seemed to see an infinite parade of trusting, upturned faces. He claims to know by instinct how to "zing up" a face, and he wonders, laughing, whether women left to their own devices really succeed in making themselves look better. "When people talk about faces being strong and having lots of character, I think they mean having lots of creases and wrinkles, and shaggy eyebrows. It's obviously no compliment to say a woman's face has character. The eyes and the lips are the most vibrant parts of the face, and it is to them that most of the emphasis should go, but the face is the background for the eyes and lips, and should not be ignored. I feel that all women should wear a base makeup, and everyone should wear a blusher, but not in an unnatural way. I believe that beauty and makeup—even when you are dressed to kill— should have something casual about it. Women with good skins—I mean neither pockmarked nor blemished—should use the minimum amount of makeup, and women with lines should use it with great discretion. Older women often make up very badly. They get used to seeing the same old face in the mirror—oh, perhaps they count the wrinkles, or watch a certain little piece of hair—but they have no real conception of their face, and their eyesight is often failing. In a strong light, in her bathroom, a woman can make believe she looks all right. It is a nervous habit to put on your lipstick every three minutes and powder your nose every ten. You need a little repair job now and again—a little transparent powder, if you're sweating, but not much more than that."

Remembering the Revson faith in eyes, I asked him about the future of false eyelashes. "I believe in them. They are here to stay. In the hands of someone who is willing to learn, they can be used for enhancement." Putting on his horn-rimmed spectacles, he rose to examine my own lashes, to see whether my doubts about unnatural aid were based on misplaced confidence in what Nature gave me. He pronounced them rather thin but acceptable, and recommended Moon Drops mascara—which, by chance, I was already wearing. Mr. Revson's enthusiastic talk of emphasizing, enhancing, and accentuating eyes and lips led me to think that he is more interested in the overt artificialities of makeup than in rejuvention or camouflage. Yet he does not always distinguish between faces and their trappings; in the discussion of false eyelashes, he did not use the adjective. Feeling rather shaky after the inspection of my eyelashes, I asked whether other women felt bewildered and uneducated about makeup. He nodded energetically. "There are so many products on the market, so many things to know. There are, however, certain rules. Don't overdo it, and never allow your face to look greasy. Make up with care, then look at yourself in a different light. If there is too much on, don't be afraid to take a tissue to it. It's terribly hard for any of us, with all our hangups and our difficulties, to be objective. But when making up you simply have to try. Women should look natural. When I say natural, I don't mean morning-natural, straight-out-of-the-tub stuff. I mean natural in the sense of not over-made-up. Some people think that the natural look means wearing no makeup, or wearing makeup to match your skin tone. That is not natural at all."

1971

Hot Pants

When a fashionable acquaintance called Le Pavillon to ask whether that restaurant admitted women in shorts, its spokesman corrected her question before he answered it. "Madam," he informed her, "you mean hot pants." Let headwaiters polish up their fine distinctions once more; yet another controversial style has come to try us. In part, it absorbs so many people because it is quite a surprise to see thighs again. But this is not the only reason for the noisy and general publicity given to shorts. (Knickers, which are almost as surprising and are seen more often at present, have never left the fashion pages.) Some of the attention is certainly caused by the appalling name with which the infant has been burdened. To a great extent, fashions evolve quite naturally. But the fashion industry is loath to see many days go by without trumpeting new eras, and whenever a style emerges, or reappears after an absence, it hurries to coin a title before shoppers can rummage sinfully in closets. Some advertisers, perhaps unnerved by reports that a Chicago consumer-research firm has declared that the name "hot pants" has no more "psychosocial acceptance" than the midi or the Edsel, have chewed their pencils over alternatives. But "shortpants," "short cuts," and "minipants" sound teenage or boring, and cannot compete with a more general and a naughtier term that has the weight of *Women's Wear Daily* behind it. That recklessly didactic, supremely fashionable newspaper has insulted the frumpy old English language even more than usual by fixing on the term and the spelling "HotPants." (After a lengthy witch hunt, it has also restored the miniskirt to a place of honor and dubbed it the "Hot-Skirt.") It has bustled its own dusty "longuettes" out of its gossip columns and replaced them with anything in "HotPants," and it has rollicked into headlines such as "Hosiery Men HotPanting" and "Hot-Pants Fever Grips Nation." It is true that the new shorts are worn by grown women in unlikely settings and seasons, and that they are found in fabrics once associated with Alpine herdsmen, cavemen, long-distance runners, and toddling pageboys at weddings. But they are still shorts.

Some men seem to like the name "hot pants." But those retailers who endorse it make what seems to me an outmoded supposition that women dress for the titillation of men—specifically, for neither lovers nor construction workers but for other women's husbands and all the other friendly strangers who might feel emboldened to voice an opinion on a woman's clothes. This is not the first time the verbal branches of the fashion industry have confused and falsified the picture. Over the past year, thinking to soothe the troubled consumer and make her spend money, they have urged her to "express herself" and offered her "fashions for all the new 'you's' in you." But the marked change in the way women dress has occurred in spite of these tactics. While there are probably fewer women who are sure of what they are than there were at the onset of this flowering of fashions, there are certainly more who know how to dress. It is to be hoped that these women will not be duped into confusing a rudely manufactured term with a style, any more than they were persuaded to buy boots that would go beautifully with their anxieties or a hat that would set off their new ambitions. They are free to reject shorts quietly or to approach them with an increased knowledge of color, accessories, and the limitations of their bodies. When women chose the new long lengths, they knew how hard they had to work to make them flattering. They added things like belts and boots, which they had never had to really examine before. Each experiment with length and shape increased awareness, and brought fashion to a point at which the restlessness of women became of far greater moment than the reaction of men.

Now that things are calmer, it is possible to see that the average woman who was afraid that she was being asked to lengthen her skirts by a couple of feet was really being encouraged to lower them only by inches. The European couture, in what seem to have been sound, placid summer collections, has placed daytime hemlines only a few inches below the knee. This may help to allay the fears of the majority. The extreme miniskirt was never a subject of debate, since those who had worn it had adopted long skirts well before last year's fuss about the midi. (The same women are now sporting tiny shorts.) Well, perhaps skirts did fall too fast. There was something violent and disturbing about the promotion of the change. This vehemence was inspired by the perverse tenacity of above-knee skirts in crude, primary colors. (The recently developing taste for strange shades and subtle combinations is probably a greater change even than the change of length and cut.) Last year, our skies rang with charges that the new lengths were regressive and inappropriate. In a sense, they may have been, but they were more natural than no change at all. It was astonishing that while women were supposedly thinking in new ways about many things, they refused to be uprooted from a uniform. As it was interpreted in this country—and one must distinguish between America and Europe, where women welcomed longer skirts without a wisp of protest—what can only be called the "above-knee look" was often a stiff, trim little dress that looked like something made by die casting and gave the liberated woman merely the choice of her fake-gold earrings and her chain-trimmed shoes. It is perhaps because mass production gained for American women the reputation of being extraordinarily well groomed that they clung to garments that were palpably its products long after the nation was disillusioned by its own industrialism.

But their reluctance to accept the change to midi was

genuine, and the industry had made investments. Women took some persuading, and it seemed that the only way to convince them they did not look dowdy was to offer them the trappings of seduction—slits up the front and the sides of skirts, low necklines, and diaphanous materials. It is precisely because men, women, and the industry then threw themselves into finding or creating titillation that a garment called "hot pants" can now be sold at all. Many of the New York couture designers use the term, and they seem to find their inspiration in its implications. The recent showings of their summer collections here made it clear that they are still struggling to get the long lengths to look sexy. It is easy to poke fun at the couture in an age of blue jeans and boutiques, when the luxurious establishments are looking to their own troubles. But their collections are worth noting because they are designed for women who like to be guided and to dress in a fairly conservative way, and because a great many women probably aspire to be their clients. The assumption of the established designers that their middle-class customer craves discreetly lewd clothes is false, insulting, and old-fashioned. To judge by all the recent showings, there appear to be two schools of fashion design—one for women who sometimes get immodestly drunk, and one for girls who have never heard of modesty and are always stoned. But since the second school— the Off Broadway of fashion—is manifestly not for most women and the revolutionary young designers have been tossing scraps of cloth at extravagantly naked bodies for years, their innocent dedication inspires a kind of affection. The more expensive houses whose designers are drawn toward prurience are a sadder case. A group of marketable and ladylike raincoats might be followed down their runways by black chiffon evening gowns with graceless slashes up the thigh and bodices designed to let no one forget that they did not cover a brassiere. Then there were shorts. They peeped from under see-through ankle-length skirts and knee-length cotton ones. Designers tried to make shorts look safe, and—unless they joined them to tailored blazers, causing the outfits to bear foolish resemblance to trouser suits without trousers—they managed to make the baggiest shorts look indecent.

The lady who enjoys being leered at, if she exists at all, is not well served by shorts. Nor are shorts made for the woman who is trying to look like a younger woman. They cannot be made to look mysterious, and must be worn innocently, or at least unself-consciously. They are quite an advanced stage in the movement of fashion toward functional, simple, and colorful clothing. The end expression of this clinging, untailored course is the body stocking. The other, seemingly opposite movement is toward make-believe, and leads us to dress up as peasants, Indians, and women of the nineteen-forties. But both moods are often found in one outfit. A leotard will be strung with African bones and feathers, or a long, ruffled skirt will be paired with a close-fitting ribbed sweater. Even shorts, which are but a step from the body stocking, have their element of fantasy, since the woman who wears them must not mind looking like a child of ten. It is the urge for practicality and ease that has led large numbers of women to trousers and caused them to invest so meekly in long winter coats.

No woman needs the prop of shameless gestures. The combination of shorts and boots should therefore be avoided. The exposure of a stretch of thigh seems consciously provocative; an unabashed display of leg does not. We have long been inordinately dependent on the covered calf, and it is certain that we will shortly feel secure enough to wear new or existing fashions without blindly pulling on our friendly old boots. It is possible to wear leg-colored tights or even knee socks with shorts, but the use of the legs as a block of color is more of a challenge. Shoes, top, tights, shorts, and belt can match or contrast in many ways. There are very brief shorts in the shops, and shorts that come almost to the knee. There are cuffed shorts, low-waisted shorts, pleated shorts, rompers, jumpsuits, two-piece suits, and overalls. Satin shorts are vulgar. Knitted shorts are nice, and crocheted shorts are delightful, but both are hard to wear. Leather or suede shorts are handsome, but they tend to be a little stiff at first. Velvet and corduroy shorts are neither too stiff nor so soft that they settle into an ugly splay of creases. It is wise to choose shorts with a few inches of extra width at the hem. When the wearer is standing up, her legs look slimmer; when she is sitting down, her thighs are less inclined to bulge. Shorts can be worn by sensible women of any age, and they have no season. But they are not for fat people, and they are more appropriate to daytime than to night.

The conservatism of employers may force some of those who are tired of hiding their legs in long skirts, boots, and trousers to return to the miniskirt. But shorts are quite apart from any question of skirt lengths. Hemline controversies have periodically troubled the Western World since the beginning of the century. Shorts spring from a far more significant development—women's adoption of trousers for evening, street, and business. The course of this revolution was so gradual and its supporters were so many and varied that scarcely anyone but bank executives and restaurateurs bothered to comment, let alone take a stand. Those dogged women who have now reached the stage of encasing themselves in trouser suits by day and swathing themselves in "pants dresses" by night are almost certainly not at the point of taking to shorts. (In fact, it is clear that many of them will overcome their fear of skirts before the autumn.) But it is those who have already moved beyond ankle-length trousers toward knickers and gauchos who are now trying shorts. If the length of skirts is to be flexible, so must be that of trousers. Shorts seem such inevitable progress that it is hard to see why they were not introduced before now, and why we were condemned to twitch at the hems of very short skirts. But shorts appear only now because however shocking miniskirts set out to be, they were still skirts, and part of the hallowed tradition of feminine dress. Not until trousers had stormed the gates could shorts skip in. Bright Young Things only sometimes wore pajama suits, and munitions workers couldn't wait to change into skirts for their dates. Society's resistance having crumbled, many women now wear trousers all the time. For the first time in the garment's relatively brief history, trousers are completely epicene. They are no longer scandalous, nor do they make women's bottoms seem particularly laughable. While shorts are fun to wear, they are not to be sniggered at, either.

Photographing
Fashion

Fashion photographs have long attempted to give concrete form to women's wispiest private dreams. Of
late, though, fashion magazines—the creators and
mirrors of these dreams—have been shuffling their artificialities
and replacing visions of lovely, unreal women with shots of
people engaged in desperately joyful activity. Their pages now
contain few formal portraits of calm, solitary, and unattainable
elegance; instead, they are crammed with lively snaps of
gregarious, gymnastic clowns. Both approaches are based on
artifice, but the second is also a pernicious falsehood. Since,
by definition, such periodicals are benders to the wind, it
must be supposed that women's ideal of feminine beauty has
changed. And so a romantic dream is being allowed to die,
while Goldie Hawn, laughing grotesquely, appears on the
cover of *Vogue*.

The few survivors among the unattainably elegant are un-
troubled by thought and untouched by the mob. They may
smile, distantly, at a palm tree or the right kind of baby, but
they are never seen to grin. Fashion and commerce spawned
them, but they stand above both. They communicate with no
one except their photographer, who can turn their loneliness to
gold. Apart from this Svengali, men have no place in their
world. These maidens' pride and confidence seem unassailable,
but their beauty can be stripped of its magic by the wrong

photographer or by the intrusion of the world upon their reverie. Few advertisements can ever capture their quality, because here a product must be made to seem more important than a face or a mood. (The most dignified cosmetics advertisements are an exception, since the product is already deep in mystery and deception and is well served by techniques that make life appear blurred.) They are aristocrats by virtue of their cheekbones and their flagrant distance from reality. Lesser females, seeing them, can feel free of prices, sizes, and envy, and settle back to dream a little.

Baudelaire, who considered any defense of nature misguided and defense of naturalness in women utterly insane, would have snorted to see periodicals start meddling with life when their strength is built on frosting. Even if the switch were desirable, they are ill equipped to make it. As so often happens when people and institutions think they hear the tumbrels of relevance, fashion photography has simply substituted a new, less dignified unreality for an earlier kind. But the move was made because many women apparently found tranquillity infuriating. It became fashionable to denounce the queenly images in fashion magazines as hotbeds of bourgeois fantasy and fomenters of dissatisfaction. Liberated girls despised decorated objects on pedestals; as they began to think, they saw how dreams had cheated them. People began to mutter that the clothes they saw were too expensive or unwearable, quite as if it mattered. As women changed, so did fashion. The idea that any part of fashion should appear aristocratic became increasingly repellent. If there were no heroes, and no artisans to serve them, why waste time with quality? Suddenly, even the rich didn't want to look rich. (One fashion magazine, in a list of questions it urged its followers to ask about their wardrobes, included "Does it look too expensive?") Fashion became democratic, and a subject upon which everybody took a tiny, dutiful stand. Badly dressed women spoke, with a glint in their eye, of putting down scheming designers. Because it seemed to represent a kind of authority, beauty had to stand in line for re-examination. In the bright light of this reappraisal, the image of perfect beauty in a perfect mood began to shrink and fall away. An insubstantial image can offer scant resistance to an onslaught of condemnations; it came to seem that cannons had been turned upon a butterfly.

So happiness is in, and muscles will be worn. It is no longer enough to be slim; you have to show the world that you can jump and click your heels in the air. Languor is quite unforgivable. Even as fashion photographs promote the gymnastic kind of life that makes frisky clothes necessary, the clothes themselves determine the way they are presented. When wearing shorts, it is best to keep moving, and it is hard to be aloof in candy-striped knickers. Today, most fashions are designed for those who are willing to laugh as they wear them. Fashion magazines are filled with pictures of girls too busy to stand mooning for the benefit of dreamers. Models rush past us, breathlessly, to share a joke with someone off the page. If they chance to remember the spectator, they give us a careless wave of their hats. Most photographs seem to have been taken in a wind tunnel; models move so swiftly that their hair streams out behind them, and skirts billow in such odd ways that they seem made for girls with three legs. Life, according to these glimpses of it, is an endless, perfect party, where each guest is programed to relate. Girls are seen in pairs, with linked arms, sharing a joke. Arrogant mouths and melancholy eyes are things of the past; all is open-mouthed hilarity. Men have popped up everywhere, bringing further camaraderie and even heartier laughs. The observer has the discomfiting impression that the photographer is having a good time, too. It is clear that the happy and healthy course is fraught with pitfalls. If the static school of lonely beauties introduced the possibility that life wasn't all it might have been, all these new get-togethers make the spectator feel flabby and left out. In a world that seems so abundantly full of happiness, she begins to feel deprived of her just share. If the new poses are intended to sell clothes, they are no improvement; calisthenics and contortions will not mask the hard truth that many fashions, and most photogenic ones, are unwearable. And while hoots and grins are sometimes heartwarming in life, they are never beautiful in photographs. It may be that elegance—

beautiful women wearing clothes beautifully—is incompatible with gaiety, since women who pin their lives on their beauty and its adornment are very rarely happy. But fashion photography concluded that beauty, after all, was dispensable and is giving *joie de vivre* a whirl.

With all this captive action, the new fashion photographs seem to play at being movies. In fact, in recent years it was the stiffer and more formal poses of fashion photographs that offered partial compensation for the loss of elegance in movies. It is rare now to see movie actresses in striking examples of contemporary clothes, and the high spots of films have long ceased to depend on dress. Garbo and Dietrich moved through almost every role with their wardrobes as co-stars; of their successors, perhaps Catherine Deneuve and Audrey Hepburn come closest to being related to their clothes in this way. But both women are more like models than actresses. Some English films in which the idea of fashion played a big part came along in the last decade, but this idea had less to do with elegance and women than with Britain's announcement that it now found finery more fun than morals. With *Blow-Up*, whose hero was a fashion photographer, movies and fashion photographs apparently fused. At the time of *Blow-Up*, a fashion photographer was indeed a filler of the void and a weaver of dreams. His images could call up something of the joy once inspired by visions of satin and chinchilla sweeping down Hollywood's interminable marble stairs. But he has since chosen to burn his books and be reduced to one of the laughing gang.

The aristocratic mood in fashion photographs is never captured by a group. It grows out of the union of two single elements—a photographer's skill and a model's beauty. Few teams have such impeccable credentials as Jean Shrimpton and the photographer most closely associated with her, David Bailey. The image they have wrought lies deep within each follower of fashion. Miss Shrimpton's pedigree is in her bright blue eyes, her marvelously well-turned head, and her childish, vulnerable limbs. And Mr. Bailey sees that she never betrays her beauty. Few observers would bother their heads with how her outfits might suit them. Her lips are always slightly parted, and she is not given to sprinting or grimacing. She is unapproachable in her diffidence and ageless in her innocence. The new photographic techniques are too clumsy and too hurried to catch the combination of child and sage that once crowned studies of beauty. Fashion magazines are more preoccupied than ever with the tricks of looking like a young woman; although they have always liked to hint that lovely faces are immortal, they now proclaim, in addition, that supple bodies never die. This forces the illusion and breaks the spell. And—perhaps it is merely that models, like policemen, get younger as their observer's age remains the same—the new grins distinctly seem to emphasize their wearers' youth. But as long as Jean Shrimpton stares quietly out from fashion magazines, they will still be purveyors of dreams. The same might be said of Naomi Sims. Her person floats far above such terrestrial matters as sales. That she is black additionally frees many of her admirers from disaffected comparisons, and forestalls the notion that if they dieted or got their hair done they might in any way resemble her. In one recent photograph of Miss Sims by Irving Penn, rainbow-colored chiffon ripples over one of her gleaming, bony shoulders and veils her naked torso. One hand is on her hipbone, the other at her waist. A golden breastplate, like a temple gong, hangs below a necklace python-curled around her endless neck. Except for some stray. delicate loops, her hair lies close to her small skull. Her face is brushed with pink, and large, discreetly contemptuous eyes gaze out through circles of lapis shadow. The kind of intelligence we appreciate in photographic beauty is a physical one: the person of Miss Sims is amply endowed with a kind of nerve-end understanding that life is often very sad. The portrait of the black American model tricked out as a bird of paradise in the idealized (and therefore inoffensive) trappings of an African tribeswoman is wreathed in ironies. But irony— a far nobler form of humor than slapstick—only makes her beauty more distinct. Age and intelligence are not as important in dreamland as they are in the world, and they are measured by different yardsticks. In that purely visual realm, a black skin is simply a challenge to the lens and a key to riotous fantasy.

In the older fashion pictures, beauties were rarely burdened with lives and names; for the greater part of their careers Miss Sims and Miss Shrimpton were not identified. But unnamed beauties are now rare in the important places in magazines, since it has become shameful to present a photograph of a girl without announcing that modeling is only a sideline with her, and that she is more interested in her life as a novelist, an actress, or the daughter of a countess. While women's interest in the images of other women undoubtedly springs, in part, from an urge to cling to the skirts of fame—an urge that led, in earlier times, to compiling scrapbooks of royalty or brooding over movie stars' divorces—this is the basest aspect of our taste for photographs, and the spectator who limits her curiosity to the way a beauty holds her head or rests her hand is better rewarded. But fashion magazines now seem to despise this gentle, visual interest. An attractive, dark-haired woman, through no particular fault of her own, united all the flaws of the newly realistic artificiality when she appeared recently in an issue of one such periodical that devoted itself to the theme of "Twenty Years of Looking Thirty." The routines she follows in order to cling to that sacred birthday—beyond which, apparently, beauty, like people, cannot be trusted—are closely described in the text: she is a former model who had the wit to renounce that drudgery in order to devote herself to other hectic interests, which include being a mother and an editor of the magazine in which she appears. In a photograph, she is caught galloping along with her two young daughters. All three heads are tossing and all three mouths are laughing.

The rules of dreamland are not inflexible. The classic portrait of beauty is usually a solitary woman, but a restrained maternity—one, that is, where the woman still looks lonely, and the infant is simply a foil or an accessory—is sometimes acceptable. But if a woman is surrounded by competitors and companions, by exuberant youngsters with mouths to feed and socks to darn, she becomes too much of a threat to peace. In the same way, while the traditional backdrop is pristine blankness or a tangle of far-flung vegetation, background may also include possessions, as long as their owner does not look too tied by them. And fame may be numbered among these possessions, as long as it is well established and discreetly worn. But the observer cannot feel at ease if full-fledged personalities come whirling down on her from nowhere. If the outsider is not to be jolted about while she is musing on beauty, the appearance of the woman observed must take clear precedence over any life or feelings she may chance to have. Henry Clarke photographed Audrey Hepburn Dotti in her house in Switzerland for a magazine recently, and Joshua Reynolds could scarcely have caught the scent of ordered indolence and the self-sufficiency of beauty more fully. The ethereal Miss Hepburn is discovered early on a summer day in her boudoir, poised among her belongings—which happen to include an infant son. Almost everything is white (including the wicker furniture and the jackets of her books) or powder blue (including the rug and the sleeping suit of the solemn child perched on his mother's crossed knee). There is no sign of Dr. Dotti. This simplicity is thoughtfully arranged—unseen hands must starch the lace at Miss Hepburn's hem, clean out the snowy cage containing her canaries, and gather the petals as they fall from the overblown roses on her writing desk— and the intimacy is something less than genuine. But in the picture Miss Hepburn remains completely private. Wealth can often secure the appearance of tranquillity, and when its presence is felt a regal mood will often prevail. (It is almost impossible, for instance, not to build a photographic dreamland around the exquisite clothes of Norman Norell; these are habitually described as "inimitable," which means very expensive indeed.) Because of this, what remains of the formal fashion portrait has by now merged completely with the portrait of the Society Beauty or the Famous Beauty. If the way of life remains subsidiary, beauty can still be pure, but a name, wealth, and even a beautiful face are valueless if style and peace are absent from the picture. The record of a Famous

Beauty in her setting has a longer tradition and may prove a more tenacious form of romanticism than the portrait of the unnamed beauty with nothing but her grace and someone else's clothes. But it is sadly possible that even the ideal lady in her ideal home will shortly be swept away, or will be joined by leapers, laughers, real children, and men. If that invasion takes place, the myth of elegance will be forever lost.

Back to Reality

American designers have been showing their fall collections, and any observer who believes that the fashion industry is a mirror rather than a juggernaut must conclude that most women in this country are not merely conservative but reactionary. The balance between the state of women's minds and those who make clothes to match it seems to have tipped, for the present, in the shopper's favor. The true picture of fashion is chaotic and beyond the reach of catchwords, and neither buyer nor seller can honestly attempt a definition of what it is that women now want. But designers realized that some approximation was called for, and have re-created what women used to want before the dark days of last fall, when they stopped spending money. Things are, to this extent, safely back to where they were—in the nineteen-sixties and even the nineteen-fifties. Women's mastery of their hem lengths has been dearly won: the rift between fashions for the young and clothes for the middle-aged is now absolute, and those who demand regression as an end to disorder have betrayed their need to be told exactly what to wear. It is fortunate that they are already quite at home with what they will find in the shops in the fall, because designers, in their eagerness to show how businesslike they are, have learned to renounce authority—lest they be accused of trying to dictate—and artistry, which might appear to have something in common with caprice. Peasants, wartime whores, and experiment are suddenly contemptible. It is fashionable to denounce fantasy and—by implication—fashion. The press, unwilling to be excluded from the new realism and responsibility, has extolled the rebirth of classicism, sanity, and a quality mysteriously referred to as "civilization." In this stern and heady new era, fashion vocabulary—which delights in wrenching words from meanings acquired in such humdrum arenas as books and history—is in over its head. The word "lady" is now synonymous with twin sets; civilization can be charged and sent; and a legion of real women, after long months of oppression, is to come into its own in the fall.

Who are these real women? The new collections suggest that they are those who felt most at ease in pencil skirts, girdles, and bouffant hair styles. They hated the midi because it made them look old, and they hate shorts because shorts make others look young. They like suits, and Lurex and brocade cocktail dresses, and heavy coats with broad, fur-trimmed collars. Their figures are flattered by firmly structured clothes and by stiff fabrics. (All the emphasis given to commonplace fabrics in the shows reflected both this need on their part and the designers' nervousness about line.) One New York department store caught the mood of the day in an advertisement that would not have appeared six months ago. "Glory Be for the Real Woman," ran the headline. "We've Never Forgotten You for a Minute." Beneath the text ("Sick of hearing about diets, exercise, and skinny girls?") was sketched, on suitably willowy forms, a vision of high-waisted corsets, long-legged panty girdles, and midriff-controlling brassieres. Real women, then, look middle-aged and fat. No amount of new wardrobes will really unshackle all those in our society who feel obliged to appear young, fit, and (since protein costs money) rich; this flowery praise of real women isn't going to change the world.

But the new focus on the middle-aged—a group, in the industry's current opinion, quite separate from youth: more powerful, and more willing to spend—is a backward step in the realm of fashion. Freedom from the significance of birthdays was just beginning to take root, and the idea of clothes appropriate to certain ways of life was already less tenacious.

The women who adopted shorts were those who worked at their figures, and those who took to the midi were willing to develop their sense of style; these were the only messages to be read in their choice of clothes. This ageless group of the slim and the stylish was a valuable bridge between the conservative and the freakish. Now, if things go according to plan, everyone over twenty-five will look much the same. Those under that limit, meanwhile, are offered a startlingly separatist course of clothes that seem intended to exclude anyone with a shred of social standing or a mite of responsibility. A young designer named Betsey Johnson—whose summer clothes now include muslin dresses the purchaser is supposed to decorate according to her individuality, and garments with all kinds of ecological themes—underlined this new division between the generations when she recently said, "Civilized relates to the fashion world. It is for my mother, who will be able to go shopping and finally find some clothes this year. But what I'm doing relates to the real world." Miss Johnson's interpretation of the real world, and that of all the other young people designing for firms with names like Hang Ups, Bananas, and Boo, is as perplexing as the one that is apparent in the collections of Geoffrey Beene, Bill Blass, Chester Weinberg, and company. But at least the young have room for a laugh or two. The Fashion Group, an organization committed to making sense of fashion for the benefit of those who work with it, concentrated on the work of young designers in a show it put on a while ago, and the bouncy, gawky young bodies wrapped in rainbow colors contrasted violently with the muted displays going on simultaneously in the showrooms of the established designers. Youth showed yellow shorts, worn with purple tights, orange platforms, and a cerise cloche; or striped pants rolled up to mid-calf, an animal-cracker sweater, and green suede work boots. Shorts and miniskirts were favored. They were almost totally absent from the couture houses, where even trouser suits were rare. The show was a hymn of praise for the very young. In spite of the fact that some styles in this show—blazers, chubby furs, and what the *compère* referred to as "the philosophy of layered dressing"—were also seen in the couture, it was clear that the two worlds were quite distinct and that the young designers had given up on all those out of school and felt free to race ahead at a head-spinning rate.

Apart from wedgies and a combination of leotard and layers of tunics that might owe something to a fifteenth-century court, revivals seem to have lost their appeal to young designers. (Campus nostalgia for the nineteen-fifties—Buffalo Bob and his Howdy Doody Show, boys with greased hair and girls with ponytails dancing together to "Blue Suede Shoes"—is, happily, still too intellectual to have caught the eye of young people earning a living by the drawing board.) But the older wooers of reality on Seventh Avenue have revived almost anything they could remember from the two decades before the midi. They adjusted skirt lengths, where it was necessary, bringing them all to somewhere around the knee for day. They indicated little interest in styles of the forties, because they remain the territory of those too young to have lived with the originals. Oscar de la Renta did show sweetheart necklines, but only half-heartedly; Valentino showed turbans and seamed stockings, but probably more out of habit than anything else. Many of Bill Blass's models wore fedoras swathed in poxy veils and carried the dangling head and paws of a fox fur over their arms, but this was all to be taken as a joke, not as a distraction from the marketable black dresses with white collar and cuffs, or the double-breasted coats in chalk-striped flannel, or the culottes, offered as an unfrightening alternative to shorts. Cocktail dresses in sparkling materials —Lurex, brocade, sequins, and beaded embroideries—are around again, with all their potential vulgarity. The Bill Blass couture collection contributed, among many other things, a cocktail dress consisting of a gold brocade skirt with a draped sash and a sweater top, in purple Lurex, that would never look quite right without a pointed bra. (This collection epitomized all the showings. Mr. Blass was *compère,* and he introduced this particular sampling of the extensive empire that is Bill Blass, Inc., by saying that, since fashion was dead, he was presenting some new clothes. He went on to explain why they were expensive. The atmosphere of the Hotel Pierre, where the show was held, and the arrangements of "Swinging on a Star" that were trundled out on a white piano were well suited to the brocade culottes, trimmed at the knee with fisher, that stalked down the runway. The collection was hailed as the one most brilliantly suited to "real women.") The established designers turned to the Eisenhower years for polo coats and their sash-belted variants, some with shawl collars, in tweed, flannel, and camel. These were often paired with jaunty little hats, so the models looked like ghosts of that lady who—in times when there were trains and redcaps to cope with a pyramid of matching hat and beauty boxes—leaned a gauntleted hand on a sheathed umbrella while she waited to board the Orange Blossom Special. The clothes of every lady in the White House since Mrs. Kennedy were also seen in the collections, but the strangest figure to float out of the nineteen-sixties was the air hostess. (This particular revival will comfort any designer who is wondering whether to wait for a style's extinction before daring to resurrect it.) As a group, air hostesses had fought furiously against the covered knee; they were justified in feeling that their trim, bright clothes, their mushrooming hair, and their toothy chic were under particular attack from those seeking to change lengths, colors, and images. At the Geoffrey Beene Boutique, the catwalk was thick with air-hostess clothes, even down to perky side-tipped felt caps. (Most of the couture houses now have two or three divisions, in different price ranges. The cheaper groups are often delegated to a disciple under the supervision of the Master; many outfits look as though no one would willingly take full responsibility for them.) Among Beene's boutique clothes were accordion-pleated skirts, black pussy-cat bows on white collars, and straight jersey skirts that, even on professional sylphs, were incomplete without a girdle. Donald Brooks, in an original way, revived things like tie-dye and nail-heads, which have been unfashionable for only six months. The European houses with American connections could not inevitably be looked to for innovation, either. The Cardin collection, with its graceless sandwich-board tunics over ski pants or miniskirts, seemed to echo Courrèges's determination, in the early nineteen-sixties, to drag female attire into the Space Age.

Though real women draw the line at looking like their children and prefer to think back to what they wore when their teen-agers were toddlers, they don't mind looking something like their husbands. Men's fabrics—gray flannel, pinstripes, window-pane and Prince of Wales checks—were present in almost all the collections. Middle-aged women do not really want to imitate clothes worn by middle-aged men, but that air of conservatism suddenly looks awfully good. Men have not yet been encouraged to seem fresh out of Sherwood Forest or a costume ball; if manufacturers had hinted at such a course, their customers would have been firm enough to refuse. Women envy the way a man can throw on a suit much like his neighbor's and then, in the certainty that he looks socially acceptable, forget it for the rest of the day. His silhouette is stable, and he is not urged to express his personality through fleeting fads; his clothes are not supposed to make a splash or even catch the eye of the opposite sex. As it turned out, women's wish for clothes rather like a man's brought about some of the finest designs in the collections as well as some of the dreariest. Where mannishness was interpreted simply as bulk that broadens shoulders, eliminates waists, and generally muffles women's bodies (polo coats reveal a vague sportiness rather than any particular gender), it was dispiriting. But where masculinity was used playfully and self-consciously—with the cheerful openmindedness, in fact, that is being widely purged—it was most effective. The Valentino Boutique collection, a light-hearted combination of schoolgirls and grouse-shooting Cabinet Ministers, looked strong and new. Black and red remain favorite colors, but this designer is now inspired by gray, camel, and forest green as well. Daytime clothes went on in layers; a silk shirt with a matching necktie, under an Argyle sweater and a cardigan jacket, might be seen with a kilt-pleated skirt or cuffed trousers. Many such outfits were topped by wide berets trimmed with down cockades and drooping pheasant feathers. While the clothes in this collection do not reveal much—hardly any see-through fabrics were in evidence this season—they are close-fitting and do not set out to muffle anything.

With some regret, I include the Chanel suit among clothes that have the wrong kind of masculinity. This suit cropped up with great regularity, and in only one of the shows I attended was it accompanied by an overt tribute to its originator. It came to seem that American designers—too timid to imitate an outfit guaranteed to appeal while the source was still active—were now expressing their liberation in this burgeoning of chains over silk shirts, straight skirts, and cardigan jackets. Chanel had the last word on real women. She never changed the length of her skirts and, as she herself would have admitted, she made the same suit for forty-five years. The Chanel suit may have attained perfection of line, but the style is now static. I would be loath to see it become a uniform once more. Styles can be revived only if they are adapted or parodied, and women of forty-five will never be thirty again. Perhaps the miasma that has settled on fashion since real women asserted their right to wear the clothes they are used to will blow over in a season. It is quite possible that these women will settle for the conservative clothes they own already and the industry will have sold its soul in vain. In time, it may even become clear that shorts are not a threat to society and that changes in hemlines are not the harbingers of anarchy.

On the Avenue

During a slow walk along Fifth Avenue on Wednesday last, many thousands of costumes passed by me; I was struck by a mere handful of costumes that had any semblance of dignity, simplicity, or taste. One was worn by an earnest young member of the Manichean sect that has temporarily abandoned its floor-length black capes and is now distributing its leaflets around Rockefeller Plaza in short-sleeved gray trouser suits. Another belonged to a follower of the Krishna Consciousness band, whose shaven heads are enviable on steamy days and whose apricot robes come into their own when they are not swathed in mufflers. My eye rested with gratitude on a nurse in an unadorned white dress, and on a fashionable young black man whose close-fitting chiffon shirt and burgundy velvet pants were worn with an easy enthusiasm as yet unshaken by lightning changes in mode. It was hard to pick out any good-looking, well-dressed girls.

I passed three secretaries emerging from a lunch-hour test of their stamina in Korvettes. The first was wearing a red sail-cloth minidress, and she looked timid, out-of-date, and frustrated by her boss's views on the subject of suitable business attire. One of her companions—the plumpest of the three—was wearing tight black velvet shorts. She typified the girls who are wearing shorts in town this summer. She was asserting her right to wear them with such militancy that it was clear she had not thought to pause and wonder whether her legs

51

would merit such display. One can almost conclude that all the shortest, fattest, and least self-critical girls in New York are wearing shorts. The style deserved a better fate. Perhaps some of the girls who would know how to make shorts outfits look elegant sheered off when they realized that all the midtown prostitutes were being photographed by the police in nothing else. The third of the girlfriends, who had the best figure and something approaching a sparkle in her eye, was wearing a polka-dotted, white-collared minidress whose skirt opened over matching shorts. Combinations like this often work well, apparently because the wearer can appear daring and fashionable without feeling reckless or hysterical.

Many of the ankle-length peasant dresses that are around are also surprisingly successful, as long as they are not worn in an attempt to hide puppy fat. I saw a young girl with shining, waist-length hair bouncing into Scribner's. Her dress was black, and printed with posies and ribbons; beneath its ankle-high flounce, her feet were clad in an appealing pair of white sneakers. Slightly shorter and more formal skirts nearly always look odd with bare legs, and mid-calf skirts can be worn with only one kind of sandal—one with a high heel and instep, of which perhaps three pairs exist to tread the streets of the city. Last year's mid-thigh-length linen dresses are still around, of course—money crops have been poor of late for the middle class—but it is hard to focus on them with enthusiasm. Yet when its skirt covers the knees, the linen dress is dignified, and stands as proof of some husband's returning financial confidence. I paused beside a linen dress with a black skirt and a short-sleeved beige bodice whose owner was absorbed in intense calculations before Mario Buccellati's vitrine. Her blond hair was held back in a solid-gold clasp, and did not depend on the sun for its careful fleckings. The shade of her golden skin, on the other hand, was clearly maintained by costly and uninterrupted exposure to the kind of sun that no one ever sees in Central Park. But the most elegant dress to brush past me was made of buttercup silk. Its silk fluttered around the kneecaps of its fortunate wearer; rippling double capelets on her upper arms were capturing the only breath of air that was likely to be felt that day in the neighborhood of the St. Regis. She was turning heads—no mean feat in times when a barrage of eccentric and revealing costumes bewilders and ultimately bores most girl-watchers. She wore high-heeled ankle-strap sandals and a red-and-blue-spotted kerchief that kept her hair off her nape. Her bag—a small mailbag—was an exception to the rule that the best new handbags are all being carried by men.

Girls tend to look happier in dresses than in separates. The assembly of a mass of ragtag parts proves exhausting to many, and often induces panic about accessories and color combinations. On a stretch of Fifth Avenue that once stood high among the world's most fashionable promenades, I saw girls in flimsy dresses worn with beetle-crusher black loafers, girls in dashikis with spike-heeled shoes, and a girl in white piqué shorts with brown fishnet tights. I watched a heavyset young woman struggle onto a bus in an ankle-length cotton skirt slit to a Hong Kong high on each side. The print was predominantly purple and emerald. She was wearing a lime-green top and white patent leather pumps, and she carried a red patent bag. At least one young woman, who was waiting fretfully to cross the street and give the crowd the chance to see her swaying walk, was not guilty of such glaring errors about color. Apart from her toenails, which were orange, and allowing for the many parts of her that were not clothed at all, she was dressed from head to foot in white. She wore a brief terrycloth jumpsuit, and her bare legs, far from being tanned, were almost blue. A crochet cap struggled to contain the recalcitrant mop on her head, and her little feet wore openwork boots that would have been tight-fitting had they been possessed of toes, heels, or sides.

By now, the covering of legs and feet presents an almost insoluble problem to most women. Even on the hottest days, many of them are still held in the thrall of boots. Some of these are the same old leather ones; others have made play of adapting to the season, and appear in canvas or white mesh, or in white leather with as many gaps and cutouts as the purchaser will tolerate before losing the comfortable feeling that she is still wearing boots. And the legs above these boots, or above shoes somehow too masculine or too feminine for the outfits they are worn with, are often sheathed in opaque tights in a wintery black or brown. These are so popular, presumably, because they are rumored to have a slimming look and because they conceal pallid bare skin. It is true that summer clothes cry out for bare brown skin; for this reason, black girls, even in the monstrous flapping white gladiator sandals that some of them like to wrap around their legs, invariably look better in their summer clothes than white girls, but untanned legs need not be punished by being covered in such gloom. Wedgies, some as high as stilts, are pounding the streets in sizable numbers. I was curiously encouraged by this fashion; it is quite as ungainly as any other form of footwear, but many of the girls in wedgies had style, and quite a few of them even had good legs.

Apart from men in business suits, the largest group of people I came across was wearing blue jeans. The kids who wear them often look as tediously uniform as their fathers; tie-dye T-shirts, headbands, and denims are, of course, blind emblems of a way of life quite as much as seersucker jackets and button-down collars. But when jeans, with their neutral color and their uncomplicated line, are used as a base for judicious flights of fancy they provide a confidence that is often lacking in those who have struggled to put together trickier and more commercial separates. I saw girls in blue jeans modified in a hundred ways: sometimes chopped off to make shorts, and edged with crochet scallops; sometimes rolled up to mid-calf and adorned with appliqué hearts on each back pocket, or belted in leather and horse brasses and paired, unexpectedly, with fragile, backless blouses made of Indian scarves, or ice-cream-colored brassieres of fluffy angora. (The appearance of bare backs and midriffs this summer marks the death of the principle that clothes appropriate to city life are quite distinct from those for the beach.) Jeans don't look or feel particularly cool, but then neither does linen, and, at any rate, their potential elegance does not depend on wealth. At the Potagerie, where I had settled to rest my eyes on soothingly simple butcher-block tables and blue linen napkins, I shifted under the scrutiny of a matronly tourist on the sidewalk outside my window table. She was cupping a heavily ringed hand over her harlequin sunglasses, framed in fake mother-of-pearl, the better to peer into my gazpacho. Her hair was big and blue. Her feet were solidly planted in yellow and white pumps that matched her self-belted dress of embossed yellow cotton and *its* matching jacket, which was trimmed around the neck with curly white braid. In the other hand she clutched a white wicker handbag constructed like a scaled-down steamer trunk. At that moment, a girl came in through the revolving door. From under her white duck sunhat, long brown braids fell to the ragged hem of her sawed-off jeans. She wore black espadrilles that laced around her slim, tanned ankles, and she was smiling.

Hats

A decade ago, millinery departments began to shrink and gather dust. Subsequently, scores of milliners, squeaking "Hats are surely back *this* year," were swept away before the bouffant hairdo and the wig. Hats were reduced to the apologetic, perching pillbox and to the even more vestigial scrap of veiling strewn with bows. Thereafter, hats were worn mainly to protect heads from sun, rain, or cold. Some few stalwart, determinedly feminine women in fedoras continued to stalk through the hatless crowd, and another handful of only slightly less imperious creatures stuck with the kind of thing described as "young" hats. These are to be found in what used to be called hat bars, whose tight-lipped informality was supposed to lure back all those who were defecting from millinery. "Young" hats include the breton, the boater, and the jockey cap. They are all disastrously, unfashionably pert, and they make women of any age—even young ones—look as though they were pretending to be young. But most women have concluded that hats, like white gloves, are boring and dispensable. Heads go uncovered to weddings, let alone luncheons. As a social object, the hat has ceased to be; as a decorative accessory, it long ago ceased to evolve.

But evolution is only one of fashion's currents. Another force—at this point probably a stronger one—is revival. And the idea of the fashionable and frivolous hat is now, like Oxford bags and padded shoulders, sufficiently remote to have been exhumed. Hats are being worn by the very young and

the very far-out. Like any other fashionable revival, the renaissance in hats is chiefly fostered by those who are too young
to remember the originals—those whose backward glance is
unsentimental and whose admiration is often tinged with
mockery. It is in the intellectual games the wearer plays with
them that the new hats—if we can consider as novelties turbans trimmer with artificial cherries, cloches swathed in
figured netting, and velvet cocktail caps spiked with a feather
that endangers bystanders' eyes—differ from any of the hats
that have survived into the past decade. The new hats are
often blocked and made of felt, and so they are unlike all the
informal, functional head coverings made of straw, plastic,
and fur to which women have necessarily remained faithful.
But however decorative and unserviceable the new hats set out
to be, they are also distinct from the structured confections of
millinery; this word is held to be laughably archaic, and the
millinery department is seen as a repository of fossils. Far from
being whisked out of hidden recesses to be placed, with
reverent ceremony, on the dignified head of the customer, the
new hats are displayed haphazardly and made to be pulled
down and giggled over. No modern girl would weep if her
husband seemed to slight her taste in hats. If, by chance, the
new hats get sat on, their fashionable uproariousness is only
increased.

The hat is gaining new supporters not because women want
to look ladylike, and certainly not because they want to look
real. The hat is gaining because it is an accessory rich in potential comedy, with a wealth of past examples to copy, and because some degree of historical horsing around is by now a
necessary element of fashionable dress. The new shapes in
hats are almost all from the twenties, thirties, and forties.
(Saks Fifth Avenue, it is true, has some splendidly hare-
brained cocktail caps by Adolfo—in black satin, for example,
decked out with a nose-length veil and a bunch of satin
poppies to nestle at the cheek—that are reminiscent of the
New Look in the early nineteen-fifties. But these are really a
milliner's wishful thought, and scarcely representative of this
designer's models, which are most often based on the thirties

cloche with a demurely rolled-back brim.) The influence of
the years of the cloche, and familiarity with knitted and
crocheted acorn caps—for the plague of which Ali MacGraw
may someday be forgiven—lead the newly hatted to pull any
hat well down toward the ears. When the brim of the hat
turns up, as it often does, the effect is Laurel n' Hardy. Even
closer to the circus and the *opéra bouffe* are the new felt hats
whose broad, soft brims are pinned to the crown in front, so
that the wearer seems to be perpetually cycling into the wind
or playing at being Napoleon. These comic silhouettes are the
base for further fantasy, in the form of decorations and trimmings that are often more important than the hat. Such frip-
peries can include a bunch of papier-mâché grapes or bananas,
a Bakelite pin in the shape of a heart, an ostrich plume, a
length of spotted net, an overblown rose of artificial silk, or a
sepia portrait, framed in leather, of some Edwardian beauty.
Many of these elements may be found together on a single
hat. They contribute to the game of make-believe, and
the wearer becomes a child again, dressing up in Mommy's
clothes. This comic quality creates the impression that the
girl who sports them is without a care; she also appears un-
committed to what she is wearing—just as the man who
adopts a funny voice dissociates himself from his expressed
opinions—and so beyond the reach of any judgment the outside world might choose to make.

Not that the new hats need be unflattering or inelegant.
Even when it is carried to excess (and viewed with irony), the
traditionally feminine trim of veils, plumes, and flowers will
still enhance a pretty face. Those who take such things with
complete seriousness may also benefit by the new life in the
hat department. If, as we are promised, veils are to make a
reappearance—*on* hats, *as* hats (and trimmed with scraps of
haberdashery), or as a simple band to tie around the eyes—
they will look as graceful on the older woman who has worn
them before as they will on the young girl who has not and
who now adopts them as costume for a role as heroine of a
romantic intrigue. In general, though, it is increasingly difficult to wear fashionable clothes—and probably impossible to

wear fashionable hats—without being well versed in the irony of such a choice. Many women, even very young ones, enjoy the trappings of elegance—soft, impractical materials and unfunctional cut; droopy, tea-gown sleeves that get caught in the typewriter; and, now, flower-trimmed felt hats that will sag in the rain—but they know that their lives are neither privileged nor leisurely, and that elegance must almost always be a pose. Two of the most consistently fashionable designers of recent years are Valentino, the Italian, and Barbara Hulanicki, of London's Biba, which is represented in a corner of Bergdorf Goodman. These two designers have succeeded because they understand that women crave graceful lines and muted colors (Valentino has become a bit louder, of late) but that these must be approached obliquely—with tempered nostalgia. It is no coincidence that they have also been materially responsible for the present rebirth of the formal yet light-hearted hat.

Valentino is unlike other couture designers in recent years in that he has shown hats that have as strong a presence as his clothes. The hats have generally had broad brims that dip, curl, or swoop. This year's version is a musketeer's hat, a foot and a half in width, which curves back from the brow and dips at the nape and to one cheek, with pheasant tail feathers arching around the brim in front. The hat, which was seen in its original form with the pageboy hair style of the nineteen-forties, has been widely imitated. So have the hats of an even earlier generation that Miss Hulanicki has contributed to the renaissance. Latterly, this designer has been absorbed by spare felt cloches that are worn low on the brow. The current Biba cloche has a narrow brim that widens in the back; the ones of recent months were decorated with felt flowers or a cutout design over one ear. That Biba's and Valentino's hats should look dignified, in spite of their modish regression, and genuinely youthful, in spite of their formality, may be taken as a sign that hats will one day reach the calm plateau where longer skirts now stand—accepted. But first of all hats, too, must live through their revival.

1972

Fitness

I n order to be fashionable—a state only tenuously connected with propriety or comfort, and one avowedly at odds with contentment—most women out of their teens need to diet and take exercise. The slim woman bent on gastronomic sacrifice is considered a fool and a bore by all but other slender dieters. Yet in her pursuit of muscle tone, even by way of obviously cosmetic calisthenics or systems based on languorous, patented stretches carried out in cozy salons, the sylph has the backing of society. We are schooled to look for litheness in our beauties and leanness in our heroes. Athleticism, or the fantasy of it, forms a part of the national character. In recent years, though, physical fitness has been gaining a new kind of disciple, drawn toward sports and exercise mainly by fashion and the desire to look young. And it is clear that supple clothes that offer no camouflage to middle-aged bulges are in style once and for all. Businessmen are encouraged to stay fit in order to improve their performance and their chances of survival. Sports such as tennis and skiing become more accessible, and bicycle riding comes daily to seem more desirable. These activities demand fitness and increase it. Many of the reasons people turn to fitness—such as vanity, aggression, tension, boredom—turn out to affect both sexes. The subject of sex and its attendant nudity pervades the fashion magazines and the bestseller listings more explicitly than ever, and this prominence leads people with faith in fashionable things to ask whether it isn't more important to create a good impression in the skin than in clothes.

A lot of normal dissatisfied souls have begun to seek in physical self-improvement a satisfaction that intellectual and social ambition appears slow to grant. Those who set off on the quest in the city will find that all strenuous activity seems artificial. They may be led to game playing, which often proves an expensive pastime, and one fraught with anxiety. They may embark on exercises done on the floor at home, starting the day with a dismal view of the cobwebs festooned beneath the furniture. Or they may venture into one of the thousands of professional exercise establishments, where they must be prepared to encounter fanaticism and, perhaps, develop it. Teachers and pupils of the many forms of exercise in New York resemble the crusaders and converts of a stern religion. They are united in their faith in its truth, but they divide into a mass of sects and schisms, and they love to denigrate one another. Dancers, not unnaturally, see themselves as the aristocrats of the muscular world, even if they are only on their second lesson. In turn, what they consider the plebeian gymnast would curl his lip at the infantile gyrations of the calisthenics class, and the voices raised against the search for perfection through yoga, isometrics, and thrumbling, pummeling machines are legion. Countless establishments specializing in unique methods of attaining fitness, based unfailingly on the movements of the galaxy and taught by skilled Europeans, escape condemnation only because no one outside of the guru and his handful of disciples has ever heard of them.

Any subject that ceases to be the property of jocks and cranks and becomes a fashionable and popular success is bound to get a lot wordier. The world of better bodies now trails a substantial literature of its own and supports a fair section of a public-relations world that was once kept busy selling us a new spring coat and a nice little hat to go with it. A figure salon without a well-publicized "personality" in charge is merely a place where women go to try to rectify the ravages of middle age; a gym without a resident philosopher is grubby, sweaty, and earthbound. Nicholas Kounovsky, the proprietor of the most fashionable gym in the city, is an elder statesman among gymnasts and—as both mystic and celebrated author—a model for the new breed of exercise teachers. His recently published inspirational work, *The Joy of Feeling Fit*, combines silhouettes of men and women in graceful poses illustrating the author's exercises, Sixometrics and Gymnaks, with exhortations on the lines of "Don't forget that your most worthwhile goal is not a perfect headstand but to live each moment of life with ease, health, and pleasure." The book makes a compelling case for the religion of the body and renders the idea of physical well-being most seductive. The author's arguments and incantations strengthen the impression that the Kounovsky method is flawless, and that newcomers will be engulfed and carried along in their efforts by such perfection. They need only obey the master and find in themselves a modicum of will.

No exercise teacher can neglect the importance of will. Marjorie Craig, in her contribution to the library of trimness, *Miss Craig's 21-Day Shape-Up Program,* ends her list of equipment ("sponge-rubber ball, ankle weights, full-length mirror") with a quality referred to as "self-determination" ("This only you can supply"), which makes the potential exerciser feel rather like a volatile emergent nation, but the firmness of the author's tone leaves readers in no doubt about what virtues they should display. Miss Craig, who has been the resident exercise expert at Elizabeth Arden's New York salon for twenty years, is now, in addition, the dean of that establishment's newly founded university of the body—an undeniably complete service known as Miss Craig's Classes. The course lasts for two five-day weeks and requires attendance two hours a day. On all ten days, the pupil spends the first hour in fairly strenuous work on will power and muscles, learning Miss Craig's exercise method. For the second hour, the customer attends a seminar in skin care or seasonal wardrobes, or she abandons the effort even of listening and submits to the variously sybaritic ministrations of the house of Arden—hairdressing, massage, manicure, makeup, and so on. Few schemes of bodily improvement will enfold the novice quite as thoroughly as this.

Any adult who begins lessons—particularly when the subject involves new physical skills—finds herself reverting to many of her childhood attitudes. The atmosphere around the powder-pink halls at Elizabeth Arden is strangely redolent of Sunday school or a genteel dancing class. Little knots of women—of all ages, and with very different shapes—scamper past in leotards, giggling as they head for their cornflower-blue exercise mats and another session with the young girl in braids who will put them through their routine. Miss Craig, a crisp and pedagogic blonde, smiles indulgently in the direction of the wriggling forms and observes—above the voice of the teacher calling "Hands-ahup-hands-together-and-over-bounce-bounce-bounce"—that her pupils seem to delight in their lessons in self-improvement. "I spend half an hour with each individual before the start of the course, analyzing her figure, hair, skin, nails, clothes, and any other problems," she says. "They listen to all advice avidly. We weigh them in each morning, and take their measurements on the first, sixth, and tenth days. We try to make a little ceremony of it. They get a report card when they graduate, but you may be sure that no one ever flunks!" Posture is, appropriately, close to Miss Craig's heart. (Kounovsky, in his more sweeping style, reveres it, too: "Control of your walk means control of your attitudes," he claims.) And although Miss Craig concedes that since most women first begin to spread in the hips and thighs, special attention is given to these parts of her pupils, she asserts that her exercise is "all-round." She sets store by perseverance and discipline, and insists on a half-hour exercise period every day for the rest of her pupils' lives; among her uncompromising mottoes are "Ears Up. Ribs Up. Shoulders Back and Down." It is the paradox of the course that these rigors are sugared by all the little self-indulgences and pamperings of the salon. Pupils appear to enjoy both the active and the passive parts of the sessions, and both parts are often new experiences. "We have certainly learned a thing or two about the average woman," murmured one member of the Arden staff. "Why, some of the women who signed up had never even had a pedicure."

Like the blurred faces of seated, watching mothers that spin past little girls in dancing class, the out-of-focus images of husbands hover around any women's exercise class. While most classes with overtly cosmetic intentions contain a few young girls and blue-haired matrons, most of those present are in their thirties or early forties, and most of them are, more or less, married. Their husbands are reported—at least by exercise teachers and their publicists—to be bowled over by wives who greet them each evening with a young girl's limberness and zest. It is even claimed that some women embark on bodily restoration at the urging of their husbands. Tantalizing as the marriages behind such enthusiasms and suggestions might initially appear, it turns out that the life a woman leads in anything but her leotard is of very little interest to her exercise companions. Life goes on in the fitness class on a few simple planes. Beyond the purely muscular and visual effects (supine torsos supporting pumping, cycling legs, or bodies formed in rubbery hoops like cards in the Queen of Hearts' croquet game), are only the highly stylized ciphers of the schoolroom—star athlete, clown, and well-meaning fatty. Fatties, in fact, are extremely rare in fashionable exercise parlors, which build their reputations largely on people who didn't need much help to start with. Many of the women who attend are maintaining, rather than seeking, what often seems to the outside observer to be taut and slender perfection. The snobbery of the fashionable exercise parlor is based mainly on physique, but—since the idea of sleekness and "good bones" is still associated with wealth and class—it also depends to some extent on what remains of the social standards of the outside world. Exercise salons rarely, if ever, deny rumors that the wives of Chicago millionaires or department store presidents frequent their halls. Women at their fashionable calisthenics are seen in few dimensions, but some of them have husbands with what their wives' gym teachers think are famous names.

The woman in search of physical improvement has many alternatives before her. Health clubs, of which there is an increasing number, will provide a multitude of services, such as swimming, sauna, yoga, gymnastics, massage, and steam rooms. These clubs are often patronized more by single people than by women papering over the cracks of age or maternity. But these establishments are highly commercial, and the prospective customer must often resist great pressure to sign away large sums for lengthy subscriptions.

A "serious" gym is another proposition, especially if it is one of those gyms that have recently been putting a dab of scent behind their ears. One such institution, under the management of Gary Novickij, a former instructor with Kounovsky, has been christened simply The Gym, but this unpretentious nomenclature does not preclude classes in judo, jazz dance, Russian folk dancing, and, eventually, yoga in the establishment's bright suite of white-painted rooms, alongside more traditionally gymnastic activities on exercise mats, rings, trapeze, parallel bars, balance beam, and trampoline. Here, men are more than unseen cheerleaders and status symbols; they, too, may matriculate, though in separate classes.

Gymnasts like to tell the world that theirs is the most dignified and human path to physical well-being, and that gymnastics offers complete satisfaction to mind and body both. Mr. Novickij keeps up his philosophical end and demonstrates a fine passion in denouncing exercise programs more specifically feminine than his. "They may work on saggy bottoms and bosoms," he observes, "but we work on backs, and fronts, and feet, and heads. With us, it's total." Amateurs in pursuit of this totality are given to rapturous talk about their gymnastic experiences—of performing impossible feats and delightful tricks, of the sensation of flying through the air, and of learning the feeling of challenge and accomplishment. "Ninety per cent of the people who come are completely unathletic at the start," says Mr. Novickij, in the face of such enthusiasm. "In the end, like any other athletes, the folks who come to gym become fanatics." Like every other exercise teacher, he will hasten to assure his female customers that their workouts will not include any movements that might develop bulging muscles. This assurance tends to be asked for and given more freely in gyms than in figure salons, because gyms aim to transcend and might seem to lose track of the humdrum question of shape. And gyms seem to be associated in the public mind with men. In fact, attendance of women has long been greater than that of men in mixed gyms. Only recently, it appears, has the ordinary, bulgy businessman come to terms with fashion, the frustrations of the sedentary life, and his vanity, and followed his wife to the gym.

1973

Style

Style is rarely glimpsed in times like these, which at best encourage its humble relative, good taste. While style and taste have been known to intermingle in the past, the currently widening gap between them reminds us once more of their fundamental enmity. The world of the merely tasteful—a trim edifice of bourgeois conformities, with narrow slots to be filled and straight lines to be toed—is bound to barricade itself, in the end, against style, which is individualistic, aristocratic, and reckless. Taste concerns itself with broad, lifetime progress, and never makes mistakes; style moves by fits and starts and is occasionally glorious. Style differs from elegance, too, yet they often keep company, since elegance is generally regarded as a prime object in the quest for style. But elegance is static and hermetic, and the moments of its attainment in a life of style are like so many cathedrals along the route of a comprehensive cultural tour. Style requires allegiance to a creed whose shifting nature makes it all the more demanding. But then style is more rewarding than the ways of elegance or taste: it is more akin to a philosophy, and it is surely closer to an art.

I have been looking at some of the photographs that have lately appeared of Mick Jagger's Nicaraguan wife, Bianca. Like a jungle orchid, she is both fragile and luscious. In her small, delicately boned face, a pair of strong black brows curve imperiously over huge, brooding eyes. Her mouth is wide and sullen, with a swollen, nearly bursting lower lip. Her resemblance to her husband is so remarkably close that it has prompted comparisons between Jagger and Narcissus; beyond that, it might be said that Jagger has completed the search for his twin soul with a neatness that would have taken Plato by surprise. But even more jolting than this likeness or her beauty is her unmistakable style. Her way of dressing and presenting herself to the world is her own. (Some deemed this originality worthy of the Best-Dressed List, to which both the Jaggers have been elevated this year. The London *Daily Mirror* duly voiced the outrage of all who believe in last bastions, alligator shoes, and the Queen's dressmaker.) In a pair of studio portraits in a recent *Harper's Bazaar*, Bianca appears first in a flapperish dress with a mid-calf hemline and deep, sleeveless armholes, from one of which an arm of almost waiflike thinness emerges, crooks backward, and ends in a narrow, maroon-nailed hand on one hip. The other hand supports a lengthy, heavenward-slanting cigarette holder. While the pose is reminiscent of a Bright Young Thing, the heart-shaped face, framed in a swelling brioche shape of dark hair, wears an expression of passionate, self-contained femaleness more worthy of a heroine from D. H. Lawrence. The second image on the page kneels at the feet of the first and turns her head away from it. Here the elfin features are framed by a gauzy, winged, and polka-dotted hat brim, and the effect is of a pale, bewildered butterfly. In other moods, Bianca might choose one of the mannish suits that are fastidiously made for her by Tommy Nutter, bespoke tailor to the trendiest Britons. With these she sometimes wears a dyed-to-match carnation in her buttonhole, and generally a hat—either a tilted, Chaplinesque bowler or a more elaborate concoction, involving feathers and veils. Almost always, she sports a knob-topped cane. On her recent visit to New York, *Women's Wear Daily*—hastily netting her for its shadowy gallery of more or less obscure "celebrities"—photographed her at an art show opening, and recorded her black velvet tailor-made, her little white crochet gloves, and her inspired black hat with a spotted veil and a white cockatoo perched at an angle on its brim. On this occasion, too, Bianca affected her cane.

It seems appropriate that Bianca Jagger should have revived for use as her mascot the Regency cane, emblem of the dandy. For she seems to exemplify many of the tenets of the cult of style known as Dandyism. The guidelines of that cult—not, perhaps, articulated by the inner circle of initiates, who were kept too busy confecting their *mots* and their neck linen— have been minutely scrutinized in literature by a series of Romantic, perfectionist outsiders. Baudelaire was one, and he saw the dandy as the disciple of a religion the severity of whose standards was an excellent discipline for the soul. For him, the dandy represented the "best kind of human pride . . . the urge to fight and destroy triviality." If the poet could have foreseen the enrollment of a woman in the ranks of the sublimely haughty souls he admired, he might have recognized in Bianca Jagger a fine alliance of the material, the artistic, and even the spiritual. She appears to be using her beauty and the garments with which she enhances it as the material from which to create a work of art. That even her most triumphant effect must be ephemeral—a unique combination of dress, light, and the evening's particular mood in her eyes—makes the undertaking superbly dandylike. The fleetingness of perfection means that it must be tirelessly sought and replenished. This is a lonely task, calling for dedication. Bianca wears a suitable air of high seriousness and of a self-sufficiency that verges on aloofness. And while she seems to enjoy admiration, she also seems at pains, dandylike, to disdain it. (Brummel put down a young buck who ventured a compliment at Ascot, re- minding him of first principles with the famous reply "I can- not be elegant, since you have noticed me.") Bianca invariably turns her loveliness to the camera lens with exquisite and regal detachment, only parting her unsmiling lips a little and widen- ing her long, dark eyes.

And yet, beneath the dandy's chilly façade, tradition has it, there beats a stormy, yearning heart. Beneath Bianca's ele- gance one senses at least a current of restlessness. Some of this, perhaps, is by association with her husband, who is Unrest Incarnate. A modicum of recklessness is the necessary electricity of style, and this quality leads, from time to time, to awkward flops and phoniness. Another photograph, taken at another party in New York, shows Bianca in a short-skirted, girlish dress whose cutaway back emphasizes her pitifully thin ribs, and jars oddly with the ever-present cane. A musty, feathered hat tops out the whole effect, which is of a drowned kitten with a dead bird on its head. A mess, in short, but still not a bore. For style must never allow itself to be a bore, and reserves its most virulent contempt for anyone who is. The disciple of style must be on constant guard, with claws of mockery sharp, against the inroads of Babbitt. This watchfulness prompted Bianca, on the night of her drowned-kitten party, to express disapproval of its site, which was "21." "They won't let you in this joint unless you wear a mink coat," *Women's Wear* sorrowfully recorded that she growled. "I hate it here." Hearing this, one might be led to wonder why Bianca Jagger, with her youth, grace, freedom, wealth, and fame, would take the trouble to make coarse denunciations of puffy, sedentary, sheeplike middle age at play. But it is because she dances on the coals of style that she must keep leaping up and sniping at complacency. The slightest softening, or a tilt in the direction of coziness or caution, could cause the death of style. The ways style finds to keep its precarious balance are often childish in the extreme. A certain childishness is deliberately courted, indeed, and incorporated in the philosophy of style; the absolute loves and hatreds of childhood are convenient judgments for the woman or man of style, because they avoid the misty middlelands of compromise and do not invite discussion. And stylish people, even if they have to force themselves, are determined to see the world in childishly bright colors. Impulse is to them the noblest guide in life, and when they are tempted to give way to weariness they must prod themselves into impulsive acts. Style rides as roughshod over party-poopers and quibblers as a fox hunt crashes through a farmer's fences. Stendhal added further chapters to the chronicle of stylishness with his praise of the impulsive élite. From his seat among his "Happy Few" aristocrats of the heart, he heaped scorn on the "desiccated souls" outside the circle. His standards were so stringent that even Byron, Romanticism's greatest, most impulsive prince and no mean dandy, proved too conventional, too much a prey to a "puerile fear of appearing ridiculous," for the Frenchman's taste. Style takes an undergraduate delight in a world divided into amusing categories—"lights and heavies," "sillies and stupids," and other variations on the theme of "us" and "them"—that represent deadly serious reflections. And it also takes pleasure in turning bourgeois morality inside out. "Spontaneous" is style's substitute for "good," and "boring" that for "bad." A touch of outrageousness, far from being shameful, is considered by style to be a moral obligation. When, after her return to Europe, Bianca Jagger lunched at Maxim's with twirling black mustaches painted on her cheeks, *Women's Wear* noted it with a squirming reproof, but she was only obeying the laws that govern her kind.

It is in definitions of vulgarity that the realms of style and taste diverge most widely. The word "vulgarity" itself is heard less often on the lips of style than it is from the mealier mouth of taste, but the concept of vulgarity is fundamental to doctrines of style. For style, vulgarity is meanness, calculation, petty-mindedness, and the base fear of going out on a limb. For taste, by contrast, vulgarity is "loudness," unseemliness, and anything that goes too far. To protect itself against the boring grown-up world, style is given to assuming an aspect of childlike purity. Bianca Jagger, in spite of the knowing sensuality of her face, wears this stylish cloak of innocence as though she had the key to a secret garden to which at any moment she might return. As one observes either of the Jaggers, questions of morality and even of theology spring into the head as they never would at the sight, of, say, Mrs. William Paley or other Best-Dressed Humans. Seeing Mick Jagger perform, you find yourself juggling, like any medieval churchman, with ideas such as demonism, possession by spirits, and satanic temptation. You might have thought that Dandyism's long flirtation with black magic would be over by now and that Dorian Gray and Huysmans's Des Esseintes were the end of a line. But Mick Jagger came along and, for a generation largely uninterested in religion and morality, breathed life into such archaisms as amorality and blasphemy.

But men and women of style needn't stray as far as the Jaggers do from the crowd for it to get wind of a difference and to loathe them. The giant forces of intolerance and conformity like to roll along unopposed and at their own pace, and they are maddened by unconventional gadflies and fore-runners. The fashions that become generally acceptable are those whose support proves too strong to be denied, and this support compels society to widen its rules sooner than risk anarchy by seeing them broken. So long hair and miniskirts, once decried as offenses to decency and even patriotism, gradually become normal in conservative rural communities. It is persistent individuality and unwillingness to be absorbed that go on being suspect. The climate is particularly uncongenial to rebels at the moment, since the world is resting up after the adventurous years of the sixties. Many of the freedoms that had crept into dress in those years have been judiciously purged. The fashion industry—both male and female divisions—in brushing aside the charades and cultivated childishness of style set out to reestablish confidence in the familiar, grown-up rules. (When the dust of confusion cleared, it turned out that some conventions had been modi-fied, and women had changed from skirts to trousers.) In-novators and nonconformists were firmly pushed out in the cold. Penitent dress designers confessed to the sin of neglect-ing the Average Woman, and stores whisked offensively unusual styles from her sight. These self-recriminations, like all arguments which hold that an informed and literate major-ity is the helpless victim of an élitist conspiracy, were fake. In American fashion, the majority has always been more powerful than the minority, and it has never been coerced by anyone. It was simply that the very idea of stylishness in-furiated good taste, and an atmosphere tainted by adventure was not one in which the middle-aged and the middle-class could relax and spend money. In fact, very few people ever strayed from the code of convention. Most men of taste went on wearing the kind of coat they wore when their standards jelled, and most women of taste went on wearing the kind of clothes worn by other women of the same social standing. Any fashion involved in their choice was passive. When the fashion industry hastily threw in its lot with the masses, who had begun to question its loyalty, it was simply reaffirming its ties with business rather than with art. There are very few successful dress designers who have a sense of style; it doesn't pay.

Tempting as it is to consign fashion in one lump to convention's camp and to leave style and art, with all their rough edges intact, outside it, democratic fashion must infringe on the aristocratic style that Bianca Jagger exemplifies. Her style works by exploiting, adapting, and anticipating the trends that course in broad, slow movements through the mass of the people. Being based on youth, beauty, and fashion, Bianca's version is perhaps the purest of all styles. Other varieties, based on talent, eccentricity, and agelessness—those of Louise Nevelson, say, or the late Dame Edith Sitwell—are subsidiary. And mature style without talent to keep goading it into ambitious undertakings rapidly hardens into the relatively sterile quality of timeless elegance. There is a cult of luxurious simplicity that is often mistaken for style, but this is only a sophisticated level of good taste. The woman who extolls perfectly plain white silk shirts and perfectly plain black cashmere pants and who expresses utter loathing for frills and ruffles almost never has real style. Her kind of simplicity is costly, and it is usually timid. Although it seems arrogant, her dedication to monochrome unfussiness is inspired by fear.

Fear also strikes the "liberated" woman, in her noncommittal, Everywoman garb of black turtleneck and pants by day and shapeless long T-shirt by night. Any more venturesome adornment of her person makes it look as though she were relying on traditional symbols of her femininity instead of exploring the newly possible outlets for her "creatvity." And yet, in this thicket of enemies old and new, style keeps on sprouting. It doesn't depend on sex, politics, or the state of the stock market. Like brilliant conversation, it is ephemeral, freak-ish, and subject to imitation by inferiors. But the flight of style's comet still lifts the heart.

Balenciaga

The Balenciaga clothes currently on display at the Metropolitan Museum of Art are as awe-inspiring as the dinosaurs across the Park at the Museum of Natural History—and as extinct. They form a perfect study in the Darwinism of style. Many of the shapes in the exhibition seem very queer to us, but perhaps not as queer as the lost environment to which they give clues. The Spanish couturier Cristobal Balenciaga retired in 1968. For the two decades after the war, he was a giant influence in Paris fashion; after the death of Dior, in 1957, he was its undisputed monarch. His greatest contribution to the morphology of woman is his definitive abolition—by means of the barrel-shaped coat and the tent, the semifitted suit, and variations on the sack dress—of the corseted wasp waist. Of all the couturiers still functioning in the mid-sixties, only he and Chanel refused to build the empires of subsidiary ready-to-wear—the franchises and treaties with department stores by which the prestige of couture is now shored up. Some months before he died last year he observed, sadly, in an interview that the gracious life that had supported couture was gone, and that real couture had become an impossible luxury.

The present exhibition is a forceful reminder of the speed with which fashion has moved since Balenciaga's reign. Even if one sets the dividing line between the old world and the new earlier than 1968—allowing for the fact that Balenciaga's work had largely ceased to evolve some years before, and for

the emergence of Quant and Courrèges in the early sixties—
it must still be acknowledged that the tides of fashion were
completely reversed in the space of a handful of years. By the
end of the sixties, youth dominated fashion, and democracy
had come to it, with its attendant choice or confusion, depending on your point of view. Balenciaga's designs are those
of an authority, aimed at mature women with a distinct position in the world. The couture, from the time of Worth,
master of the crinoline, had never concerned itself with un-
married girls; neither did Balenciaga. Because, despite his acceptance of such novelties as boots, "chic" raincoats, and
trousers, he was rooted in the traditions of the couture. He
believed that within his realm he had an obligation to provide
leadership. He would not have grasped, any more than would
Poiret, in the nineteen-hundreds, the idea that a new generation of ready-to-wear designers—the closest thing we now have
to fashion leadership—would take pride in interpreting the
often contradictory inclinations of the masses rather than in
commanding a receptive élite. The idea of couture depended
on a structured society with a privileged few people worth
emulating. The nature of this élite often changed, depending
on the kinds of government in Europe and on their relation to
America. And the role of the couturier changed, too. Worth
thought of himself as a tradesman, and could never have been
invited to the glittering Second Empire receptions for which
he provided every gown worth looking at. At the peak of his
career, Balenciaga stood at the top of a pyramidal fashion
structure that now seems as alien as a feudal court. Beneath
him stood the slightly fuzzier couture talents. Beneath these,
in an order determined by the modernity and/or nationality
of the observer, were ranged the patrons who could pass for
leaders of society (precedence was given here to those with the
dash to be leaders of fashion, too) and the warring baron-
esses—the more or less "legendary" female editors of the
powerful "glossies." In spite of Balenciaga's contempt for his
publicists—he often banned even slightly critical journalists
from his collections, which he put on at deliberately in-

convenient times—his fate was inextricably enmeshed with fashion journalism, which was at its most powerful in the postwar years. The techniques of fashion photography were at their most sophisticated, publicity was not yet moving at a speed that human beings could not control, and the avid curiosity of the public was as yet untainted by rebellion against the iron will of commerce that was behind the velvety purrings of tirelessly enthusiastic prose. It was Carmel Snow, of *Harper's Bazaar,* who first took up the newly launched Balenciaga, and it has fallen to Diana Vreeland, former editor of *Vogue,* and probably the last fashion editor to cultivate the "legendary" manner, to organize the present posthumous tribute in her new job, with the Metropolitan Museum's Costume Institute. The authority of the glossy magazines was vested in them by business. In the context of the Paris couture, this meant the stores and the firms of copyists who came from America to carry off the *toiles* that would serve as patterns for custom-made reproductions for the benefit of wealthy women who couldn't get to Paris. Women who couldn't afford the custom-made models bought off-the-rack copies in department stores, and so on down through the wrong end of the telescope to the base of the fashion pyramid, where a lot of ordinary girls dreamed of marrying a prince, as Grace Kelly had, and so getting to wear Balenciaga clothes. This trickling down from Paris constituted Fashion; there wasn't any other kind. When Europe was cut off, during the Second World War, and while Parisiennes were cycling around in hats made from wood shavings, American designers got along on their own remarkably well. But once the war was over, the combination of verve, good public relations, and general Europeanness of Paris couture again proved as irresistible to wealthy American women as it had in the time of Edith Wharton and Henry James. A Victorian fashion writer remarked that if the campaign for "rational dress" had been led by a respectable member of the British aristocracy instead of this dubious *American* called Amelia Bloomer, the whole scheme might have stood a chance of catching on. The belief that nothing good in fashion could ever come out of America was so prevalent among American couturiers that it was not until the nineteen-sixties that they began to hold their heads high. By then, unfortunately, all couture was doomed.

The exhibition reminds us how thoroughly fashion has devoted itself, since the miniskirt, to the semblance of youth. It is not that the Balenciaga clothes could never be worn by young women but, rather, that they could clearly be worn with great distinction by those who were no longer young. This failure to exclude middle age is today a striking and unfamiliar quality. Here are clothes for women with hips and bosoms, even the odd bulge or two. ("M. Balenciaga *likes* a little stomach," one of his fitters said.) Many of his inventions distinctly benefited the older woman. Waistlessness was flattering to her, as was the blouse-back sheath, which concealed the lower back, whose curve is attractive only in the very young. Balenciaga's way of setting the neckline away from the neck and shortening the sleeves to three-quarter length led the eye to the back of the neck and to the curve of the wrist, both of which can be quite as graceful at sixty as at sixteen. This paring away of cloth also gave room for pearls and bracelets; his was an age in which rich women wore costly jewels without embarrassment. It was an age of hats, gloves, and perfect grooming, a time for the mature and womanly woman. When we now see photographs of the mannequins of the fifties, with their French twists, heavy brows, and precise lipstick, we marvel at the way they seem to have striven to look twenty years older than they really were. "Younger Set" departments in stores specialized in young women's clothes that differed from those of their mothers only in that they avoided assertiveness and authority—attributes then thought to be inseparable from elegance and incompatible with youth. Balenciaga's clothes have a structure that is often more significant than the body they cover, and a dignity that could make up for any that might be lacking in a stocky dowager with a pouter-pigeon chest.

The relation between clothes and the figure in Balenciaga's world goes very far toward being the exact opposite of the contemporary ideal. Today's unstructured styles depend not only for their best effect but for any effect at all on the kind of perfect, youthful body that looks terrific in a bikini. The success of Halston's soft sportswear and diaphanous caftans shows how far the emphasis of luxurious dress has shifted, for his expensive, effortless styles are intended to be subsidiary to the even greater luxury of the meticulously tended body beneath. Balenciaga's clothes, by contrast, have distinct forms in their own right, and are often made in what now seem stiff fabrics, such as his favorite, silk gazar, which has the weight of fine cardboard. He was the last representative of a traditional couture that believed in a freedom of invention more or less unfettered by the lumpy forms that nature has lumbered women with. His right to ignore or play up any part of the anatomy was unchallenged. Behind him we can look down the mirrored halls of Couture Past and see a procession of women variously hobbled, S-shaped, flat-bosomed, square-shouldered, or fiddle-shaped, according to fashion, by which each of them is held in thrall. Aside from Balenciaga's own sack, the years spanned by his career saw the New Look, the H-line, the Y- and A-shapes, the trapeze, and the matchbox—before the advent of the mini, trousers, and the midi. These last three represent the decline of the couture, because they all came from the people previously at the bottom of the fashion pyramid—the young and unestablished, a group still referred to by the old-guard couture faithfuls, with an ancien-régime contempt, as "the Street." There are a couple of Balenciaga minis in the exhibition, including a strapless gray organza number that hits four or five inches above the knee, but this is insubstantial, like an epic poem written in invisible ink.

Balenciaga's talents were contemporaneous with a less earthbound school; and his clothes were most successful when he felt free to sculpt and drape as he was moved. His strong, independent shapes almost never look contorted, and his tunics, chemises, and sack dresses are finely proportioned. (They are particularly effective in black.) His turtle-backed dress, with its great swoop of gathered fabric from nape to half-belt, is a marvelous study in line, like his one-seam coat and his coat with puppy-skin folds at arms and shoulders. A couple of examples of the classic semi-fitted suit, with jacket vaguely snug in front and vaguely convex in back, are included in the show, but these have been so widely imitated—virtually every woman of the right generation has worn some version of it, and its popularity is unabated among the patrons of the fustier kind of Madison Avenue specialty shop—that the originals have lost their vitality.

Balenciaga's daytime shapes may have had a more lasting effect on women's wardrobes throughout the world, but it is in evening clothes—to which the show gives greater prominence —that we see his inspired sense of line soaring unrestrained through all the shapes of nature and history. Here, once more, we are reminded of a different fashion planet—a place of galas, tiaras, and twelve-button gloves, inhabited by a race of women who had not yet learned to think social substance an enemy of fantasy. Some of the dresses on display more closely resemble events or experiences than garments. There is, for one, a short black taffeta dress with the kind of utterly guileless top—in this case, bateau-necked and kimono-sleeved, but more often strapless—that is almost always, in Balenciaga's evening gowns, a prelude to the zaniest kind of carrying-on in the skirt. Its skirt is sculpted in an astounding way into the shape of a spinning top, and formed from row upon row of pinked ruffles, so that the legs would seem to grow out of its heart, like stamens from a black chrysanthemum. To contemplate this dress is to feel an irresistibly mounting gaiety, and finally the viewer is impelled to utter a sort of snort expressing satisfaction in a world that had seen the birth of such a piece of work.

Some of the shapes demand considerable adjustment of an eye accustomed to the sight of blue jeans. The harem skirt of the early nineteen-fifties qualifies as such a shape, and certainly as one of the most extraordinary fashions of all time. How did one sit in these bloomer-hemmed balloons, which look like giant puffballs that have settled around the legs?

There is a knee-length version in the show, and one whose puff is formed by a detachable balloon skirt, which doesn't advance it much in practicality. And then a third compounds its eccentricity by reason of the split-level hemline to which Balenciaga was tirelessly drawn. Many of his skirts are knee-high in front and anywhere from ankle-length to a full-blown train in back. It has been said that Balenciaga's passion for the undulating hem led to the evolution of the model's backward-slanting walk. At any rate, like surprisingly many of his fancies, the hem made sense: the feet, after all, point forward, and in the fifties feet were particularly pointy and apt to get trapped in hems. The notion had come up before—in the period of transition between the short skirts of the twenties and the longer skirts of the thirties—but it was the Spaniard, with his memories of the flamenco skirt, who made it his own. The influence of the designer's native land would be unmistakable even if the visitor were not primed by the exhibition's piped-in click of castanets and by the presence on the walls of masterpieces of Spanish art. There is a group of tight little velvet jackets, embroidered and trimmed with jet, that owe much to the matador's traditional suit of lights. There are dresses with the characteristic east-to-west farthingale of Velázquez's Infanta, and there are the magnificent black lace dresses that take their cue from Goya's *majas*. But in his admiration for, and flattery of, the back of the neck, Balenciaga was positively Japanese. The pair of great curved evening capes that flank the entrance to the show—one of rows of ruffled black lace, the other of bois-de-rose ribbed satin—take their inspiration from the costumes of the Kabuki theatre. Then there are velvet evening coats with gathered backs and barreling, overstuffed sleeves, for all the world like a Renaissance chamberlain's, and a taffeta gown with something closely akin to the bustle of a *fin de siècle* "stunner." The harem skirt after all, had had a vogue under Marie Antoinette, as had what was then the "sacque" back, which came to be known as "Watteau folds," because of the publicity given them by the eighteenth century's Avedon. It was largely left to Dior, in the postwar era, to recapture many of the crinolined effects recorded by the Empress Eugénie's pet artist, but Balenciaga went through his own Winterhalter phase just before the war. As it happens, though, the one example of his work of that time to be seen in the exhibition is a very simple strapless dress in white silk with a smudged gray Paisley print, dating from 1937; of this dress one could say with greater confidence than of any other on display that it would not go amiss this evening at dinner in New York.

When uppity young ready-to-wear designers pillage fashion archives, the process is dismissed as a nostalgia hangup; when the old-style couturiers dipped into the past, that was known as happy inspiration. Balenciaga was as unhampered in this by questions of expense or practicality—at least in his evening gowns—as were his ancestors in the couture, and so was better than his juniors at reinterpreting the past. It was as if the whole panoply of luxurious costume were his, a fief held by divine right, and he approached the past with confidence and dignity, not as a petitioner from a lower class snickering nervously behind his hand. He was heir to the ancient craft traditions that formed the bulwark of the French couture. He drew freely on the experience of the great French silk weavers, and we are reminded, in the exhibition's catalogue, of the old, romantic names of tulle, zibelline, bomazine, cloqué, matelassé, taffeta, broché, organza, marquisette, and point d'esprit, and of a time, before blends and synthetics, when a heroine could tell her maid to "lay out the bayleaf faille." He could command that the stuffs be dyed to any color in his mind's eye. (It must be said that some of his more vibrant visions jar a bit: American Beauty is now an alien hue. And some combinations of colors are very dated: lime and shocking pink in a print jostle each other unpleasantly, and we are baffled by the idea of softening a black dress with touches of baby pink.) Balenciaga inherited a mighty force of hand laborers skilled in the painstaking application of beads, paillettes, and pearls, and in working with fine lace. By now, economic necessity has caused a shift in attitudes, and most rich women are no longer willing to advertise their exploitation of a poorer woman's eyesight. But in many of the Balenciaga gowns trim still takes precedence over form, much as it did when the only fashion news concerned the way a crinoline would be decorated. There is a coat that is covered by separate ostrich feathers, each sewn on upside down, so that it wafts and quivers with every breath, and there is a strapless black dress thickly encrusted with black stones and bouncing jet beads so fragile that a score of them would be crushed each time the wearer sat down. Presumably, both these garments would be returned to the atelier the morning after a ball for the seamstresses to replace shed feathers and crushed beads against the next time. But alongside the more grandiose follies of trimming there are dresses in which, as in the modern style, shape has taken precedence over trim but into which the lingering old conventions—fussy, droopy bows, fastenings like ribbon bellpulls, and other extinct furbelows—still creep to mar the effect of stark and often revolutionary line.

Balenciaga was the last couturier for whom the old view of fashion continued to hold good. For him, fashion was a matter of cut, fabric, color, and line. It was also involved with the murkier concept of prestige, but it remained, at base, a question of women and their clothes. His work was not supposed to reflect the public mood or to tie in with fashions in movies or books. "We didn't talk about trends in those days, and there wasn't any *rush*," Diana Vreeland has said of the era of postwar fashion—a time she sometimes refers to as "the Great Adventure." This lack of rush, together with the self-sufficient, hermetic quality of the old kind of fashion, leads to a strange, floating chronology within Balenciaga's work. Broadly speaking, it is possible to say that the most startingly free inventions date from the fifties, when Balenciaga was an experimental young lion, rather than from the sixties, when he was an established old master. But the visitor to the exhibition is often fooled into thinking that a dress dates from, say, 1945 when it was in fact made in 1954 or 1967. The dress could perfectly well have been worn in any of those years, provided that there was still a marble staircase and some chandeliers. This lack of strict position in time has led to the claim that Balenciaga's clothes are timeless—the quality of timelessness was much admired by the old fashion school—and to an emphasis on their eternal, sculptural nature. Meanwhile, though, a newer school is joyfully discovering their historical context. Some of those who visit the exhibition are too young to have any interest in the names of the rich women who have lent the clothes, and too young to be made nervous by the shapes of the fifties. One of the ironies of the show is that it will certainly add fuel to a revival that has already gained enough momentum for the young ready-to-wear designers in Paris to be showing styles directly inspired by Balenciaga. The barely forgotten master is on the point of being fashionable once more.

Denim and the New Conservatives

For years, some people have been saying that blue jeans constitute the one fashion of any significance in America. But only of late have any really fashionable people begun to support the assertion. Unprecedented honor is being given to denim—whose support is already so widespread that a blue haze floats above the pavements of the world— by two distinct and fashionable élites who have established particular ways of wearing the uniform of the masses. The first group consists, broadly, of the middle-aged, the middle-class, and those who are still in revolt against the old sartorial rules but continue to be concerned with the way they dress. The second, and more exquisitely fashionable, group is slightly younger, though well out of its teens (the very young have no impact on fashion anymore), and its members long ago turned their backs on the idea of "fashionable" clothes. The first group continues to move vaguely toward self-expression; the second, and more evolved, group is in retreat from the flamboyance it courted some years ago. The first seeks out denim under the illusion that denim brings freedom; the second, more self-conscious, adopts denim precisely for its uniformity and as a purge.

The denim wearers of the first group remain within the orbit of the fashion industry, which has set off after them with renewed vigor—one of the most bizarre twists of the whole extraordinary saga of innocent little denim and the giant, Commerce. From the beginning, this story has been one of impossible contradictions and ironic twists. The huge numbers of people in blue jeans proved a source of great profit for the sort of big business many of those people professed to despise. And then shops discovered that they could make money not only by selling many inexpensive versions of blue jeans to a lot of these people but by selling a few costly versions; the fashion industry, spared the painful decision between catering to fickle trendsetters and to sheeplike followers, was able to trundle after both with piles of denim. In the past few years, the cult of denim has extended not just to Watkins Glen but to the salons of couturiers and to furriers who sheared mink and dyed it in the sacred hue. And some of the most expensive versions of the All-American denim theme have come bouncing into our stores from European manufacturers. The irresistible pull of both European fashion and denim means that American customers will pay large sums for, say, French blue jeans despite the galling knowledge that fashionable young people in Saint-Tropez are only imitating young people in America, a country that can and does produce better and cheaper blue jeans than France. Not the least of the ironies associated with denim and business is the question of recycling. It has always been the thing to own battered and faded blue jeans that got that way in the wearing rather than by bleaching and other ways of precipitating maturity. As a result, a pair of blue jeans now costs more when it is bought secondhand than a pair of blue jeans that has never been worn by anybody. A taste for intricate and fanciful embroideries and nailhead arrangements of cabalistic symbols worked by hand on those worn-out pants sometimes brings the price, for those who cannot find time to sew, to hundreds of dollars.

The litany of marvels that touch on the subject of denim is interminable, and much of it is familiar. What does seem new, though, this fall is the fervor with which "chic" women pursue blue jeans and their offshoots. One of the most curious derivatives of blue jeans, the skirt made of old blue jeans that have been opened in the crotch seams, had a considerable vogue this summer in the most expensive resorts. On Madison Avenue, one now sees rich women who continue to care passionately about the status value of their clothes staring coolly at their reflection in passing shop windows and at their well-cut, pressed, and embroidered denim outfits. Such women wear denim on days when they are not wearing silk, cashmere, and tweed, and no doubt they consider it an extension of the "classic" look advocated by the fashion press. This variety of denim enthusiast wears her jeans tight enough to show off a well-groomed figure. She is, in spite of her enthusiasm for what she takes to be the latest fad, a late bloomer in the denim world. Her approach to denim identifies it with the creaky notion of "throwaway chic," and it is a dated one. She is fashionable in her denim, but only in an old-fashioned way.

The other camp of denim wearers is more complex, and more disturbing. These people, who are probably much more in tune, with fashion—in the broadest sense—than anyone else, care so little for faddish finery and competitive display that they seem to prize utter sameness in dress. Their refined fashion sensibility is not immediately apparent, because their denim is, superficially, the humblest denim the world has seen since the stuff appeared only on the shelves of the general store. The denim style of the more sensitive enclaves of the Village, the West Side, and SoHo is the style of the purist and the neo-ascetic. Unlike the "chic" devotee of blue jeans, this loyalist often wears positively baggy denims, and scorns such travesties as embroideries and nailheads. To underline their association with honesty and toil, the denims of choice are often overalls. At best, among the denim-clad souls in this group, one sees a man who is distinguished from his fellows by the single gold ring in his ear, a girl with Brünnhilde braids on top of her head, or someone in a pair of overalls that has a set of drab patches at the knees. Theorists of blue jeans in the sixties claimed that one's individuality was made more apparent when it was contrasted with the sameness of denim, and that the malleable clay of blue jeans brought out the touching differences in human bodies. But in those days self-expression, in the form of headbands, beads, badges, and so forth, was still permissible. The new style eliminates virtually all such frivolities. The almost fanatical rejection of color and individualism in dress by those in our society—people in their twenties and thirties—to whom such things have generally meant the most is a further reminder of the passing of an era. The new, uncompromising denim uniform belongs to a post-war generation involved more with introspection and intimacy than with society at large. In the late sixties, blue jeans were to a degree an emblem of militancy, an indication that the wearer wanted to end the war and change the system; they are now to be seen as an expression of the urge to lie low and keep out of trouble.

This new style of denim wearing—what could be termed the totalitarian mode—might not make the casual observer feel that it has anything at all to do with fashion. In fact, though, the people you might see in rumpled overalls on a Saturday afternoon in SoHo, shuttling—like prisoners in a yard—among the fire escapes and gutted warehouses, are mostly very fashion-conscious. A negative reaction to clothes is part of a fashionable life style. If, in these most progressive circles of denim wearers, it is unfashionable to be "into" clothes, it *is* fashionable to be "into" good taste and the good life. The new denim fits into the world in which former members of S.D.S. take up the art of wok cuisine; in which décors involve stripped floors, stripped walls, and stripped oak iceboxes; in which restaurants painted chocolate brown have amplifying systems that pipe Beethoven cello sonatas and early Aznavour. Denim is valued as one of a number of textures—wicker, chromium, bare wood, brick, and Lucite among them—to which the most refined modern tastes are sensitive, and which are endowed with an almost religious significance. (Perhaps this unthinking veneration of surfaces and substances is related to the use of drugs.) Like other modern textures, denim is imbued with a moral value and is regarded as being both honest and true. It represents a return to first principles and mislaid paradises. But it deliberately does not pretend that it is a fashionable style of dress. The fact that in the new refinement of fashionable aestheticism there is a greater freedom in what people hang on their walls than there is in what goes on their backs is fresh evidence of how the torch of fashion has passed from Seventh Avenue to the art world.

Unlike couture customers in recycled denim, people with the real scent of fashion do not slip lightly into hypocrisy. In their world, sincerity is "in." They are, in theory, quick to spot fraud or exploitation; their materialism is nothing if not high-minded. But once the elements of this kind of fashion have established credentials for honesty, they are subject to no further scrutiny. The trouble with bulldozing all the old things and leaving the new, bare essentials is that weeds invade the wasteland which remains. Self-regulated conformists, unencumbered by the need for choice, forget how to choose and are thus in a vulnerable position. The clean slate the new blue denim typifies is irresistible to any dictator of taste who happens by and leaves his mark—be it camp, neon sculpture, or the color chocolate brown—on the package accepted by a docile crowd. Perhaps the wearing of nothing but denim by people who ought to know better will quite soon come to an end. Before it's too late, it would be good to see taste struggle out from under the uniformity of fashion and back into the jumble of civilized life.

1974

Biba:
Fantasy Emporium

The new Biba department store, in London, has deservedly been described as the most exciting store in the world, and it is also a place of multifarious ironies. One of them is that an establishment counted among the forerunners and scant survivors of the wave of trendy young boutiques of the sixties, and one of the most consistently influential, should choose to make its move to adult quarters now, just when older department stores have nearly worn themselves out dividing up their acreage into imitation boutiques. Barbara Hulanicki and her husband, Stephen Fitz-Simon, the creators of Biba, opened their first little shop nearly ten years ago, and with it set in motion revolutionary changes in the way shops and girls—then, in time, men, children, and houses— looked, both in Britain and the whole world. Among these changes were semi-darkness and near-deafening music in shops; a new appreciation of such "muddy" colors as mauve, black, brown, puce, rose, purple, blue-gray, gray, and rust; and the spread of these "Biba colors" to unexpected surfaces—through cosmetics to eyelids, lips, and fingernails, and through paints and paper to the walls of bathrooms and bed-sitting rooms. The staidest provincial living rooms in England are hung with mushroom-shaped, Biba-Edwardian lampshades in naughty satins and velvets that drip with shivering fringe like lanterns in a gypsy fortuneteller's booth. Virtually single-handedly,

Biba kept the idea of hats alive for the young and put every-body into boots. The Biba Look and derivations of it gave much to the Pre-Raphaelite air that marked British fashion so strongly in the late sixties. And the style of the old Biba shops —with a wealth of peacock feathers, potted palms in brass spittoons, and neoecclesiastical wood paneling—played a great part in the wide popularization both of Victorian clutter and of Art Nouveau curves. With its latest move, and without entirely shedding its allegiance to the combination of music hall and mosque that made its name, Biba has progressed enough in time to encompass the nineteen-twenties and thirties, and is now proceeding to open unprecedented numbers of eyes to the joys of all things Art Deco.

The new Biba also performs the valuable service of raising fundamental questions about what a department store should be. Is it not, as a public place, a unique synthesis of promenade, living theatre, gallery, and classroom of taste as well as marketplace? Why is it, when all this vitality is possible, that so many of the department stores everywhere are so wretchedly dull? Most establishments give more thought to things in stock than to people passing through, and feel that the role of management is catering to the most timid common denom-inator of taste. With a predictable banality not unmixed with envy, department store minds more conventional than those at Biba have sneered at its elaborately fanciful décor and the spaciousness of its marble halls, claiming that only the cus-tomary counters laden with goods can bring profits, and that generous aisles are wasted space. The Fitz-Simons positively relish this tedious criticism, and have long been pleased to swim against the mercantile tide. They believe that people quite as much as the things they might buy attract other peo-ple to stores, and that a lively, congenial crowd—a group well disposed, incidentally, to spending money—will be drawn to an amusing and even controversial setting. The belief in the significance of people is such in the new Biba that the space next to the ground-floor windows—a part of the building that would generally be dedicated to displays of goods intended to serve as "magnets" to passers-by—is given over to the comfort of customers who have already committed themselves to Biba's portals, and who are encouraged to wait for friends or read their newspaper on a sofa from a nineteen-twenties Pullman car in the shade of a potted palm. In a more mature exchange between management and customer than is usual, both parties at Biba contribute more to the experience of shopping, and they expect more of each other. The shop lays its own lively, eccentric, fantastical, and sometimes even disturbing taste on the line, and makes unmistakable demands on the customer's judgment and emotions. The décor—particularly on the main floor and in the Rainbow Room restaurant—takes a lot of living up to. The vivid images of Busby Berkeley's sequined choruses fanning out kaleidoscopically from behind Biba's mirrored islands of display, or of Fred Astaire and Miss Rogers whirling down the aisles, conjured up by normally pedestrian journalists at the opening of the new Biba attest to its stimulus. To some early visitors to the store, though, it seemed a disagreeable, vaguely threatening stimulus. "Everything looks like an imitation of something," one shopper complained. "It's like a theatrical set with nobody to watch the performance." Controversy is not often associated with department stores, but Fitz-Simon enjoys it. In an invigorating reversal of the anxious ecumenicalism of most department stores, he has said, "Unless we have a large number of people hating us, we can't get people to love us."

The new Biba is to be found in seven-story department store premises in Kensington High Street designed for Derry & Toms, the previous occupant, in 1932. The building originated, then, in an epoch when the idea of modernity held a romantic appeal for decorative artists, and when the stylized system of artistic themes expressive of faith in the future showed up in shop design as well as in every other branch of the arts. And in shops, as elsewhere, those themes were carried out with all the benefits of now defunct craftsmanship and luxurious materials. *Building* of May 1933 said of the original store: "If we required proof that woman has at last entered her heritage, we should have it in the new store of Derry & Toms at Kensington. It is a monument to her emancipation and a tribute to her influence."

To the Fitz-Simons and to Steve Thomas and Tim Whitmore, the two designers who collaborated with them on the work of conversion—none of them out of their thirties, and all young enough to have artistic sensibilities more tuned to the past than to the future—any traces of the optimism of the building's origin and whatever grace remained to it after years of indifference were touching and exhilarating. In recent years, Derry & Toms, its customers, and the world had deteriorated sadly from the happy state so comfortably discerned by the gentleman from *Building*. By the time it closed its doors, Derry & Toms was reduced to sorely faded glory. Dowdy merchandise, largely ignored by saleswomen and customers alike, lay jumbled around. A stale smell of fish-and-chips clung to the restaurants on the upper floors, where elderly waitresses trudged past with tea-time buns for silent couples in damp mackintoshes. But some part, at least, of the delight in the new, supremely fashionable Biba must derive from contrast with the old, superlatively seedy Derry's. For to the designers of Biba, as to the whole generation who grew up after the war in Britain, faded glory is fertile loam. When they moved into their new home, the Biba team lovingly restored the most distinguished Art Deco of the building. And then they went a stage further and gave it exuberant, exaggerated new life.

The Rainbow Room restaurant, on the fifth floor of the Derry & Toms building (to allot precedence to the focus of Biba sociability), has long been acknowledged by experts to be a gem of period architecture in a class with such masterpieces as the Chrysler Building and Radio City Music Hall. Biba's crew first stripped off layers of ugly paint, whose muddiness was more army surplus than Biba-like, and repainted in a gently retrospective peach the room's meticulous curves and finely engineered proportions. An oval ceiling rests on oval columns smooth as eggs, and rises in progressively narrower tiers above the heads of the diners, so that they seem to be sitting inside a porcelain jelly mold. Or, rather, to employ

an image almost certainly intended by the architect, who was
of an era with a passion for streamlining in all forms, from
airplanes to borzois, the diners seem to be looking up, with a
buckled, hall-of-mirrors perspective, at the pale, stepped decks
of an ocean liner. As if the artist had not thoroughly established himself to be a modern-minded man with this reference
to Cunarders, he threw in the rainbow. Concealed strips of
neon lighting—then in its infancy, and viewed as an artistic
medium of dignified potential—in the colors of the spectrum
light up each tier of the roof in bands of pale, viscous fire. To
all of this found grandeur the Biba people joined their own,
more whimsical pomp. They took thousands of yards of pale-
peach cut velvet—one of the many exquisite revivals of Art
Deco textile patterns commissioned for the new store—and
recovered the room's original dining chairs, new banquettes,
and plumply curving sofas, where, among more jungle palms
and chromium ashtrays on pedestals, a chap can while away
the moments when his sugar keeps him waiting. The newcomers installed sparkling lengths of bar counter, in peach
mirror glass pieced together like the prismatic spheres that
twirl above dance floors, and trained a bartender in the mysteries of the *Savoy Cocktail Book*. Then came the girl in fishnet tights, with her tray of cigarettes; a white grand piano of
enormous length, and Sunday-afternoon tea dances; and an
army of ebonized lamps shaped like naked nymphs on tiptoe,
with globes of light at the end of yearning, outstretched arms.
The bank of lifts, another of the distinctive original features
of the building, was given the same enthusiastic restoration as
the Rainbow Room. The new owners replaced chipped and
missing bits in the bronze trelliswork on the glass doors and
in the fine woodwork of the interiors, then polished up the
bronze panels above them—splendid pieces in the style of
Edgar Brandt's ironwork, with a quintessentially Deco relief
of stylized fountains, soaring birds as stiff as rockets, and spiky,
leaping gazelles. And then the lift attendants were dressed up
in funny-colored satin shirts, with bow ties so hugely wide
that one expects them to start whizzing into propeller motion,
like prank-shop neckwear. Some of the lift boys even cry out

"Gayohing ahop" with the authentically swooping, Etonian-cockney diphthongs of the prewar Jeevesian school.

One reviewer characterized the process of transformation that went into the new Biba as "turning an Art Deco master-work into a masterpiece of Art Deco pastiche," but Biba's most irrepressible Art Deco pastiches are in fact not imposed on the restored "masterwork" of the Rainbow Room but created from scratch on the ground floor, where little of the original gran-deur remained and all the majesty is Biba's own. It was Biba who installed the sumptuous marble floor in the color of pastel mink, and smooth enough to skate on. At generous intervals in this satiny sea, in the subdued, sepia light to which Biba would have remained faithful even without the present curtailment of power, there loom those islands of display, many of them Art Deco in inspiration. Above a counter selling hat veils, hatpins, embroidered gauntlets, brocade umbrellas, and other singularly Bibaesque trinkets, a ceiling-high, fan-shaped structure of tinted mirror glass lends its imperious facets to the many yards of sparkling images of itself that Biba offers at each turn. A second giant chunky crescent shape in glass, this time in awning tones of white and emerald, holds sway over a flower stall with gaudy banks of real and artificial flowers. A Cubist-patterned carpet runs right up over the counter in the shoe department, much of whose stock still looks made for pert little moppets out of Norman Rockwell covers playing dressing-up games in Mommy's closet. The same Cubist rug clothes the bookstall—a raised nook with maple carpentry and a very *raffiné* selection of works about obscure movies and Japanese screens, and Peter Cheyney in hardback. This corner, a studied reproduction of a private library in the Aldous Huxley years, is described by the Biba team, whose sense of this kind of distinction is keen, as a *deliberate* pastiche. On the ground floor, as on all the others, man-high black loudspeakers, built like nineteen-thirties radios—sometimes even shaped like Aztec temples, with zigzag lightning flashes across their grilles—feed into the air an even burble of music in a furiously eclectic choice from every decade in living memory. (Perhaps with special emphasis on the palmy days of early rock 'n' roll, when Elvis could drive them wild just by swiveling his knees in baggy trousers as he sang of diamond rings, kisses, and junior prom infidelities.)

The second floor houses women's clothes, and, as perhaps befits the center of Biba's world, it is fairly straightforward in its décor; or, at least, with its penumbral reaches, dotted by bentwood hatstands hung with hats and clothes, it is familiar to fans of earlier, smaller Biba shops. Biba clothes are designed by Miss Hulanicki—now with some assistance—and they have had an enormous influence on fashion in the past decade. Like much about Biba, they are to be loved or hated, but they are unique. Over the years, they have been fairly consistent in shape—high of armhole, birdlike of chest, often wide of shoulder pad, and often with long skirts that give play to such typically soft materials as crêpe and jersey—and in their inimitable mood, which combines a tongue-in-cheek romanticism, whacky "glamour," and the innocence of a Mabel Lucie Attwell illustration. All this in Biba colors, with shifting hints of the thirties, forties, or fifties, and at prices well within the range of girls in their teens and twenties, who form the core of Biba's support. The same distinctive Biba cut, hue, and tone show up in clothes for men, boys, pregnant women, infants, and Lolitas of ten to fourteen, on other floors that abound in witticisms of display. The men's floor is enlivened by such Jazz Age impedimenta as monocles, hair pomade, ankle-length coats of fake raccoon, and top hats; by a bowling alley; and by a boisterously tasteless corner, dubbed The Mistress Room, where an array of erotic female underwear is draped around a leopard-covered bed. A playground atmosphere prevails on the children's floor, where there is a Wild West saloon, a moated castle, a merry-go-round, a snack bar with toadstools to sit on, all scaled down to make children feel at home, and a maternity department with outsize furniture, to make pregnant women feel small. The basement food hall is also a playground of a kind, but a more successful creation because it is designed by adults for adults, and so without the overtones of coyness and patronage that mar the children's floor. Belowstairs, a tall black unit with shelves of crispbreads and grapefruit juice rises in slender reproof beside its shorter, dumpy neighbor, whose shelves groan with pasta and other fattening foods. (Charles Rennie Mackintosh beside Antoni Gaudí, one observer remarked.) The food displayed is made doubly appetizing by the briskness of the setting's wit. The fish counter is in a fishing boat, the wine in a stony cellar like something from an opera set; tinned foods are on shelves inside ten-foot tins, including a familiar red soup tin labeled "Warhol's Condensed." The dog food is on shelves inside a monstrous, crouching replica of the Fitz-Simons' Great Dane.

All of Biba is an exploration of the idea of a department store as entertainment, but it falls to the household floor in particular to investigate the meaning of taste. Not for nothing has this floor been likened to Mae West's broom closet: there is an almost overwhelming gusto in the way it presents what might seem to the uninitiated to be the most abysmal taste. But nothing here should be taken at face value. The onion layers of Biba sensibility are at their densest in this assemblage of household things that have caught the highly evolved, highly idiosyncratic fancy of Miss Hulanicki, whose own taste is especially visible on this floor. Objects have significance beyond mere appearance or convention. Satin sheets, tinfoil wallpaper, ostrich feathers, and all the other tinsel comforts that the Biba follower may dwell on at home as she drinks her cocoa by the gas fire of a shared and drafty flat have special value as the accessories of make-believe. Into Biba's choice of won-at-the-fun-fair china in gawky floral patterns or glassware straight from the years of postwar rationing there goes a quasi-maternal satisfaction at the rescue of such hitherto unloved, unwanted stuff from certain neglect. An ebullient and passionate enthusiasm for burlesque marks to some extent the choice of each object, and rules completely in the "kitsch rooms," which take their place alongside only slightly more orthodox room sets. In these shrines to camp, some of the more uproariously ghastly household gods of the world beyond the pale of Biba taste—pictures of poodles in 3-D or of the Queen in coronation dress, or clothes brushes shaped like guitars and ice-cube makers shaped like naked women—are set up to be picked off, more to amuse the crowd and keep them on their toes than for profit. The kitsch rooms also serve to remind those who need reminding after making their way through the rest of Biba that every taste in the world is relative. But then, Biba is an accomplished and flexible juggler of shifting contradictions. At its most impassioned it is somehow most puckish, at its most retrospective most modern, and at its most sophisticated most naive. And it is the only department store in the world daring enough to offer us life, spoof, and romance, too.

Recession
Dressing

Call it inflation, recession, or simply jitters, there is something in the economic air these days that is making women think hard before spending money on clothes. The old interest in the cautious principle of spending more on fewer clothes of better quality is back. Unfortunately, though, quality is more elusive than ever for those of middling means. The dwindling supply of skilled labor in the fashion industry and astronomical increases in the cost of cloth mean that an investment which seemed only recently to guarantee quality now insures progressively inferior goods. It is a reflection of this and other dismal dilemmas of those who cater to the middle ground that among all the designers who presented collections in recent months—collections conceived under the full onslaught of economic anxiety about energy—the surest voices in America came from the two extremes marked by James Galanos, who lives by the most costly high fashion, and Clovis Ruffin, who produces some of the least expensive designs.

Alongside the current renaissance of the ideal of high quality in the puffs and downdrafts of the Western World economy there is also a growing pride among the privileged few who know that they alone hold the key to high quality— hard cash. (One indication of this surge of Money Pride is the breathlessness with which the peregrinations of jet setters

and their gigolos to ostentatious parties are being chronicled
again.) Wherever luxurious clothes continue to exist, they can
be sure of support from rich people whom the times are making
richer as well as from those whom the times make insecure
enough to prompt them to show visible proof of their wealth.
Even rich young girls, it seems, are shedding their blue jeans
and their scruples about extravagance and discovering the
couture. The Paris couture, which bloomed all through the
Depression and the rise of Hitler, is looking less nervous this
season than it has for years. With a sigh of relief, it has let its
Maoist work clothes and other dabblings with the unsettling
present go hang and is lining up with Beauty and the Idle
Rich. With a studiously complacent languor, it is reproducing
the sort of thing it made so exquisitely in the nineteen-thirties
(which comes now from Saint Laurent and Dior) or the confident years on either side of 1960 (at Givenchy and Patou).
America's closest approach to the Paris couture, James Galanos,
is feeling quite smug about the market for his two-thousand-
dollar dresses, too. The California designer—virtually the sole
survivor of a whole group that flourished around the Hollywood lovelies of the nineteen-fifties—recently presented his
enormous summer collection at Bonwit Teller, and his dreamily
elegant tone comes straight out of race meetings, garden
parties, tea dances, and those other pleasant aspects of the
nineteen-twenties and thirties that today's consciousness has
conjured up in the interests of romance. The great majority
of styles in the Galanos collection are gowns for evening or
"late day," with skirts falling either to the ankle or to the
bottom of the calf. This low-calf length is dubbed the "restaurant length," suitable for dining in the remaining deluxe
restaurants of the world, which, in Galanos's opinion, deserve
to be visited by people in more sumptuous attire than dungarees
and khaki. Many of the dresses, which were shown with low
cloches and T-strap shoes, involve crêpe de Chine, layered
silk chiffon, or feather-light silk failles from the Swiss firm
of Abraham et Cie., which may be the last manufacturer of
really magnificent fabrics in the world. Some of the stuffs have
hand-screened prints of hothouse flowers and tea roses, or

revivals of Dufy prints from Abraham's archives; other Galanos outfits are simply a gauzy cloud of almost foolishly beguiling white. Delicate silhouettes are the sum of countless little tricks of flattery—slender, low-waisted bodices ending in points above a wafting, bias-cut skirt; the softening effect of tucks at the breast, capelets on the upper arms, and discreet gathers at the waist; and bias-cut cape backs to float out from the shoulder blades in graceful, mobile folds. The gowns are finished with elaborate, meticulous care. After the show at Bonwit's, Galanos picked up one of the airy silk creations of his workrooms and peered appreciatively at hand-rolled hems; hand piping and hand facing; a cuff cut on the bias to move with a gesture of the wrist; a cobweb chiffon lining; and a bustline gently molded rather than forced into an ugly dart. "If women want luxury, they shouldn't go looking for feathers and sequins," the designer said, with a superior smile. "*This* is what luxury really means."

Galanos, from his ivory tower, takes mischievous delight in observing that women get better value for money in a dress from Sears, Roebuck than in "an average seven-hundred-dollar Seventh Avenue dress, which is a manufactured product, designed to a businessman's formula." Certainly, to judge by *their* summer collections, the top Seventh Avenue men who compete for space on the rung of the financial hierarchy somewhat below Galanos are nowhere near as sure as he of what can be offered to whom, or why. Instead, they choose to offer something for everybody (except, perhaps, for fools old-fashioned enough to want to stand out in a crowd), and they succeed rather well in coming up with some nice, wearable clothes. Whether these are worth the money you might pay for them is a very different matter. The qualities that used to justify the high prices charged by illustrious designers—originality and authority of conception and impeccable construction—will almost certainly be absent. These qualities fell by the wayside in the past few years, during the period when fashionable women went one way (to imported clothes) and other women went another (into pants), while American designers got lost in the dust kicked up by their own mad scramble to keep up with every side. These continue to be difficult days for even the most famous of all those Famous Designers department stores persist in offering us as bait. The ranks of the mighty are frequently shaken by news of partnerships that come unstuck (Donald Brooks, Inc.) or fears of financial failures (Chester Weinberg, Ltd.). On the twenty-four floors of 550 Seventh Avenue, which is regarded as the *crème de la crème* of addresses for the sort of house that makes seven-hundred-dollar dresses, the showrooms seem to change hands with alarming speed.

It is not surprising that there is a loss of heart among American designers of anything more challenging than sportswear, which doesn't need to be designed in any sense that might justify old-style ballyhoo about the "personality" behind the "creations." Nor do business suits (however revolutionary the cut of their lapel or radical the choice of their plaid), suitcases, sheets, and even nightgowns really call for the talents of a "designer." Yet without all these undesigned, money-spinning extensions of their empires to serve as buttresses, designers might find that the idea of their "prestige" had collapsed completely. Of late, top designers have been obliged to re-evaluate the market value of their own "prestige." Many of them were so guilty of abusing this golden goose in recent years that it may never recover. They came to see prestige as a license—quite divorced from the obligation to provide high quality or originality of design—to impose a surcharge on the price of clothes. Many Famous Designers have brought trouble on themselves by their greed in tapping the fount of prestige and by persistently overestimating the foolishness of their customers. By now, there is increasing support for the theory that it might have been better if more of the top-drawer designers had had the courage to do a single collection and do it well, instead of attaching their names to all the second-string "boutique" and "sportswear" collections of the past few years, too. The evolution of these collections has often been embarrassing, and has reflected persistent miscalculations about the direction of fashion. For a long time, it was clear that designers saw the customer for their "couture" collections (with the possible exceptions of Galanos and Norell, they were never more than semi-couture) as a middle-aged woman of formal, conservative tastes, while the second-string choices were supposed to find favor with her daughter, or with herself in certain rare and clearly defined moments of informality. As a result of this misconception, the senior clothes went on looking too stiff and precisely tailored and the junior clothes too perky and cute long after really fashionable women became far more interested in wearing comfortable clothes that showed off a good body than in dressing according to their age or social standing. In many cases, the second-string collections were not even designed by the Famous Designers, who contented themselves with lending the "prestige" of their names to the efforts of unpublicized assistants. This hoax further weakened respect for the designers' "prestige," and it became easier to question the voice of authority when it spoke in tones alternately booming, squeaking, and—in really bad years—pleading. Among women who care about fashion, respect for and loyalty to uncompromised designing talent is probably as great as it ever was, but their reaction to the mercantile abstraction of "prestige" is far more cynical now than it was five years ago.

In part, though, the designers who came to power in the past twenty years were innocent victims of history, and their prestige was a burden forced on them by their position as members or direct heirs of a generation of American high-fashion design hellbent on proving that it was just as good as Paris couture. Even into the nineteen-sixties there was a widespread assumption that it was up to the French to be seized by flights of fancy, while it was up to Seventh Avenue to copy them or, wherever the notorious timidity of American women made it necessary, to tone them down. Understandably, American designers came to resent their inferior relationship to Paris—a relationship that had remained essentially unchanged for well over a century—and to feel an urge to show themselves capable of having an idea or two of their own. As a result, all through the nineteen-fifties and sixties, while a booming America settled into the shoes of giant world power, Seventh Avenue experienced its own particular wave of commercial chauvinism, with manufacturers, buyers, and the so-called fashion press rallying round to hoist onto pedestals any designers who looked lively enough to cock a snook at Paris. In time, lulled by automatic encomiums from the press, those designers came to believe in their own deification a little too well, and got out of any habit they may have had of putting their ear to the ground. The American semi-couture went on creating elaborate meticulous fancies and asserting its equality with Paris long after Paris had surrendered the role of innovator to the prét-à-porter and had ceased to be a threat. When their Gallic sparring partner withdrew into a respectably regressive semi-retirement, the American designers were left with a stultifying acceptance of the techniques perfected by the Paris couture, overlaid with a certain red-white-and-blue crispness in design but without any proper sense of direction. A further legacy of the years of putting up a united front against the French, I suspect, is the monolithic character of top American design: from that period on, it was taken for granted that every house, at every season, should come up with styles that were, in all but details, exactly the same.

Meanwhile, beyond the range of this transatlantic windmill-tilting, women and their lives were changing, and a new, distinctly American kind of fashion was beginning to emerge. Emphasis was shifting from a basically formal view of clothes and the importance of their shape and fit to a more informal style of dress that began with bodies, to whose shape and movement a soft, "unconstructed" garment remained subsidiary. Halston's grasp of this shift in priorities made his fortune in the past few years, and all the anti-Paris chaps, locked up in their respect for hidden facings and unseen linings, could only shake their heads enviously over the popularity of Halston dresses with no more tricks about them than there are about a cashmere sweater or a chiffon scarf. The success of Halston—which may owe something to his background as a milliner and consequent freedom from preconceptions about how to construct clothes—signaled the end of designing in the way the old-guard Famous Designers understood it. Halston is, in fact, an anti-designer, whose chief contribution to the history of American style has been to liberate fashionable women from the conventions and unnecessary artistry an earlier generation of designers had fettered them with, and to give presence to humble shapes like trousers and trenchcoats by making them in luxurious materials. The price of those materials and the sameness of his styles have made Halston a rage among status seekers. But when he ventures beyond uniform shapes and into more ambitious attempts at "designing," the results are often ungainly or derivative. Stephen Burrows, another key figure in the development of the "unconstructed" mode, took its modernity a step further by exploring the aesthetics of technology. Burrows was the first designer of note to employ frankly machine-made, highly visible zigzag stitching simultaneously as hemming, seaming, decoration, and trademark. And although his designs are sometimes carried out in silk chiffon, Burrows makes his clearest statements in synthetic jerseys, with their dense, animal movement and their eerie, big-city sheen.

The supple, "unconstructed" style, like the blue jeans to which it is close kin, is perfectly adapted to mass production. And there is no earthly reason that it should cost a lot. It has now become clear that this more comfortable style, calling for no costly craftsmanship, is where the future of fashion lies—or, at least, the future of clothing. Fashion, in the sense that Seventh Avenue seems to understand it, may not have much future. But the singular dilemma of the high-fashion houses in these days of transition is that the better they keep up with the "unconstructed" times and the smaller their effort is seen to be, the more they are forced to rely for justification of their high prices on the creaky old notion of "designer prestige." As styles get simpler—not just with a cunning impression of simplicity, à la Vionnet, but *actually* simpler—the more ludicrous it becomes to pay enormous sums for the sake of the name behind the "design." An unadorned Halston caftan, made of a single layer of silk chiffon, and only "more or less" hand-finished, can cost as much as five hundred and fifty dollars. A pair of little-nothing evening pajamas from Oscar de la Renta—a sack top above a pair of baggy, Asian-peasant pants—is around six or seven hundred dollars. A few ostrich feathers to trim it would add a couple of hundred more.

A representative price for a day dress from the summer collection of Ruffinwear, designed by Clovis Ruffin, is forty dollars; an evening gown is about sixty. Beyond their price, though, and the already remarkable fact that they are *dresses,* and so a bright spot of confidence in a still uncertain, uneven field, Ruffin's offerings are distinguished by a balance between design and lack of it which seems exactly right. They never overwhelm the wearer with the designer's superfluous fantasies, but neither do they surrender the female form to the merciless silhouettes of T-shirts and flour sacks, as the extremes of "unconstruction" will. Like appliances by Braun, they unite elegance and functionalism, and make a strong case for living in the present. And they are very honest clothes. At Ruffinwear prices, fabrics involved are inevitably synthetic (in this collection, Dacron jersey in various weights, and the silky fabric known as Nyesta), and the designer has a happy understanding of what such fabrics cannot do and what they can do superbly. Almost everything in the collection is machine washable, and the dresses are mainly in clear, spring-bulb colors or in very simple combinations of such colors. (Prints on synthetic jerseys still tend to look garish.) There are no belts or formal buttons, because these would betray the cost of a dress at Ruffinwear prices, and because no one needs them. For the same reason, there are no zippers; Ruffinwear appeals to the sort of people who are not frightened of pulling things over their hairdos. The collection ranges from frisky cousins of the basically Ruffinian, flippy T-shirt dress to the shoulder-baring majesty of long gowns that include a black shaft in neo-Grès style and a reedlike column of white with a plunging back and a cowboy-scarf cowl at the breast. The choice in between includes the suavity of a zabaglione-colored shift, cut high in the shoulders but with a shrug of matching cardigan, and the wispy charm of a bias-skirted dress in dusty, white-veined pink, with a shirred and strapless bodice and a separate triangular fling of stole.

At twenty-seven, Clovis Ruffin must be the youngest successful designer in America. The self-assurance with which he employs the "unconstructed" manner shows clearly how his generation of designers sees the style not as a bandwagon to jump on but as the only language it has ever understood. Not that the style is exclusively for the very young. On the contrary: the exhilarating novelty of Ruffinwear lies in its agelessness and classlessness. Ruffin's dresses are worn by impecunious young office workers with cheap sandals and plastic bangles, or, by the likes of Mrs. Onassis, with handmade shoes and diamonds. Recently, Ruffinwear took up residence at No. 550 Seventh Avenue.

1975

Paris

Today, the spirit of change moves more in a slow, inevitable current than in the plunging cataracts and stagnant pools that marked its course some years back. But few formerly accepted authorities—whether governments, economists, courts of law, and churches or, on a traditionally feminine scale, husbands, lovers, and the world of fashion—have escaped the scrutiny of increasingly critical followers and subjects. France, historically crucial to any definition of Western civilization, has certainly not been immune to the effects of contemporary change. The near-revolution of May 1968 still reverberates. Army conscripts have lately taken to the streets of barracks towns, in protest against discipline for discipline's sake; universities are still in a state of considerable disarray; and many children in once authoritarian public schools now call their teachers the familiar *"tu."* Supermarkets and fast-food shops are gaining great ground, while what were some of the most distinguished names among Bordeaux wines, together with the wine expertise that failed to nose out the adulteration of those wines, are eternally discredited. The government of Valéry Giscard d'Estaing is committed, if perhaps not to any really perturbing reforms, at least to the whole intoxicating idea of a modern French society, smoothly run by public relations and technical know-how. Market research, business school methods, the polling of public opinion on every subject from abortion and homosexuality to singing in the bath—all these enchant the French, who are not yet inclined to be as wary about advertising as we are, and whose politicians have yet to learn how badly a public relations machine can misfire and how changes of the electoral heart have a way of lying deeper than the soundings of the polls. Giscard's administration gave France, in the person of Françoise Giroud, Secretary for the Condition of Women, official recognition of the unspecific new yearnings and the specific old grievances that French women, like women everywhere in the world, are learning to voice. Meanwhile, amid talk of changes on the part of the government and talk of crisis in the press, the average Frenchman—who is of a line accustomed to living with crises at least since 1789, and who is, after all, of quite a Latin temperament—takes his pleasures much as he always has. He drives his car as often as ever, especially on *autoroutes* at either end of *"le weekend,"* because the President's instincts (as well as his pollsters) tell him that nothing is closer to the manhood of a Frenchman than his automobile, unless perhaps his *bifteck pommes frites,* and that it is politically wiser to ask for economies of heating oil than self-discipline about gasoline. Some French pleasures were actually stepped up this winter. Long lines snaked around movie theatres in Paris, and hard-pressed waiters with loaded trays dashed about through laughing crowds in late-night restaurants. The quantities of food consumed in France over the Christmas and New Year's holiday probably surpassed all records for national gluttony.

Fashion boomed. Last fall, when attendance in most fashion shops back here was pretty thin, shops in Paris were jammed with women investing heavily in *"le look"* of the season—long, wide layers of skirts, dresses, coats, capes, and shawls, whose combined effect was so utterly novel as to oblige a complete overhaul of accessories, and to make women compound initial folly with the purchase of a pair of costly new boots. Mme. Giroud's suggestion that French women not let their heads be turned by the fashion for voluminousness, and that the nation's economy was ill-served by the consumption of such unprecedented yards of imported winter fabrics, was ignored by all but the French garment industry, which greeted the Secretary's counsel with howls of outrage. A few of the more analytical victims of the fashion frenzy sought to justify it by calling it insulation, proof against potential heating cuts. Others explained that, because of the camouflaging effect that women inside the new width found comfortable and many men observing it apparently found infuriating, what was involved was a laudably feminist fashion. Perhaps it was, in a way. But independent-mindedness can scarcely have been the chief reason for the spending spree on rust-colored boots with sky-scraper heels and on billowing raincoats, or for women's eagerness to lose themselves among the ankle-wobbling creatures that teetered down the more fashionable streets of Paris like columns of khaki-colored pup tents. This looked suspiciously like the old-fashioned, slavish sort of fashion—the delight of cartoonists, the despair of husbands, and the key that unlocked some dark, lunatic impulse even in normally sensible women.

A like impulse toward this or any other fashion was not felt in New York last fall, nor—in spite of the wishful thinking of our manufacturers who visit Paris and return with heads full of the delightfully profitable fashionableness of Parisiennes and with suitcases full of Paris fashions—will the impulse toward the new width be felt here this spring in any significant number of women. In some cases last fall, perhaps, American women temperamentally inclined toward the latest fashions may have felt restrained by the fact or the feeling that they did not have the money to fritter away on such extravagances. But the support for new fashion per se is dwindling here faster than it is in France, less for reasons of economy than because, without French women's heritage and temperament to slow it, a tendency to buy clothes first for reasons of logic and practicality and only occasionally on the impulse to be fashionable has advanced more freely here. Given other opportunities for self-expression, American women will take them at the sacrifice of fashionable clothes. It now appears to be more admirable here to spend time dressing up one's home than to be seen to have spent time adorning oneself. Women with careers tend to go for comfortable, unstriking, easily accessorized, vaguely uniform clothes that resemble in tone the business suits of their male colleagues—suits that may be a bore but that *work*. Many of the Parisian women who invest in the latest fashions have careers, too. More women of the French middle class have jobs, proportionately, than such women do here: by one estimate, 20 percent of France's lawyers and 12 percent of her doctors are women, compared to 2.5 and 8.5 percent here. But neither a career nor a "raised consciousness" necessarily means a rejection of fashion for French women. It is a cliché for them to explain with considerable smugness that feminism should not preclude femininity, and that the liberation of French women is proceeding on a serene course, with none of the "inelegant demonstrating" or "unfortunate man hating" that, French women would like to believe, mars the women's movement in America. In France, style in dress is simply another aspect of a powerful middle-class tradition of living graciously with choice objects, a part of being a "cultivated" person. And, while the discriminatory laws of the Napoleonic Code may be under fire, the value of pleasing and seducing men—*"l'art de plaire"*—is really not in question, even for women judges or Cabinet Ministers. The subject of *la Femme,* whether as a glacial ideal or an erotic object, or at points in between, has been of continuous and consuming interest in France, and women's influence on thought, society, and language as well as their relation to men, love, and marriage have shown up in French literature from chivalric poetry—by way of the Petrarchans, the *précieuses* whom Molière ridiculed, and the heroines of Mme. de Staël and Flaubert—to the present, post-Beauvior age. This attention to womankind has fostered the traditions of fashion, too. The more puritanical and less intellectual society of America early became accustomed to look to France for messages about both women and style. There has never been any sustained rivalry to challenge Paris as the center of the world of fashion. America is too big and too diverse to produce the sympathetic audience and the sense of artistic camaraderie that designers in Paris find stimulating, and by the time a market with the taste and money for high fashion developed over here, America was too developed to create the pool of hand labor, in small ateliers flexible enough for the fast execution of new ideas, that backs up designers in Paris.

Paris fashion was in origin a celebration of femininity, of beautiful shapes, fabrics, and workmanship; American fashion developed more as a manufactured product, to be sold, by way of the most ingenious and intensive Madison Avenue methods, to an audience relatively lacking in conviction about the product's usefulness. The Paris definition of fashion, wherever it still exists, is eternal; the American variety of fashion, whose methods are now often applied to fashions produced in Paris, too, has a very uncertain future. American women have a lower tolerance than French women for fashion, because, whether or not American women are more "liberated" as women, as Americans they are more evolved as citizens of the modern world. They have witnessed the souring of hopes built up by advertising, the shattering of the consumer dream. Perhaps the citizens of France may be able to escape the worst of the pains that follow mindless materialism because their slower change from a peasant economy to an industrial one kept them closer to those "fundamental values" that America is now trying so fumblingly to reconstruct. As profoundly materialistic as the French are, they never completely fell into the trap of believing that happiness meant a color TV; instead, they held stubbornly to the impression that happiness meant being in love or joining the family at table to enjoy a good meal. A slower evolution in French taste may also be detected in the greater respect still given to the theme of modernity in the most refined sort of Parisian interiors; chromium and glass functionalism, called *le Design,* crops up often inside the ancient houses of Paris, while a cluttered, eclectic scheme of plants, baskets, and hand-printed Provençal fabrics—intended to convey an impression of the inhabitants' endearingly muddled humanity—is more common within the new apartment towers of Manhattan.

Representatives of the fashion industry of the world, whether department store buyers from Osaka or women's page journalists from the German provinces, flock to Paris regularly to marvel not just at the fancies of her designers but at the willingness of at least some ordinary Parisiennes to wear those fancies on the streets. Part of the legendary reputation of French chic is indeed true. Women in Paris are as skilled as they are cracked up to be in the tricks of tying a scarf. Many of them have a good sense of color, and a firm belief in the need to keep their clothes pressed, their figures trim, their skins clear, and their heads well coiffed. Most, rich or poor, are extremely judicious shoppers, and they will buy a dress only after assessing and usually trying on many alternatives. Women of a broad span of age are susceptible to fashions which might be adopted in only slightly different ways by a student of twenty with no position in the world and a woman of fifty-five with an important job or a prominent husband. The idea of who is in the world and who isn't remains on a small enough scale to be real in the tightly knit world of Paris society, which unites the kind of power that in this country is spread out between New York, Washington, and whatever remains of Hollywood. By the standards of New York, faces are so like one another on the streets of Paris as to seem like those of cousins, and, in addition to the narrower range of types, there are no real extremes of wealth and poverty. This broadly middle-class atmosphere of Paris is clearly one in which the traditional kinds of fashion, based on slight variations, thrive more readily than among the wild and kaleidoscopic parade of New York, where a merely elegant, discreetly modish woman is barely noticeable. Indisputably, fewer distinctions are drawn in France than here between women simply on the ground of age. Young girls dress up more there and so look older than their contemporaries here, and French women over forty often seem positively blooming. France is clearly less gripped by the tedious *Playboy* creed that only young girls are sexy: "older" French women appear to have more self-confidence than their contemporaries here as a result of the greater open-mindedness of French men. French women reveal their age quite freely, and because they are not obsessed by the thought of looking miraculously young, they often do.

In addition to these uniquely French qualities of the feminine character and life, though, French women share many of the opinions and values that are common to all active minds in the Western World, and that traverse frontiers with extraordinary freedom. None of the shifts in our own common values would seem to threaten fashion more directly—even, in the long run, fashion in France—than our disillusionment with novelty. Viewing innovation with suspicion, which used to be characteristic of conservatism, has for some years been evident, in tangible matters at least, among those who might have been expected to concern themselves with inventing and forging ahead—the young and those associated with the arts. Among these, the urge to recycle materials and objects was accompanied by the urge to recycle time, which led to the curious phenomenon of nostalgia for the unlived and unremembered. Although rivaled among French fashion enthusiasts by the army surplus mode, the flea market school of dress, picked up at *les puces,* is still considered to be of great significance in the Paris fashion world. (The latest army surplus vogue in Paris, the hundredth or so in a perennial international plague, is to blame, together with pathetically imitative manufacturers here, for the miserably unflattering khaki and olive drab that is flooding the stores yet again.) What the support for flea-marketry represents more, perhaps, than affection for the secondhand is the desire to find style, but obliquely, and splendor, but tackily, and so put an ironic distance between the wearers and the fashionableness of their clothes. The ironic approach is an essential part of style in clothes by now—an air of saying something often quite intense but only in a footnote. This approach has grown up out of flea market and "nostalgic" fashion, but it is interesting to observe how historicism itself—for so long the code of youthful consciousness in dress design, and so upsetting to a generation old enough to remember the authentic styles of the thirties, forties, or fifties—is now too obvious to be of value. But the earlier tradition of fashion based on the invention and promotion of novel ideas, for its part, seems more outmoded than ever. Many of the gratuitous biannual inventions of Paris fashion seem like indefensible demonstrations of mindless wastefulness, an anachronistic remnant of the discredited business principle of planned obsolescence. The fashion of tireless novelty still finds an audience among nations or social groups where a shorter experience of attempting to buy "the good life" makes for an unripened sense of disillusion. The young in Japan, for instance, will still unite passionately behind the latest Paris fashion fads. But in truth, in spite of last fall's temporary and local indulgence in fad, its power is fading even in France. And the two organized branches of Paris fashion—the ready-to-wear, or prêt-à-porter, designers, and the remaining score or so of houses that constitute the haute couture—have already adjusted themselves to changing attitudes, changing audiences, and the growing disenchantment with the new.

The future of fashion lies hidden. But it is a measure of how much the old ways have been left behind that the most influential Paris fashion this winter is insignificantly novel; instead, it holds suspended within extreme simplicity of design an infinity of delicate emotional and intellectual messages, so highly refined as to utterly and perhaps intentionally elude the heavy-handed instruments of advertising and fashion journalism that were developed to promote the fashion of novelty. The spirit of tense tranquillity that seems so exactly matched to the present era of transition in design is found only outside the confines of the haute couture, except in the case of Yves Saint Laurent's couture collection, in which the spirit is captured, but intermittently. The haute couture environment seems to inhibit the individuality and artistic integrity that show up so appositely in the work of such famous prêt-à-porter figures as Sonia Rykiel and Karl Lagerfeld, of the boutique Chloé, and in the lesser-known designs of Anne-Marie Beretta and of Sabine Lamorisse and Patrice Bry, of the boutique Les Années. In the creations of such designers we witness fashion pausing to wipe clean the slate of much of the gadgetry of the past, and allying itself with a greater serious-mindedness, a more generalized aestheticism. The designers working within this mood are inclined to dismiss the importance of innovation and, to a large extent, that of changes in shape; what is respected is color and texture of fabric and purity of tone. Since the best fabrics are invariably costly, and such an intangible as purity defies transmission beyond the designer who captures it, the fashion that depends on such factors cannot be copied successfully in cheaper materials. Sonia Rykiel's deceptively simple little sweaters, for example, have been highly susceptible to imitation, but cheaper copies are conspicuously lacking in the presence and meaning of the originals. It is no coincidence, I think, that the designs of Kenzo Takada, the Japanese designer who is often viewed as the brightest star of the Paris prêt-à-porter, lose far less of their essential style even in markedly inferior reproductions, of which many are in existence. This designer's work seems to me marred by restlessness, too dependent on dynamic and novel "ideas" to be precisely in tune with the times. At the moment, designers who succeed in finding the exact balance of modernity and refinement become fashionable by demonstrating their desire to stand with first and permanent principles, beyond the reach of "fashion." Saint Laurent has for some time been fond of denouncing *"la mode qui se démode,"* or the variety of fashion that goes out of fashion because it is intended to do so. Sonia Rykiel echoes the denunciation of fashion that depends on constant acts of unfaithfulness to last season's favorites, and prefers to think of her clothes lasting for years as a comfortable, neutral frame for the individuality of the wearer. Lagerfeld, for his part, admires the artistic principles embodied in the draperies of classical statues, and is absorbed by the idea of allowing fabric to retain its integrity, without suffering the violence of being chopped up too much and forced into artificial shapes with complex seams.

The history of this welling up of refinement in design is as far from being simple as the "simple" clothes it has produced. The designers of refinement belong, broadly speaking, to the "younger generation" of Paris fashion; Sonia Rykiel, who is in her forties, is the oldest of their number. The new tone has strong roots within the group of young designers of the nineteen-sixties, the *stylistes* (a word of disputed meaning, but generally used to describe propagators of fashion "ideas" rather than artists), who set out, democratically, to bring interesting, often inexpensive design to far greater numbers than those touched by the haute couture. But while the most successful heirs of the *styliste* explosion continue to voice contempt for the ivory-towerism and gratuitous invention of the old haute couture, and speak up boldly on the side of "real life," this is only a schematic alliance, a vestigial code; the designers have grown into artists, speaking a developed and hermetic artistic language to a particular élite. Just as the *stylistes* sprang up to sweep away the notion of an élite based on wealth—the foundation of the haute couture—with an élite of youth and zest, this in turn is now being succeeded by an élite of good taste. (Like all fashion shifts, this one is demographic and sociological: the population is getting older and more educated.) And the "new" good taste is always a step away from joining up squarely with the old wealth. Sonia Rykiel and Lagerfeld have established themselves as designers for the emerging élite of rich good taste, and they are, in effect, today's equivalent of the haute couture. Their clothes may be untailored and unburdened by inner structures, and worn by the sort of modern, fashionable body whose likeness to others makes the interminable fittings of the haute couture unnecessary, but a humble Rykiel sweater-jacket can cost three hundred dollars, and the simple, off-the-rack styles of Lagerfeld's recent collections are translated in such luxurious fabrics as to cost just as much as more complicated, made-to-measure styles in some houses of the haute couture. There may be a philosophical difference in the mind of the designer; there is certainly an emotional and social difference for the rich client of the prêt-à-porter who feels that it is no longer the thing to *look* rich in the way the haute couture knows how to make its clients look, but there is no significant political difference between the old haute couture and the upper echelons of the new prêt-à-porter.

One thing that does distinguish the best of the prêt-à-porter from virtually all the haute couture, though, is an impression

of awareness—if not anything quite so specific as thoughtfulness—given by the ready-to-wear creators, who seem to share
a keenly nervous and thoroughly modern turn of mind. Their
clothes often convey apparently contradictory, ironic messages,
and have layers of significance behind their often insubstantial and subdued exteriors. They are never exactly what
they seem to be. It is sometimes said, for example, that Sonia
Rykiel and Lagerfeld are masters of fashion for private and
personal lives; more accurate, though, would be a description
of them as masters of the more intimate and informal public
lives of society women. Both designers have abolished hems,
and are interested in the technical improvement of dress-
making construction, but what really interests them is the
idealization of technique, the *idea* of breaking with tradition.
Sonia Rykiel was impressed recently by the observation made
by an admirer of her clothes that they looked tinged with
humanity, as if, though new, they had, in some mysterious
way, been worn beforehand. There is a curious truth in this
impression, and Mme. Rykiel's exquisite silks and cashmeres
carry within their folds some infinitely distilled and wispy
essence of the campy, already humanized splendors of the
fashion of the flea market. But this lingering essence is almost
entirely masked by an over-all effect of propriety and femininity, which is what has made Sonia Rykiel replace Chanel
and, to a large extent, Saint Laurent in the hearts of the well-
groomed, rather antiseptic-looking ladies of *le tout Paris*. Underlying much of the more refined sort of prêt-à-porter seems to
be the theory of adjusting the balance between creator and
customer once and for all, in accordance with what is supposed
to be women's greater desire for independence; the shapes and
personalities of women are henceforth to take precedence, the
theory runs, over the constructed abstractions of designers. In
practice, though, the experiment in partnership founders, perhaps because it is based on the ideal of a woman with both a
superb, well-tended body and a confident sense of her individuality. (In reality, the two assets usually prove to be
mutually exclusive.) The artist, who may be quite laudably

bent on suggesting rather than imposing, and quite nobly uncompromising about the ungimmicky simplicity of his unconstructed style, still ends by leaving less than perfect bodies
uncharitably unflattered. Women, instead of using utter simplicity as the designer intended—as a blank page on which to
fill in their own unique style through little personal touches
of jewelry and accessories—demonstrate an insecure eagerness
to soak up every last button of the designer's style, and turn
themselves into walking advertisements for the designer's
systematized whims.

The dilemma implicit in the idea of high fashion as a neutral
uniform—an idea with rational origins not unrelated to blue
jeans—is that when the uniform is both recognizable and
costly, it attracts followers more interested in demonstrating
their wealth than their individuality, and so makes a far from
neutral statement about class and culture. The useful, sensible
systems of Saint Laurent's ready-to-wear clothes have been
diminished by having fallen under this pall of status, which is
now falling over Sonia Rykiel as well. (Lagerfeld is less
affected, because he does not promote a complete, widely
adopted package of style with "obligatory" shoes, hats, and
jewelry, as Saint Laurent and Sonia Rykiel have done.) It
has been said that the huge success of the luxurious Parisian
ready-to-wear designers this winter has been created precisely
because they were so expensive, and that while they may be
on an ideal quest for the sort of artistic integrity that has been
crushed by the self-exploitation of the couturiers, the customers for the newer designers are simply in search of the
same old status that they once found in the haute couture.
In truth, the artists of refinement are hedged about with traps.
Fashion is an impure and fleeting art form but a very big business. What begins in the artist's eye as an exercise in style
moves out into the world on the backs of status seekers, and
success produces new temptations and paths to a designer's
destruction. Like the haute couture, the prêt-à-porter is now
well organized, and goes in for press shows and twice-yearly
fanfare that create and feed the appetite for novelty which the

best designers profess to despise. And, like the designers of the couture, the successful designers of the formerly rebellious generation have learned to sell their names for products secondary to their "ideal vision" of fashion. Sonia Rykiel has already launched her perfume on the world, and Lagerfeld is in the process of launching his: the familiar cycle of exploited talent begins again.

Couture

The haute couture is a degenerate institution propped up by a sycophantic press. When the couture houses of Paris make their twice-yearly presentations for the benefit of the world's fashion journalists—although some of these have defected and now attend only the shows of the more dynamic prêt-à-porter, around six hundred devoted followers remain unswervingly loyal to the haute couture—the two sides are in cahoots to get outsiders to believe that something is going on that is not going on: novelty. This first deception is compounded by a second: neither side really believes that novelty is valuable, even if it *were* what they were both launching with such ritualistic fuss. Despite the battle cries of journalists and the caprices of designers, the principle of a sensible, "evolving" wardrobe, with basic pieces and layers that carry women through from season to season and from year to year, is now widely accepted—at least in theory and in private—even by journalists and designers. But these sensible wardrobes, calmly acquired, do not generate publicity, which provides the direct livelihood of most fashion journalists and the indirect livelihood of all couture houses. This publicity often proves mystifying to an observer from the world outside the couture citadel. The recent revelations about the spring collections of the Paris couture are a case in point. Weeks before the showings, carefully orchestrated rumors were put about, originally by French fashion journalists and then by their colleagues elsewhere in the world, all more than willing to let it be known that they had access to inside secrets and were onto a "scoop," that there were going to be some "dramatic changes." Fashion was about to undergo a transformation, the newshounds' message ran, from the long, wide, and tentlike to the shorter, slim, and tubelike. Such announcements made weird reading, particularly on this side of the Atlantic. The width that was soon to be consigned to oblivion because "everyone in Paris was bored with it" (actually, the style had been in evidence only for some three months, worn by a fashion-conscious minority in a few corners of that city) had barely crossed the sights of even fashion-conscious women in America. But American manufacturers, as ever dazzled by *anything* at all that had caught on in Paris last fall, had already put many versions of voluminousness into the pipelines for the spring and summer seasons, and fashion publicists gave birth to one of their finest barbarisms—"The BigLook"—to describe the coming style. (In spite of all these preparations, it is by no means clear that American women will buy up all the smocks, tents, and maternity shapes they are supposed to. What goes down in Paris in the fall isn't necessarily going to go down in an American summer.) The prospect of a precipitate halt in the advance of width and the impending arrival of "the tube" seemed to mere outsiders a nightmarish return to the days when couturiers sat around scheming up shapes to substitute for those of women.

As it turned out, though, the fashion press was leading its readers through the looking glass to inspect the emperor's new clothes—and not for the first time. At the spring collections, Dior's Bohan came up with some pretty, if untubular, dresses quite like pretty dresses he has come up with in the past; Ungaro bared the knee, but listlessly, in what looked like hairdressers' gowns; Givenchy showed straight-skirted gabardine dresses in the style that conventional, middle-aged women throughout the world have never ceased to wear. Most of the remaining twenty or so houses, each of whose presentations every fashion journalist dutifully attends, showed clothes that were merely boring. But some of them succeeded in demonstrating, simultaneously, contempt for the women they supposedly design for, by way of skirts you couldn't walk in, and such absurdities as a sundress made of tweed, and contempt for the women in the audience, by way of shabby and unprofessional presentation, and parades that were completely unedited grab bags of different themes or interminable repetitions of a single theme. The show by Yves Saint Laurent could not be faulted in the way it was presented. But it contained the group of dresses that were apparently the origin of all the pre- and post-collection mumbo-jumbo about revolutions and tubes. There is nothing either *new* or extraordinary about these dresses, but by the time the journalists arrived to view them they had fallen victim to their own predictions of novelty and were unable to put on the brakes. The dresses sent some fashion editorialists off into the sort of ecstatic prose that no fashion magazine has felt sufficiently authoritative to indulge in for several years. They burbled recklessly on about how all women were going to want to see themselves in dresses in the Saint Laurent style so much that by fall they would undoubtedly want to change their figures, if necessary, and get themselves in trim for the new millennium of fashion. Saint Laurent's dresses are elegant enough—but only on a sylphlike form— and they have an uncompromising purity and simplicity of taste that seems right for the times. But then so have T-shirts, which are what these dresses are based on, and whose anti-fashion character they share, except they happen to be translated in hugely expensive black-and-white-striped silk jersey. In all but this fabric, the Saint Laurent dresses resemble, in their several lengths and variations, such well-established favorites over here as Clovis Ruffin's fifty-dollar dresses in stripy nylon knit; those Lacoste chemise dresses with the crocodile trademark, which are washable and good for golf; and all the hundreds of thousands of ankle-length T-shirt dresses that tanned young matrons with good figures have enjoyed wearing for at least five years as they pad around barefoot in their patios.

. . .

There is perhaps more excuse for fashion journalists' participation in this and a host of past conspiracies to fool the public about what the haute couture produces because they sense—probably with justice—that if they allow the idea to die that fashion is ceaselessly new and always obligatory, many of them will find themselves out of a job. For the couture houses to sustain the myth of novelty is more cynical, though, because they now survive and thrive not through innovation at all but simply by promoting their prestige—in other words, by convincing customers that what they are spending so lavishly on is guaranteed to be the same, "established" old thing. In many respects, the haute couture is far from being what the careless scanner of fashion pages—with memories of the legendary postwar artistry of Dior, Balenciaga, and Fath; of the Space Age, early-sixties energy of Courrèges and Cardin; even of the conscientiously "relevant" styles that came from Saint Laurent five years ago—might believe. The launching of new styles and their reproduction to the measure of private clients—the strict definition of haute couture—are now only the largely unprofitable tip of the couture houses' surprisingly diverse business empires. There are no longer enough private customers to make up for the losses incurred in the production of some two hundred samples a year—many of them intended merely to help out journalists who cover the shows by providing striking photographs and spice for jaded copy. The losses from producing these samples are written off because the press showings at which they are displayed result in such spectacular free publicity for the couture name that is borne by a swarm of secondary products. Most couturiers now also produce ready-to-wear collections—often for men as well as women, and with accompanying accessories—on the side, and these are distributed by way of boutiques that spread the couturiers' fame throughout the world's most lucrative markets. Sometimes these subsidiary collections are actually designed by their namesake and produced under his watchful eye. More often, though, they are designed by someone else, then manufactured by a completely separate concern, often far from France, under a system of foreign licenses that are sold outright by a couturier or from which he collects royalties. Some couturiers take pride in their reputation, and make a conscientious effort to leave a mark of their personal taste on products that bear their name; other couturiers are greedy and careless, and permit their name to appear on ugly, badly made goods displayed in grubby shops.

There is wide disagreement among couturiers about how far the idea of products related to the couture can be stretched before the name that has been so liberally scattered is debased, bringing the whole golden edifice of prestige crashing down, amid public derision, around the ears of couturiers both good and bad. Pierre Cardin is often singled out for criticism because he lends his name not just to predictable articles like sweaters, neckties, and necklaces but also to a seemingly endless list of products that range from candies and kitchen equipment to bicycles. The name of Bohan is found on sheets, and that of Saint Laurent on shower curtains; Givenchy's name is on sunglasses, and Balmain's name on wigs. In several cases, the name on which all the couture profits pivot is only a name. The house of Chanel, who died in 1971, is kept going, in a harmless but rather creepy fashion (the journalists' sole criterion is whether "Mademoiselle" would have approved of the tiny departures her assistants make from her basically unchanging suits), because the financial house that owns Chanel perfumes deems a semblance of vitality useful. The case of Dior is even odder, because Christian Dior has been dead since 1957. Marc Bohan has designed the couture collections at Dior for nearly fifteen years, but it is Dior's name that still appears on some seventy products, from lipsticks, luggage, and lingerie to scarves, shoes, and shaving lotion. Few, if any, of the couturiers are independent, or even substantially in charge of their houses' purse strings. The perfume side of the Dior empire is owned by Moët-Hennessy; the perfume side of Saint Laurent is owned (so was his fashion, briefly) at one remove by Squibb. L'Oréal owns half of Courrèges, Baron Bich (of Bic pens) owns Guy Laroche and—by a wrinkle peculiarly French—the backing for the couture house of Jacques Esterel comes from a Communist millionaire. The exports for the couture empires of such companies are rising by leaps and bounds, helped rather than otherwise by financial insecurity in the world, which seems to make the rich richer and to make the nouveaux riches—whether on Fifth Avenue, the Ginza, or the Faubourg Saint-Honoré, or in the Arab countries, West Germany, or South America—more in need of the reassurance of their wealth and taste that they believe they find in a little label with a big French name.

One can't help admiring the transformation of an ancient craft industry that, unaided, would almost certainly have died. By subjecting the couture to rational business methods and developing its potential in an abstract management-consultant fashion, its backers have pulled off a triumph of what the modern-minded French like to call *"le marketing."* But it is a characteristic of the most skillful kind of modern marketing—whether of an industry, a product, a policy, or a politician—to enlist "the media" as its more or less conscious publicity arm. The world's fashion press, whenever it prates on about the divine new tendencies in a couture collection, is simply serving up propaganda for a group of successful international corporations.

The French fashion press, at least, has a direct sentiment of commercial chauvinism to justify its attentions to the haute couture; still, the alliance produces some curious and paradoxical effects. All journalists in France, even those concerned with fashion, tend to think of themselves as political creatures, allied with the left wing, the right wing, or—more commonly —some fraction, subdivision, or splinter of a wing. In France, both Socialism and Communism are part of established society in such a significant way that it would be unthinkable for them not to be present at the collections of the haute couture —another important part of established society. Two boutiques in the old working-class quarter of Paris around the now demolished Les Halles—a neighborhood that, like SoHo, houses a community of earnestly tasteful young people, with the same international libraries of picture books on Garbo, the American Indian, and the Pre-Raphaelites—furnish what, together with clothes from the flea market, has become the uniform of Parisians who are both fashion-conscious and committedly left-wing. The shop called La Maison Bleue was founded by an intense young man with a Ph.D. in sociology who thought that his shapeless flannel flour-sack designs would be just the thing for "The People." (Except that the clothes proved quite expensive, and "The People" turn out to have a stubborn loyalty to such unreformed fashions as miniskirts and double-knit pants suits.) Globe, a neighboring shop, is an even more unremittingly ideological spot with a few bleak gray metal filing cabinets in an aircraft hangar décor, and a few dismal piles of secondhand army surplus clothes—British desert shorts, Foreign Legion jodhpurs, Balaclava helmets, and Vietcong pajamas—that are carried off by the most attractive young fashion journalists and model girls in Paris. And in the magnificent rococo or Second Empire salons where the collections of the haute couture are unveiled one sees an incongruous parade of the more cerebral French fashion journalists, clothed by Globe or La Maison Bleue, with Moscow street-cleaner kerchiefs over orphanage-style pudding-basin haircuts, wending their way to a spindly bamboo-turned gilt chair and an honored place in the couturier's front row. Here they may come across a photographer from the Communist daily press, making sure of a good shot of the latest examples of haute couture evening gowns, one of which still costs—as it did in 1900—about the equivalent of a year's salary for the seamstress who made it. But whenever left-wing French fashion journalists show signs of chafing at their support of a capitalism that allows a handful of rich women to spend more than the price of a family car on a single dress, they are firmly reminded by couture interests that the system they are thinking of tearing down supports fifty thousand French workers. And whenever supporters of the Giscard administration voice doubts about covering couture shows as if they were news, officialdom draws attention to the splendid effect of the couture empire on France's balance of payments.

The idea of independence never got much of a foothold in fashion journalism in any country. Reporters of fashion "events" share with motoring critics and State Department correspondents the humiliating need to depend on those they write about for information that is never—unlike books, plays, or news—to enter into the public domain. Most newcomers to these semi-private fields of reporting grasp the conventions so rapidly that authority rarely sees the need to remind its dependents of the unpleasant consequences of a withdrawal of such privileges as access to a test model, a background briefing, or a good seat at a fashion show specially mounted for the fashion press. (Some years ago, when an American fashion columnist felt stirred up enough—and powerful enough—to describe one couturier's collection as "frankly ugly," he made her pay penance for her unprecedented and unrepeated moment of rebellion by not inviting her to his shows for several seasons.) Like other industries and governments, the fashion industry knows how to bind reporters closer with a few judiciously placed confidences, and it fosters dependence on press releases. The usual justification for such releases is that they are an aid to reporters who must insure that rivals do not beat them to a deadline with the story of a unique event. But this excuse seems foolish when the reporting is of couture shows, for an opinion about the couturier's "new ideas" is mutually arrived at by the journalists present, often with the friendly help of the couturier, and the clothes on display will not be worn until six months later, anyway.

Like any other social or professional group—although perhaps rather more slowly, because all the powerful branches of the fashion industry, even when they are vociferously bent on a show of novelty, are fundamentally conservative—the fashion press is being gradually transformed from within. It is debatable, though, whether it can change significantly before it simply peters out. The whole idea of "women's news," dealing with subjects beyond the ken of men, has been under serious challenge for several years. And as opportunities develop for women in careers outside the traditionally "feminine" and "intuitive" fields such as retailing, fashion, public relations, and journalism, recruitment to fashion journalism must fall off. This independence gives women new possibilities in work and more confidence in their own taste, so the job of fashion adviser and the need for fashion advice must decline together. That the Paris couture, which is no longer synonymous with originality, quality, or artistic integrity, retains any prestige at all is a tribute to the still vibrating waves of the energy generated in the nineteen-fifties and sixties by a generation of ambitious and aggressive women—often English or American —for whom, when they embarked on their careers, fashion was one of the few possible openings and Paris and the continent of Europe were still exotic, relatively untrammeled territory. The modern, promotion-based couture industry has its origins less in artistry than in a classic exercise in the carving out of a kingdom of power by the relatively powerless—women journalists and homosexual designers. A younger generation of women, less interested in power or interested in new varieties of power, is less willing to spend long, often poorly paid years in apprenticeship as they wait to join the "editors" in front-row seats at the pompous rites of fashion shows. Those younger women who do break into the circle seem not as eager as their seniors to spin outrageous tales about how designers' "novelties" are greeted with "ovations," and their reports are not as likely to be distorted by the urge to possess expensive clothes. In time, this may have an effect on the widespread convention among fashion reporters that they should get the clothes they publicize, if not for nothing, at least at far lower prices than those paid by readers who take their advice.

Fashion reporters are beginning to pay at least lip service to the theory that they ought to be allowed to function at fashion shows as theatre critics do at first nights. This principle of free speech has no support of any consequence among designers, most of whom offer their collections to the press not for judgment but for approval, and who see themselves as hosts of private parties to which they graciously invite a few loyal friends. Criticism by guests is not called for; the only possible reaction is wild enthusiasm or merciful silence. Even if objectivity were tolerated or encouraged, it is not at all certain that the fashion writers would know how to exercise the prerogative. There have been so many years of trotting off, lemminglike, to Paris, to play a well-defined part in the ceremony of whipping up group enthusiasm in order to return and whip up more enthusiasm in a bigger group—the readers at home. Hints of critical opinion *have* surfaced in fashion reports of late, but the tendency is to apply it only to the weak or the far-distant, while continuing to accord automatic admiration and sympathy to the most powerful designers of the hour and to advertisers at home.

Still, even a minute, inadequate rebellion makes a useful dent in the theory—apparently so widely adhered to by manufacturers—that fashion is a variety of religious faith, a worldwide web of mindless enthusiasm, and that if any part of the whole is damaged by scrutiny, the structure will collapse completely and women will give up buying any clothes at all. This fear of individual opinion is like that of a hidebound cardinal halting debate on a trivial point of doctrine lest it lead to questioning the existence of God. In fact, like all outmoded authorities and discredited creeds, the haute couture variety of fashion is well on the way to destroying itself. Autocratic fashion systems adopted by slavish followers are no longer the source of real fashion. Most women now want a fashion that reflects them—and there are enough varieties of women to keep a thousand national garment industries afloat without the aid of abject publicists. Slavish women still exist, of course, and there are still those who swallow whole each of the series of latest "looks" the fashion magazines come up with, but few sensible women envy these walking mannequins or seek to copy them. Even those who go in for the complete anti-fashion pattern of denim or army surplus look pathetically robotlike; they are a sadder lot than those who dress up in expensive packages of status symbols, because the rebels put more thought into their choice and a higher level of self-deception is involved. The time is past for the fashion that comes tied in neat, biannual bundles, trailing coordinated accessories and enthusiastic adjectives, and for the commercial ballyhoo about big looks replacing little looks and bringing new personalities to "every woman." All this nonsense only clutters up our lives unnecessarily and unsettles women by suggesting that something is going on in fashion that the initiates know about but that is beyond an amateur's comprehension; and the simple, personal pleasures of dress—for drama, comfort, flirtation, as a cure for gloom, or out of peacock vanity—are thereby robbed of their inestimable worth.

1976

The
Fashionable
Mind

Many societies have been openly dominated by fashionable people, but our society is quietly permitting itself to be dominated and transformed by fashionable minds. The word "fashion" (with "fashionable") isn't heard much anymore, and even its successors "trend" and "style" have come to seem a little tasteless and passé. But fashion is everywhere around us just the same. It's there wherever political strategies are planned, movies made, books published, art exhibits mounted, critical columns turned out, dances danced, editorial policies formulated, academic theses germinated: wherever people think, speak, or create our shared forms of self-expression. Fashion usually is neither named nor noted but is simply the lens through which our society perceives itself and the mold to which it increasingly shapes itself. This hidden, powerful, mental sort of fashion is thus worth taking stock of. In spite of its great parade of intellect, its support in influential places, and its mellifluous accompaniment of self-promoting public relations, the new variety of fashion pretty much shares the creed and the limitations of the frivolous, pirouetting old variety of fashion—that of dress. The shared creed is materialistic, and holds that appearances are of greater significance than substance. Among the shared limitations are fickleness, a preoccupation with descrying the will of the majority in order to manipulate it or pander to it, and a concern with the accumulation or protection of power and profit. Although all fashion looks mobile and rebellious at times, its roots are surprisingly constant: to think or act for reasons of fashion in any given field is to support that field's established centers of power. The character and the ancestry of mental fashion become more difficult to detect as it increases its power and its pretentions by annexing "better," previously impregnable departments of society, and converting "more serious," formerly independent minds. In this way, fashion succeeds in fobbing off on more and more people its own distorted imitation of life.

Mental fashion, like any other kind of fashion, is by nature restless—bent on promoting, and profiting by, constant novelty. It is always on the move. It is no longer content merely with slick, razzle-dazzle opinion making and smart, comet's-tail trend spotting—the social and external side of mental activity. Such preoccupations were sufficient for fashionable minds in a nation concerned with foreign affairs and public scandals but were not wholly satisfactory later, when the individual citizen withdrew into himself to search for fulfillment through jogging or *cuisine minceur*. So mental fashion turned inward with him, and started to seep down into the realm of those profundities, verities, and values which used to be called moral and spiritual. It is scarcely an improvement that the fashionable mind is beginning to weary of the appearance of cultivating maturity and introspection. Having witnessed fashion's corruption of our definition of the world, we must now sit by as fashion subverts our definition of the self. In advertising, we can see fashionable intellectual hubris at its crudest and its most absurd. Copywriters pepper their prose with references to "individuality," "taste," and "quality," all of which abstractions are taken to be suddenly and deliciously "in." Even if one dismisses the intellectual pretensions of advertising style as harmless shadowboxing, one must feel depressed to see how fashionable minds in more significant fields blur the distinctions between real and spurious quality, between actual life and make-believe. The newly profound faddishness may be daily observed in the work of commentators, critics, editors, artists, television producers, and the like, who presumably transmit its influence to the general public. The sort of people who ought to be professionally protecting real quality and fostering genuine individuality—not just the image of these, or the toy-town versions that advertising fools about with—seem ever more inclined to present thoughts, facts, and values, and human beings, too, simply as fashionable commodities, much like the season's new hats of old. Everything is to be dealt in, acquired, used, promoted, and, in time, inevitably cast off. Sometimes, as if by chance, merchants and promoters of mental fashion throw their weight behind what really seem to be works of quality and originality, and, consequently, of uncertain popularity. But these are presented with such great self-laudatory cymbal clashings and heavy underscorings that the original spark of worth and talent ends up looking feeble and somehow disappointing.

Our society is neither so naive nor so cynical as to hand itself over to fashion without in some way believing that fashion is a worthy guide. We have long had an interest in pretending that fashion is something more dignified and substantial than it really is. The new status of fashion became obvious some years back, at the time it changed its name to "style" or "trend." There came to be widespread recognition that fashions of any kind were not merely esoteric and self-contained trinkets but a part of life. They were seen at first as visible, bobbing markers of the otherwise hidden course of some of the great currents of the times, and later as instruments to aid in the interpretation of those currents. From this function as instrument, fashion grew until it came close to being equated with intelligence. In the amount of respect we accord various intellectual attributes, a nose for trend now rivals the power to analyze the present and has surpassed the ability to store the past memory. Perhaps the fashionable influence in thought has gained power less by its own intrinsic vitality than by the default of competitive influences. Maybe technology and its accompanying calculators, computers, and scientific polls caused the solid, reasoning, "masculine" side of our mind to atrophy, tipping the scale further toward the licensed gadfly that is the intuitive, "feminine" side of our mind—the origin of fashion.

However it develops, the excessive use of fashion as a framework for perception will ultimately warp that perception and, with it, any reasonable picture of the world. The greatest drawback of an overfashionable perception is that fashion is concerned, virtually by definition, with surfaces, images, appearances. This drawback is painfully plain when the fashionable mind is supposedly employed to get at the heart of things, or when the conclusions it reaches may have a lasting effect, as in the reporting or interpretation of national events or the definition of "good" and "bad" art. Fashion is well equipped to pass on to us how things look or seem, and is often good at making assessments peripheral to appearances, such as how much money they are worth, but it is not equipped to tell us what things really are. When the mind surrenders itself to fashion, the first casualty is objective judgment—which is, to all intents, the mind itself. Fashionable perception is incapable of discerning any fixed truth about an object or event, and so leaves the object or event at the mercy of the observer and of the time and circumstance in which it is observed. A fashionable mind is often distracted from thorough concentration on its object by the question of timing, and will wander into self-congratulation on the observer's impeccably fashionable chronological instinct and into overweening claims to have known and appreciated fashions long before they became widely fashionable. These intrusive assertions of pre-fashionable familiarity with a subject—hyper-fashionableness, in other words—crop up frequently these days. Fashionable observation is very far from being self-sufficient, and is highly self-conscious about the company it keeps. It is inclined to rove jumpily around the edges of its object, like the eyes of an ambitious guest roving beyond a conversation partner at a cocktail party full of powerful people, and is distracted by its attempts to encompass the comings and goings of others. To the absolutely fashionable mind, an opinion, a taste, or an enthusiasm is of significance only for a particular, restricted moment—a moment when it is held in common by some right-seeming group of fellow-souls, just before it is adopted by large groups of followers.

Fashion as it exists now, whether in literature or in kitchen equipment, in neckties or in ideas, is intimately connected with money and power. This basis is by no means always apparent, and our careless inherited assumption that fashion is spontaneous, amusing, innocent, and amateurish is likely to keep us from examining or questioning the ways in which it has evolved. The part that commerce plays in fashion is something we are often led to overlook, for the fashionable mind is well practiced in masking a general allegiance to commerce and the status quo behind what seems to an outsider to be an appealingly individualistic enthusiasm for some particular novelty. Fashion is a skillful master of enthusiasm, and of a Pavlovian discernment of certain correspondences—between a current best-seller and a potential successor, for instance—but is an inadequate touchstone in the search for honest, disinterested distinctions. These are born of an isolated, dogged, unfashionable side of the mind—a sort of gawky mental provincialism.

It is important to remain aware of the flaws of the fashionable perception, because that flawed perception is capable of influencing and changing the world it perceives. Fashionable minds and their backers do not just absorb the world passively but, if it is necessary in order to create the trends they seek to promote, actively distort it. Fashions, quite simply, do not exist until a fashionable mind is turned on them. Only in that fashion is free to conjure up the previously nonexistent and is unfettered by the need for consistent loyalty to any client does it distinguish itself from the fancier echelons of the public relations business. In these, as with fashion, underlying commercial and corporate purposes are often suavely concealed beneath a sincere, personal veneer. Fashion and public relations share a charter to turn life to their own advantage, to make malleable and commercially useful the naked human perception. Both interests consider life too small, dull, and colorless to get itself sufficiently noticed without the lobbying efforts of professionals. The mind attuned to trend setting and trend spotting has no regard for the objective, independent pulse of life but, rather, will recklessly declare that trends exist, will invent catchwords and categories for those trends, and will proceed to stuff poor, unsuspecting life and muddled old culture down into profitable slots.

In order to make a real mark, of course, the manipulative, subjective, trend-bent perception loosed on the world must be a corporate subjectivity, and not merely an isolated, personal one. The reason that some phenomenon or other is declared to exist as a trend is that powerful interests have invested in that existence. (The "media event," which is no event at all until the network camera crews tramp in to make it so, is one example of the attempt to shape the world to subjective corporate fiat.) The fashionable outlook never permits itself to wander far from the path that will bring in big-business profits, and is also susceptible to the temptations of personal financial gain. For fashion of all kinds is fundamentally materialistic and utilitarian. Its tendency is to view perception and reflection as commodities, ideas as merchandise, and words as promotional tools.

In spite of its allegiance to the material and its leanings toward the superficial, among other barriers to wisdom, fashion is now setting out boldly to colonize the world's mysterious islands of individuality and the hitherto unexplored territory of the inner life. Thus, trends that look like trends—broad, uniform, and public, that is—are now less fashionable than trends that can pass for the spontaneous impulses of the private mind. Fashion now pivots on a show of the personal and the sensitive, on feelings, values, an air of education, a sense of fine distinctions, and a great play of self-confidence and independence—on what is packaged commercially, in short, as the Quality Life. The increasingly estimable-looking camouflage that fashion is taking on makes the process of detecting its presence and influence infinitely more complex, and makes anyone seem churlish who takes issue with it once it is detected. Is one entitled to complain about the end of quality just because it arrives still trailing a few wisps of the promotional straw it was packaged in? The fact is, though, that the dilemma of withholding admiration from excellence simply because it has been given the backing of fashion rarely comes up. Fashion tends to diminish all that it touches, and what might fool the cursory glance as being genuine and good often turns out on closer inspection to be a mirage of authenticity and a mutated, pastiche version of the good. The paradigm of the fashionizing process is the New York commonplace of a fashionable young man taking over from an unfashionable old man the ownership of a real nineteenth-century saloon, tearing out its insides, and replacing them with a stylized imitation of the insides of a nineteenth-century saloon. Because common sense has been drugged by fashion, albeit the "good" fashion for the solidity and workmanship that originally endeared the premises to the new owner, no normal instinct survives to question the destruction of the irreplaceable, or the validity of the fake that pretends to improve on it. The most tasteful kind of fashion almost always proves the most destructive, because it sets its sights on the worthiest targets.

The dimension in which fashion operates is an amalgram of the mental and the material—a miasmic half-world where ideas have functions and prices, while objects are hung about with thoughts and dreams. The acts of buying and selling have in recent years become more and more densely shrouded in a fuzz of references to individuality and thinking, probably in deference to the college-educated, reputedly self-aware and independent-minded survivors of the tumultuous nineteen-sixties who are now peaceably earning and spending money. These form the natural market for products wrapped up in a fashion whose object is the self—for a materialism that is twined appealingly around unmaterialistic, or even anti-materialistic, thoughts and values. Advertisers, who once sold cars and shampoos by playing on mindless romantic dreams of moonlit tides and slow-motion flowing manes, now play crisply on their audience's complacency about its enlightened consumerism. The habit of cigarette smoking is twisted to become a demonstration of maturity and ratiocination. Clothes that will make people into comfortable carbon copies of their peers are described as inimitably suited to the unique personal style of each of the thousands who buy them. And it is scarcely necessary for advertisers to spell out the notion that a certain codified, ritualized pattern of furnishing a house with homespun textures and materials indicates the vitality and honesty of the inhabitant's mind.

The blurring of the distinction between people and products has led to an assumption that is often voiced these days— that clothing, furniture, and possessions of all kinds are, or ought to be, a form of self-expression. If the premise had remained on an amateurish, human scale, as a declaration of the right to privately enjoy and freely control the props and costumes of one's own little stage without regard to the dictates of social circumstance, it might have had some value. But when fashion took up the originally sound impulse, it perverted that impulse, as is its way. Commercial interests gleefully exploited the notion of self-expression through spending, foreseeing that the path to self-knowledge—the necessary prerequisite of self-expression—must mean false starts and wrong investments by customers, which would prove profitable to business. Still, the invariably disappointing faith that people are what they own and will be better fulfilled if they own better things spread steadily. It is not difficult to resist conversion to this faith when the stereotyped and materialized presentation of a "distinctive" self is made in a clumsily worded advertisement for mass-produced perfume or some part of the denim uniform. It is more tempting to accept this false self when it is encountered further up the scale of worldliness, where materialism looks more incorporeal and fashions look a lot like ideas. A definition of the self as being fixed by a carapace of possessions sits more cozily if those possessions are thoroughly imbued with intelligence and taste.

Americans, acting under the combined influence of rampant acquisitiveness and psychoanalytical self-absorption, seem particularly inclined to mesh possessions with their sense of self-esteem, and to view them as social signposts and emotional milestones. One may see in this country all stages of evolution of the identification of the individual with his goods—from the simplest level of the immigrant who thinks he must be someone because he can now afford a secondhand Buick, through the second-generation status seeker who concludes that he must be someone impressive because he can afford what his friends will recognize as being from Vuitton or Gucci, to the fashionable pinnacle where the most confident and established citizen *knows* that he is someone because he has the good taste and education to possess a particularly fine example of a Coromandel screen together with the self-assurance to take it for granted. If more and more people aspire to belong to this last category, the basic misapprehension remains the same at every level of acquisition. Certainly, though, materialism is upwardly mobile now, causing fashion to try to look as permanent, respectable, and lifelike as possible while status moves on to reside less in the act of buying than in the fact of long-term possession. And today it is not enough even to possess things; you have to be seen to be the sort of person who appreciates their finer points. Shabby chic has been more highly valued than mere chic for some time, but the most fashionable things of all today are those that look not like fashions but like aspects of a completely independent mind.

It is fashionable to give the appearance of being unique—that is, to demonstrate the uniqueness of one's acquisitiveness—by being a connoisseur of some sort and possessing a "collection" of objects. Truly fashionable collections tend to fall into a curiously restricted number of categories; antique corkscrews, miniature shoes, old baskets, and Oriental lacquered boxes are among the current favorites. (The shift away from diamonds, Georgian silver, and other objects of intrinsic monetary value to objects admired for their warmth, their quaintness, their good design, or some other subjectively defined virtue is part of the present fashion for humanized materialism.) Occasionally, to save their clients time, interior decorators assemble collections for them. As it is with such instant collections that supposedly "accessorize" a fashionable individuality, so it is with the individuality itself. The intention is deceitful—designed to trick outsiders into being impressed. The slow, genuine, stop-and-start process of accumulation is circumvented, and the end result is a stereotype. If inanimate objects are left to stand in their world, and are not invited out to mingle with our sense of self, they will quietly console and delight us. But to bind possessions up closely with the mind is less than fair to both. And the more fashionable it becomes to protect a self-conscious individuality, the more surely fashion will erode real individuality. A fashionable individuality has a way of turning out, on further scrutiny, to look less like an individuality than like a fashion.

The fashion for a schematic individuality that begins and ends with the image of one's material circumstances is the domestic aspect of what becomes on the grander and glossier public plane the cult of "celebrity." The promotion of a certain controlled and stylized public personality and the acceptance of this surface as a definition of worth increasingly form the vital motive power of our culture. The cult has spread outward from the performing arts—where a visible face and even an openly displayed private life are part of the job—into fields where personality used to be considered background and best left unemphasized or unseen behind the finished product, such as writing books or communicating the facts of the news. Celebrity, the public side of "individuality," is ostensibly human but really a part of fashion, and, like other aspects of fashion, it operates in a dimension that runs parallel to life and often apes it very closely but is not the same as life itself. Like other aspects of fashion, celebrity specializes in blithe manipulativeness and outrageous volte-face, and operates according to completely self-contained, self-perpetuating criteria. Underlying facts and underpinning fixities, often unattractive or tedious, belong to the real world but not to that of celebrity, where all is bright, swift, and palatable. It is of no significance, for example, whether a man actually has the genius, or even the readership, to lay claim to the title of "distinguished author" as long as he understands the knack of projecting himself in that role within the hermetic confines of the celebrity world, where humanity is less significant than its image. The variety of individuality which is handed down by the mechanism of celebrity proves as disconnected from real individuality as does the hypothetical mass-market self whipped up by advertising or the assembly-line uniqueness summed up by a fashionable collection. It is clear that celebrities do not exist as ordinary people do, by virtue of drawing breath on earth (regardless of who may observe them doing so), but are manufactured and promoted like commodities and fashions.

Fashions in famous people, like every other kind of fashion, have begun to look more educated and discriminating, and to succeed in tricking a wider audience into believing that the world of celebrity is just as admirable and just as real as life itself. The supposedly private, un-celebrity face of the famous has never been spread out before the public with as much intimacy as it is now. The spotlight of publicity swings quite as often, these days, to "serious" people as to the posturings of spangled starlets. And a special subdivision of celebrity, dubbed "eccentricity," has been cooked up by some of the more broadminded celebrity makers to encompass people like Sarah Caldwell and Woody Allen, who fail to pass the stringent test of physical uniformity which continues to be generally demanded. This category of self-sufficient or unconventional-looking characters represents people-fashion's nod to the "high-class" end of fashion, where reside "quality" and "style."

Sometimes the cloak of celebrity falls over genuine talent and real originality, and sometimes a lack of these is concealed behind a cunning imitation of them. Ideally, talent survives perfectly, in total mastery of itself. But the danger of life's swathing itself in an accessible, simplified, public relations version of itself is that original talent settles down to fit the comfortable shape of its public image or withers away unnoticed behind it. The public, meanwhile, distracted by a host of shadows and substitutes, is deprived of art. Literature, for instance, has been irrevocably diminished in past decades. More than by the ascendancy of image over print, the damage has been done by the transformation of culture into a fashion-based industry. In fact, by now the association of literature with celebrity faddishness is so far advanced that the general assumption is not merely that literary creators are significant primarily as celebrities and talk-show guests but also that their literary creation should itself look familiar with and know how to harness the money-spinning power of fashion and celebrities.

The criteria of fad and of the celebrity cult do more than mold our opinion of this season's literature; they also determine how much attention and value our society will accord the literary figures of the past. The hagiological-scatological web of biographies and commentaries-on-commentaries and movies-of-the-book which our culture has woven around the Bloomsbury group, F. Scott Fitzgerald, and Ernest Hemingway, among others, is inspired less by any particular respect for the brilliance of the artists' *work* (although the unexamined presence of that brilliance behind the visible and entertaining mound of gossipy secondary information soothes the cultural conscience of the audience for literary best-sellers) than by the seductiveness of the luxurious conditions and the aura of celebrity surrounding the artists in their *lives*. The various literary cults of today illustrate characteristics common to all fashion, and show how, if fashion has a chilling effect on contemporary talent, its power to diminish is all the more discouraging when it is turned on the talents of the past. In addition, literary-historical fashion-mongering, with its concentration on particular "in-groups," shows how all fashion is naturally drawn to discern or create patterns of social or personal power, and how the dimension of fashion tends to seek its frame of reference within itself. It continues to promote, even generations later, those who always made that dimension their home. More often than not, it emerges that the key figures of popular literary history were celebrities and self-publicists in their own day.

The new, thoughtful-looking, lifelike breed of fashion has been fostered by a generation (linked in common cultural impulses, if not necessarily in age) whose perceptions are attuned to and often blunted by the transient images of television and the movies but who also have college educations that have left a taste for the sensation of intellectual activity and a nostalgia for the literary enthusiasms of studenthood. The verbal appetite of this group is powerful enough to send advertising copywriters scratching out their polysyllables and newspaper editors scrambling to fill up their Op-Ed pages with a show of "provocative" thought, but is not discriminating enough to care whether words are being employed in the service of fashion or to advance our understanding of life. This group, in its instinctive use of material possessions as the prism through which it views itself and the world, is middle-class. Here is the natural market for surfaces, fashions, and the patina of culture. In literature, this market picks out work furnished with appealing objects it can fantasize about possessing, "atmospheres" to which it can surrender itself and in which it can happily bathe. Just as this market is willing to accept the décor of its living room as an expression of its inner self, it is inclined to accept the decorative parts of art as art's essence.

The machinery of fashion-making which has been developed to feed an essentially materialistic audience the appearance of opinion, perception, and talent it has learned to demand is profoundly destructive of just such intangibles. Fashion takes up with originality and talent because it knows that these often prove profitable, and also out of its characteristic compulsion to replenish itself by ceaselessly devouring the new. But as soon as fashion adopts its latest find, this is transformed into fashion's creature, existing by the grace of fashionable attention, and drained of the qualities that proved so fatally attractive in the first place. If, as an ambitious fashion increasingly demands, those initially attractive qualities were real independence and integrity, the tragedy of their fall is the greater. Fashion hurts most what it professes to admire most, and does most damage to the best; the fate of mediocrity has never mattered much. Fashion exerts a harmful pressure on the intellect, which either cravenly caves in and accepts the soothing notion that "quality living" means a discerning collection of gouaches and a rather nice taste in wines or chooses to resist the tide of fashion and attempt the perpetual effort to separate truths and values from both parasitic public relations gimmickry and the scent of power. This resistant mind often wears itself out or falls into a habit of stylish ironical dispute and self-conscious enthusiasms felt *in spite of* their being fashionable or *because* they are currently unfashionable. It is evident how this sort of attitude (which brought us kitsch) can very easily flip over into being the trendiest mind of all.

The fashionizing of intellect hurts the society in more ways than by depriving it of the unfashionized intellect's clarifying and constructive influence: the society actually learns to pattern itself on fashion. It has come to be acceptable that the Western democracies should give supreme political power not to the candidates with the most honesty, ability, or character but to those with the most skill at manipulating images and convincing voters that an imitation world—based on power, and self-contained, self-interested, and self-deceiving—is the same world as the voters' own. The rules of politics are rules of fashion. Political minds, like fashionable minds, rarely look hard at themselves or at the real world. Instead, isolated by vanity and celebrity, they search for the latest fashion in issues and slogans, hoping to latch onto it in time to turn it to their own advantage. Like fashion, politics is learning to *look* less superficial: the "in" thing that all politicians yearn for is no longer the image of "charisma" or "pragmatism" but the image of "leadership" and "integrity."

The arts are in danger of being submerged by fashion, and are increasingly subject to critical definition—their cue for self-confidence—based on frivolously determined opinions of whether this branch or that is "in" or "out." Fashionable critics endow with the magical "vitality" now representational art, now the avant-garde theatre, now dance; and then, sooner or later, withdraw their accolade with a yawn and leave talent, which had its head turned by the praise and money that gushed over it in good times, bewildered and excluded in un-merited bad times. The greatest disservice that fashion does is carelessly to turn life's most precious and fragile assets into marketable products of transient worth. If a great, dark locust cloud of fashion settles upon our world, upon our dream of quality, upon our humble individualities, we must fear that its passing will leave behind a ravaged field of empty gestures. While the rush is on, fashion is good for business, but it is hardly beneficial to society, talent, or the mind. And in the long run fashion may prove very bad for life.

1977

Fall Collections:
Form

Working way ahead of mere shoppers, as ever, the New York designers have been giving us their tulip-time display of what they hope to see us wearing in the fall. The collections have never before been so numerous, so elaborately presented, or of such generally high quality. Yet, although the best of the new clothes are profoundly satisfying, they do not set out to be exciting. Clothes that consciously cultivate excitement look dated now. They continue to form at least a part of collections at both ends of the fashion spectrum—from the old guard, schooled in an earlier tradition of drop-dead glamour, and from those of the younger generation who have not grown out of their years of startingly anti-establishment rebellion. In the grander category, John Anthony's satin evening gowns that expose bosoms and lengths of thigh; Halston's cruelly revealing chiffons and his skintight satin leotards under open taffeta skirts and saloon-girl boots, which all seem designed to prove that ladies are really whores at heart; the steely glitter of a Bill Blass or an Oscar de la Renta, who sums up the ladylike sterility of the Washington-ballroom mode; and Pauline Trigère's fox-trimmed opera suits, with their echoes of Walter Winchell at "21"—all these appear to fall outside the imaginative focus of designers with a proper sense of the fashion that is right for now.

And the old symbols of excitement and liberation developed by the younger generation as a challenge to their elders also look flat and conventional whenever they crop up these days. Carol Horn's styles, influenced by the Third World, non-tailored tradition of dress, and depending more on wrapping and draping cloth than on cutting and shaping it, no longer evoke our instinctive philosophical sympathy. This designer's passion for versatility within a single garment (hoods transformed themselves into off-the-shoulder necklines in her show, and diaperlike pantaloons turned first into mini-length, then into knee-length, and, finally, into calf-length balloons) resulted in a tiresome orgy of unwrapping and rewrapping that no longer seemed particularly valid. Stephen Burrows, for his part, bears the unforunate burden of having not just his designs but his whole career serve for many as a symbol of American new-wave fashion excitement. His career has come full circle now, from a triumphant launching at Bendel's seven years ago, through a painful period of insensitive treatment at the hands of big-business Seventh Avenue, to what has been billed as a triumphant comeback at Bendel's this season. But neither the saga of his career vicissitudes nor the standard of his show was quite sufficient to bowl us over anymore—and we had been somehow encouraged to believe that nothing less than wild enthusiasm would serve. A couple of other "younger generation" shows I saw, which included European designers seeking to launch themselves on the New York market, underscored the curiously irrelevant quality of clothes that bear too obvious marks of youth. Cygne Designs and Dianne B. showed selected styles by some designers—mostly French—of what is viewed as the younger school. A youngish crowd, keyed up to witness galvanizing new fashion, jammed itself into a stylishly renovated midtown bistro to see the show. A pair of mystically robed youths sat on a magic carpet and provided musical accompaniment, sometimes by singing in falsetto. The parade of fashions was interrupted at one point while a girl in an Afghan wedding dress and a barefoot young man wearing a green cloak and a ruched gold jumpsuit performed a tremblingly cabalistic dance. The fashions included coats with designs like playroom murals, a few miniskirts, and gauzy garments of Moroccan or Indian inspiration. All this let us know that we were in the presence of the younger generation, and so did the audience, whose members simply oozed individualism, wit, and "style." They all looked to be around thirty. Somehow, the whole occasion didn't quite make sense. The audience had come to see thrilling young fashion, but its members—with their amusingly scavenged clothes, their thigh-high boots, and their hair tied up in beribboned, clownlike tufts—already represented it better than the clothes they saw modeled now and would be able to buy in shops, at considerable expense, in the fall. One costume appeared on the runway with the model carrying a metal toolbox for a handbag. But what lesson about the freedom to wear anything that strikes the fancy and the possibility of self-expression through humble found objects had that toolbox to teach one not atypical girl in the audience? She had already made her way to Forty-fourth Street wearing, on her head, a gold-painted creation that looked like a cross between Aladdin's lamp and the prow of an ancient Egyptian barge.

The whole experience left one with a feeling of uncertainty and gloom about rebellious fashion now that the nineteen-sixties generation has grown up. Is this all that kind of fashion added up to, after all? Was this what those years of quickening pulses were leading to—a group of grown-up people, with a code of individualistic "style" in dress that was not so remarkably different from one exponent to the next, gathering to applaud a toolbox, a miniskirt, and (most perplexing of all) a pair of gray flannel pants? A second show of young European designers I saw—a dozen were represented, in this case, both British and Italian—had more gusto than the Cygne show. The models did some lively capering in their miniskirts, and in place of mystical warblings there was the loud, lascivious pulse of a song that seemed to be called "Do It to Me, Superman." But this show, too, gave one an eerie feeling of revisiting the nineteen-sixties without itself bringing to the fashions of that time the psychological baggage that inspired them then—the driving impetus to feel free and to rebel.

Some of the young designers came up with restrained, crafts-manlike styles of vaguely Art Deco inspiration. These were the conservatives of the group. Others showed full-blown psyche-delic-playtime styles: a mini in canary-colored teddy-bear pile, worn with matching Courrèges-length boots; balloon-shaped minis, like those Kenzo had shown earlier in Paris, and worn with boots that looked made of the same pink plastic as babies' rattles; and mad, brilliant-colored Pierrot outfits with giant clownish spots, worn with hair styles that were a bouncing mass of multicolored antennae. After the revivals of the modes of the thirties, the forties, and the fifties, here was a complete expression of nostalgia for the sixties. As with the other re-vivals of earlier decades, it was undoubtedly designers too young to have remembered the originals who were now ap-proaching the styles with such verve.

This show was also noteworthy for having a miniskirt that was the most uncompromising and unmistakable miniskirt seen in any of the recent shows. It was that of a blousy, tunic-like dress, worn with natural-colored pantyhose and short, cuffed, high-heeled boots, and it was sported by a young model who appeared to relish the way she looked. She looked very good. The subject of miniskirts is a loaded one in fashion at the moment. They showed up in the fall collections in Paris—notably at Kenzo, who is considered to be very influential. Virtually all the New York designers showed at least a token example of a miniskirt, although the majority of hem lengths ranged from below the knee to the ankle. But when mini-skirts were shown they were generally accompanied by a whole panoply of leg-disguising tricks—high boots; socks rolled over boots; socks rolled over other socks; kneewarmers; legwarmers; and tights and shoes whose color merged with that of the dress —that will, it seems, play a part in fashions of all lengths this fall. The effect of short skirts over real legs is thus considerably watered down. The fashion industry and the fashion press ap-proach the prospect of drastically shortened skirts with a cir-cumspection bordering on fear. At least, designers feel that they are on an even keel again, evolving confidently and calmly from one season to the next. The trauma of the midiskirt debacle, now seven years old, still haunts them, and they do not want to risk worrying their customers—who in the provinces of every country have only recently consented to drop their skirt lengths (when they wear skirts, and not pants) to below their knees—with even a hint of dramatic change. But in spite of attempts to play the mini down, it is around again. It is showing up in both London and Paris, where there is a generation of restless and fashionable young women who have been stuck in long skirts for close to ten years, and a still younger group who never had the fun of wearing miniskirts at all the first time they were around. And the miniskirt is beginning to show up, at least in the discothèques, in New York.

That sole self-confident minidress held the key to the success of the new fall fashions in any length or style. It wasn't making a political statement or skulking about timidly trying to pretend it was other than itself. It was primarily an enthusiastic piece of design, standing on its own terms. The best fashion now is neither noticeably establishment nor strikingly rebellious. Like other aspects of society and the arts, fashion reminds us that, however indefinable the spirit associated with people who were broadly of college age in the late nineteen-sixties, it was a strangely potent phenomenon and its representatives are now coming to positions of actual power. The ball of that group's generational values, or what remains of them, has now rolled firmly to the center of the fashion stage. One often has the feeling that the best work is being done by designers who are in their late twenties and early thirties—or by those who empathize with them. The most sensitive of the older group of designers are strongly influenced by the silhouettes and the sense of whimsey—what might be termed the "Annie Hall" style of comic elegance—that developed naturally among people in the thirtyish category. There doesn't appear to be a truly original or cohesive style growing independently in the generation below that—among people who are now in their early twenties or younger. The fashion tone of the sixties generation prevails in a modified form, though, and has shed its original restlessness and frenzy. Beneath the most successful new fashion, one may detect the symbolic generational base of energetic idealism, but its surface appears to be at ease. When it really works well, the new fashion has a distinct air of peace.

To produce a self-assured and fashionable-looking collection today, a designer must thread a path through a thicket of paradoxes. Chief among these, perhaps, is the premise that the most compelling professional effects are those that draw, at least symbolically, on a style that was invented by amateurs. In recent years, "the girl on the street" who knew how to put an outfit together with flair—with old and new ingredients and often from sources outside the traditional fashion industry—became a more powerful force for change than any designer. And that prototypical girl on her mythical street is far from the same as a model in a fashion show. Even *Women's Wear Daily*—a publication dedicated to bolstering the confidence of the fashion industry—tacitly acknowledged in its review of a recent show that official fashion often lacks a certain vital spark. In giving an encomium to the collection, and struggling, with obvious sincerity, to convey the point that *this* praise was genuine, unlike some of the paper's dutiful bombast, the reviewer noted that the show had "such smashing originality that every model who came on the stage sparkled with the mood of real-life fashion." Real-life fashion is based on the moods and fantasies and self-image of the women who wear it. Fashion that looks too much based on the moods, fantasies, and self-image of designers doesn't sparkle, and it won't sell, either. Fashion designers are themselves aware that their success and their economic survival depend on their discerning and anticipating the image that their customers have of themselves. There is much talk in the fashion business of capturing the elusive winning "mood."

Good professional fashion must give at least the illusion of being on an individual, even intimate scale and must be a refined version of the amateur fashion assembled by women for themselves. It must also recognize the reality that people do not throw out their wardrobes each season and start afresh. The notion of wardrobes that evolve—taking into account both the expense of a succession of radically new styles and the way one gets attached to clothes that have become part of one's personality over the years—is given as much play in designers' written releases these days as the significance of "mood." But it is a further paradox of fashion today that as its context becomes quieter and concerns itself more with development than with revolution, its presentation—the medium of the fashion show—becomes more public, more bent on generating a near-hysterical sense of excitement, and more anxious to create an illusion of earth-shattering novelty. Fashion shows had never before been as elaborately staged and as uncomfortably overcrowded as they were on Seventh Avenue this season.

For the reporters, buyers, and hangers-on who follow the full course of the fashion show period, it is primarily a test of physical and emotional stamina. It is as though their task of looking at clothes also trained them as extras in a disaster movie. Conscientious attendance at the industry's showings can continue from breakfast to evening with barely a pause between. The pack of followers—of shifting size but with a core of real faithfuls, whose faces, like those of the top models they watch, acquire a familiarity that haunts one's dreams as the sessions progress—moves all over town, from shows in showrooms, ballrooms, and department stores to shows in discothèques, restaurants, and lofts. The participants are pushed and shoved into and out of elevators so crowded that bodies are propped upright with their trampled feet far out of line with their center of gravity. Designers' guests are stabbed by camera equipment and jabbed in the backs of their knees by Vuitton carryalls stuffed with order books. They are driven to undignified brawling over their right to a seat, and, once sardined in place, they are subject to terrifying hazards in case of fire. The feverish search on Seventh Avenue for novelty and for sure profits has come to rival the showings of the Paris prêt-à-porter, which have long been infamous for the discomfort they inflict on those who visit them from all over the world. (Teams of Japanese businessmen with cameras, a familiar sight in Paris, are now much in evidence here, too.) The remark most frequently overheard among the distracted and weary crowd was "This is getting just like Europe," and, indeed, many of those who suffered on Seventh Avenue had only recently returned from a similar fray in Paris—and often in London and Milan as well. To the high level of anxiety imposed by physical conditions is added a psychological stress created by the peculiarly self-conscious and competitive nature of many professionally fashion-minded people. Even as a professional fashion woman elbows another in the ribs, she narrows her eyes to take in the details of her victim's cunningly draped Parisian shawl. Even as she glares down to see who has crushed her toe, she assesses the style of her assailant's shoe and the color of her hose.

The competitiveness rampant in these gatherings turns on a prerogative that might puzzle an outsider—the right to see the clothes. Fashion shows have moved more and more, latterly, to larger and more appropriate viewing sites than showrooms. Often, in the case of these alternative venues, there is a raised catwalk, so that even those seated at a distance are able to get some general sense of the styles that parade along it. But the designer's showroom, set up with rows of chairs along an aisle at floor level, remains the most common arrangement. It is in the interests of those in charge of allotting seats —they have as finely tuned a sense of power and its shifts as any maître d' in a fashionable restaurant—to flatter the front-row people by making them feel that they are not merely big spenders but also celebrities. People in the second row see the clothes from the waist up, and if the chairs are not too tightly packed together there is an occasional glimpse of feet and hems between the shoulders of the row in front. People in the third row see hats and heads, and people in the fourth and fifth rows, if fourth and fifth rows exist, see nothing at all unless they stand up, but a lack of floor space often precludes that. That these arrangements persist is dramatic proof that the majority of those who attend fashion shows are content to see little of the clothes as long as they are given the feeling of participating in an "event."

Clothes are on their way to becoming subsidiary, insubstantial elements of professional fashion shows. That audiences should accept and designers—by their increasing preoccupation with the theatrical effects surrounding their creations—should encourage this withdrawal of emphasis from clothes as such reflects part of the thinking that has led to the conclusion that the "mood" of the customer is vital. The old authority of fashion, with its confidence in itself as a minor art form, has vanished. Clothes exist far less in the eye of the designer than in the emotions of the beholder. This truth, which has been dimly perceived by customers for some years, is now being translated by designers into the way they present their fashion shows. Clothes have a mysterious and human life beyond their tangible selves. They are fragile ideas and symbols, subject to loss of vitality under the wrong circumstances and to increased value under the right ones. It was inevitable that designers should become concerned with manipulating the aura around their efforts. Clothes presented in a genteel showroom do not look the same as they do in a discothèque, to a background of hustle records and flashing lights. An outfit looks different on a model who jogs down the runway with flying hair and in the company of a lumbering English sheepdog from the way it looks on the same model moving with the traditional gliding walk and glassy eye. Clothes don't look the same under different circumstances, and they are not the same.

At the moment when clothes are launched in a fashion show, the experience is so compressed and intense for spectators that their all-important perceptions teeter in precarious balance. Seating arrangements complicate impressions that are already being played on by music, lighting, and other aspects of a theatrical production style. The experience of being invited only to a secondary show or seated in some subsidiary area at the first forcefully brings home the way the same clothes can be diminished from one occasion to the next, or even in the brief passage between one room and the next. From some windowless rear stockroom, guests experience only at a distance, through the sound of clicking cameras and the pattering of enthusiastic applause, the supreme moment of an outfit's novelty, which takes place in the room up front. After what seems an age, the outfit appears in the back room. Both the garment and the girl modelling it have become infected by a sense of second-classness and fatigue on the way. The girl, responding instinctively to her clothes' loss of worth, tones down her arrogant or coquettish performance of the earlier room. She goes through the perfunctory motions of her turn and hurriedly whisks herself away.

The attempt to create consciously an aura of excitement around fashions—especially those in the natural, easygoing style—can backfire. As the audiences for fashion shows swell; as settings become more majestic; and as lighting, music, and the performance of the models draw more on the techniques of the theatre and of dance, the gap between the shows' form and the clothes' content can widen into absurdity. The more that professional fashion seeks to cater to "real life," the greater are the hazards of overpromotion and the weirder the effect when its clothes are launched amid the deliberate illusion making of a theatrical presentation. One designer hired Roseland and a large band for his show, then showed to the assembled crowd a banal collection of blazers and sportswear. Diane Von Furstenberg's humble wrap dresses in T-shirt fabrics, with their winning combination of P.T.A. neatness and sensuality, look fine in suburban shopping malls, no doubt, but when they were viewed en masse in a giant, multimedia presentation at the Pierre, with a flashy, stop-and-go slide show taking place around them, they were dwarfed into something like silliness. Ralph Lauren, in his turn, staged another of the season's largest shows—in the Grand Ballroom of the Biltmore. Over a thousand people were present: faces lifted to a raised catwalk stretching below the noble chandeliers, with more eager faces drooping down from the balcony that rings the chamber. The music was on a grandiose and trumpeting scale, and spotlights powerful enough to pick out enemy aircraft were aimed from on high to follow the models' parade and play dramatically over the crowd. Down the catwalk came Lauren's fashions. These are not banal, but neither are they, by any stretch of the imagination, to be classified as art. They are wearable, stylish, practical translations of the All-American look—of preppiness and of L. L. Bean. They are certainly close to being a certain kind of real life. The audience saw girls with squeaky-clean blond pageboy hair pass non-chalantly by in trim little sweater-dresses and flat shoes, as if their noses were in the air of some Ivy League campus in the decades before blue jeans. A lean black model loped along within the searchlight's pool dressed in tight velvet jeans, a workman's watch cap, and a navy turtleneck sweater that might—for all the eyes in the balcony could make out—have come from an army surplus store. A redhead strode down with an air of studied introspection, her hands deep in the pockets of the sort of comfortable-looking cardigan that Virginia Woolf threw on when she was struggling with a novel in her country cottage. The models were clearly inspired by the blown-up attention they were getting, and they performed some brilliant mimicry of ordinary women carelessly getting on with their lives. But there were always the searchlights and the thousand faces, and ordinary women they were not. The whole performance was strangely jarring, and it certainly added nothing useful to one's perception of Ralph Lauren's clothes. If one saw a beautiful, long-legged girl in a turtleneck sweater and a pair of tight jeans walk by in a setting more natural than a darkened ballroom—running her dogs on the beach, say, or swinging down a city street—that girl would be more appealing and her clothes, unencumbered by fake significance, would look their best.

The audience on such an ostentatious fashion occasion is so lulled into bonhomie by its free glass of white wine and then so well whipped-up to expect novelty and excitement that it rarely realizes that what it is watching is perfectly mundane. But some subconscious awareness of the absurdity of staring solemnly at a pair of jeans with the aid of searchlights seems indicated by the crowd's reaction to the appearance of styles with more inherent glamour. Whenever an expensive-looking long-haired fur coat came down the runway (the models sometimes tossed Lauren's fur designs over his comfortable, casual clothing), a spontaneous animal roar rose from the thousand throats. The clothes were shown for what they were, then—uniforms for ordinary and private people. But the furs were symbols of money, power, and drama: a spectacle that the watching crowd knew, at heart, to be worthy of the arena.

Fall Collections:
Content

With all the theatrical fanfare that launches collections these days, how is one supposed to assess the curious hybrid that is the dramatic new fashion show? To apply the standards of the theatre, the dance, or the art gallery is patently absurd, however designers may seek to cloak their efforts in the trappings of grander and more widely respected art forms than the craft of clothing manufacture. The form whose criteria would seem most applicable is the public relations happening, but this is scarcely a helpful guideline, having historical roots even shallower than those of fashion shows, and being a genre that by its nature makes no provision for critical analysis on the part of its audience. One is supposed to have one's attention alerted (often in some very nebulous way) by a P.R. event, or perhaps to be staggered by the expense it involves, but one is not intended to judge it, compare any one with any other, or refer to a tradition. Each example bubbles up and then sinks back into its own moment.

But as one experiences the motley events that are the new fashion shows, one aspect of the whole does seem to present itself as a valid object of critical scrutiny—the performance of the models. This is a surprising development, because no spectator at a traditional fashion show was ever particularly tempted to think of these young women as performers, let

alone as people bent on expressing themselves. Their emana-
tions, when not completely neutral, used to be vaguely animal-
like. They were gazelles and, in some cases, jungle tigresses at
first; when, five years or so back, they started dancing down
the aisles in youthful-looking fashions instead of gliding by in
mature ones, they became more like puppies. But now models
seem anxious to be seen as human beings, in some direct and
equal relationship with the human beings who come to gawk
at them, and they are encouraged—in varying degrees, according to the designer's taste—to project their personalities.
Fashion shows have become more elaborate in part because the
job of modeling, within its own peculiarly circumscribed
range, has started to evolve. It was perhaps inevitable that in
our age of individuality and "creativity"—and long after
practically every other kind of woman has learned to stand
up for herself—models should begin to assert their right to be
more than objects, and to behave like people. In the field of
fashion photography (a career separate from showroom modeling, although the same woman is sometimes in demand in
both), the new concern for the model's self-respect is reflected
in current talk of listing—along with the photographer, the
designer, and the manufacturers of accessories—the name of
the woman who is shown wearing the clothes. It is now common to see showroom models greet friends in the audience
they parade before; and at the end of the show they gather
round the designer to bill, coo, and applaud his work as
affectionate show-business equals. Even designers who used
to be known for the sedateness of their clothes now permit
models to prance, flirt, mime, jog, or ham things up with
spoofs of the model's traditional struts and turns. Watching
the show put on by Carol Horn, one felt like some indulgent
nanny on the sidelines of a creative playground where models
got up to a hundred cutely self-expressive stunts, from playing
the flute, knitting, and waving lighted flashlights to applying
lipstick to each other's mouths.

The show presented by Anne Klein and Company in the
Grand Ballroom of the Plaza was one of the most comprehensive of the season's examples of the new fashion spectacle.

Throughout the show, the senses of the huge audience were remorselessly manipulated by dramatic changes of lighting and music. (The first group of clothes appeared in a semi-darkness that was chopped up by the flicker of one of those discothèque light machines which make their victims feel they have a terrible malfunction of the eyelids or have wandered into a Buster Keaton film.) And the models in the show were given a lavish opportunity to spread their performer's wings. Complex choreography sent them out in groups, weaving in and out in a Busby Berkeley flow, or else captured them temporarily in static spotlit friezes of kneeling and stretching poses, like figures on a Grecian vase. The show's finale wholeheartedly abandoned the pretense of making the clothes look remotely the way they would look on Anne Klein customers in their normal lives. The models—or, at least, those among them who were capable of taking a stab at such activity—were transformed into ballet dancers who happened to be wearing Anne Klein designs. This was clearly the model's big moment. Each in turn got to make a dramatic entrance, leaping out from behind the gold and white Ionic columns of the ballroom's stage; to flit down the long runway essaying balletic twirls, twists of the wrist, and chassés; and then at the end to retreat into the wings with a ballerina's limpid lingering backward gaze. The audience, which thought that it had come to see a mere fashion show, rooted valiantly for these more high-flown performances, and it seems a mite churlish to observe that most of the models made simply awful dancers. (Among the few things that inspire the same sinking feeling as clumsy dancing are an ice skater coming a cropper and a horse misjudging a fence.)

One sometimes yearns, as one trudges round the collections from this extravagant entertainment to that stimulating performance, for the days when fashion shows were fashion shows, and models, instead of performing other jobs with an amateurishness that is supposed to be endearing, did their own work with a superbly professional grace. They are beautiful women, for the most part, with elegant models' bodies, which are of quite a different build from the bodies of dancers.

But the psychological tide may have turned for them irrevocably; it is probably impossible for them to put on a completely bland act again. They look really happy now only when the show is grand, the crowd is huge, and they can feel themselves to be the active stars of a noisy success. In smaller, more traditional shows, when they are simply walking down the runway in new clothes, their expressions betray the prickly defensiveness characteristic of people who feel overqualified for their job. But, in the end, the possibility of models' developing themselves through their work will always be limited. Even though attempts are being made to emphasize their personalities, models must always remain subsidiary to the clothes they display and serve as litmus paper for the designer's tone. One of the most interesting aspects of attending lots of shows is witnessing how utterly different the same top models, who go the rounds of them all, can look and behave in different circumstances, according to their outfits, their perception of the atmosphere around them, and the degree to which they are encouraged to display their newly discovered sense of self.

While it seems futile to judge fashion shows solely on their presentation and difficult to judge them solely by their clothes, it seems fair to demand that there be some semblance of harmony between the two. One of the most charming of the season's smaller shows was that given by the designer Joan Vass—it was her first such effort—in her own apartment, on West Twenty-fifth Street. Mrs. Vass's clothes are all made by hand on cottage-industry lines. Many of her styles are given names, as though they were family pets—there is the Alexander Nevsky coat, the Sierra Club muffler, and the Christopher Robin hat. Her show was on an equally intimate and human plane. The apartment where it took place is a huge, shabby penthouse, a cross between an artist's loft and a greenhouse. The "models" included her daughter and her three sons and a group of young dancers whom the designer had discovered in Riverside Church. These dancers had their own inexperienced and very free interpretation of what was called for in displaying clothes. Their spontaneity made a welcome change from the artificiality of the models the audience had watched for hours and days at a time in other showrooms. The dancers were not exactly the same as average women, but they had, in several cases, the rounded curves that ordinary customers are often endowed with and real models never possess.

Along with harmony between form and content, the audience at fashion shows ought to have a right to expect some consistency of tone and some evidence of editing in the designer's presentation of his styles. Many shows are unnecessarily padded out with multiple examples of the same idea or with styles that will never actually be produced for sale in the stores. But this season Perry Ellis, Charles Suppon, Bill Haire, Richard Assatly, Gil Aimbez, and Alice Blaine (or the firms who employ these designers) were responsible for sound and generally well-edited collections. Their presentation was often fairly lavish, but the clothes were usually able to match the vitality of the display. Giorgio Sant'Angelo presented a hopelessly rambling show, yet he may be excused for that, because he is among the few really artistic talents around, and his collection had some perfectly brilliant ideas in it. But my favorites of the several dozen shows I saw were those of Calvin Klein, Geoffrey Beene, and Mrs. Harriet Winter. Each of these collections had a markedly different tone, but among them they sum up the new fall fashions at their best. In all three cases, the clothes had a private, unostentatious character and were presented with relative modesty and restraint in the designer's own showrooms.

Getting in and out of the Calvin Klein show was one of the most nightmarish experiences of the whole season, and the near riots that erupted in the aisles and at the elevators on that day have become notorious in the annals of the fashion world. But once the audience was squeezed into the room (at least, those of the invited guests fortunate enough not to be blocked in the lobby or trapped in the elevators) it saw a show whose models instinctively comported themselves to match the clothes they wore—with a fine combination of delicacy and arrogance. Klein's style is more controlled and conservative-looking than either Beene's or Mrs. Winter's, but his work has developed and lightened considerably from the strictly tailored sportswear with which he rose to prominence—a tailoring that used to seem too cramped and inhibited for my taste. A general feminizing of Klein's tailoring was exemplified in this collection by the little jackets with which he has replaced his famous but more masculine-looking blazers. The Klein jacket is narrow-torsoed, squarish-shouldered, singlebreasted, and short—of a length somewhere between bellhop and hipbone. It is a silhouette that flatters more women than the longer, double-breasted blazer does. Although any mention of thrift shops is as taboo in the professional fashion world as the irresponsible boosting of miniskirts, the pre-New Look fashions to be found in such places have certainly had an influence in the reshaping of contemporary jackets. And Klein's extremely feminine, beautifully detailed blouses, used in combination with relatively masculine tailoring, are a modern version of a fashion idea that is several decades old. Sometimes his jackets appeared with skirts that fell to some three inches below the knee, but they looked their self-confident best in combination with sinuous, long-legged pleated-front trousers. (Klein's loyalty to the elegance of well-cut trousers is refreshing at a time when other designers are to be seen turning resolutely to skirts for their greater "softness" and "femininity"—the often mindlessly employed shibboleths for the new fall clothes.) Outfits were assembled in gentle combinations of the colors of nuts and fruits and in interesting textural contrasts—tops of velvet, fine tweed, or cashmere over blouses of cotton, silk broadcloth, charmeuse, or handkerchief linen. Blouses had delicate tucks and discreet ruffles, or more of the scalloped collars and cuffs that Klein used so successfully in his spring collection. Often, these scallops were turned down at the waist to extend beyond a jacket sleeve and frame the hand, or turned up at the collar and ringed round by a silk kerchief for a swan-neck effect. This was tied in a bohemian bow tie that

Klein's written release characterized as "very George Sand." Other new-looking toppings included hipbone-length cardigan jackets that were collarless and buttonless and had the savoir-faire of early Chanel; body-hugging wraparound sweaters of fine cashmere; and cashmere pullovers with necklines that followed the collarbone. All these trim sweaters held their own against the big, bulky, hand-knitted monsters one saw in profusion elsewhere around town. I had less sympathy for Klein's cashmere serapes, slung pointlessly over one shoulder (shawls of every kind will be seen ad nauseam in the fall, it seems), and for his use of foulard-printed challis, which also threatens to be part of the obligatory uniform of slaves of fashion. I liked the way Klein used charmeuse in blouses combined with tops and bottoms of more robust textures but relished the fabric less when it appeared alone for long or short evening gowns. This slithery, satinlike material was used in many of the collections, and designers often played up its overtones of boudoirish sinfulness. To Klein's credit, his choice of colors and style generally mitigated the lingerie connotations. In the main, his collection was notable for its dignity and clarity.

Geoffrey Beene's collection differed from any other by a quality rare among fashion designers, who are on the whole an instinctive breed. (The innovators, of whom there are very few these days, create with instinctive flashes of inspiration. The assimilators and imitators, who form a far larger group, react instinctively to those flashes of inspiration and pass them along at just the right moment.) The distinctive quality of Beene's work—which at the same time reflects an immediate sensuous response to the color and texture of beautiful fabrics —must be characterized as a variety of intellectualism. This is of a kind different from and more deep-seated than the smattering of cultural crosscurrents which has become common in the written releases and statements of "philosophy" that many designers now launch on the world together with their collections. Such releases draw on increasingly ambitious sources these days in their attempt to interpret as well as describe new clothes. Designers rightly perceive that the psychological and cultural atmosphere attaching to an outfit is of as much significance to shoppers as details of its shape, hem length, and color. This atmosphere is what will first capture the customer's imagination and put her in the mood to buy. Descriptions of clothes released by designers have become more fanciful than ever in an attempt to conjure up symbolic images and correspondences between clothes and the arts. At the simplest level, this greater literariness gives colors more inventive names. Perry Ellis's clothes came in, among other things, "pink dust/blue ridge" hopsacking, "birch" melton, "quail" corduroy, and "truffle" tweed. Bill Haire listed his outfits as "movements" in "Copen blue and ash" or in "port and clay," and labeled his pastels "Monet blue" and "Degas pink." Devotion to the ballet, fascination with Byron and Shelley, and the influence of Dumas's *Three Musketeers* were listed as the sources of inspiration for the designer's collection. Credits these days no longer restrict themselves to the names of those who provide shoes, makeup, and hairstyles for fashion shows but stretch to include those responsible for their "poetry" and "choreography" as well. Donna Karan, one of the designers for Anne Klein, referred not to groups of clothes but to various "idioms" and "moods" and she gave credit to Martha Graham and Jane Austen. Before long, we shall doubtless see designers' programs filled with academic footnotes, and their clothes described, like Whistler's paintings, as symphonies in color. But Geoffrey Beene's brand of thoughtfulness goes beyond semantic dabblings and historicist parlor games. It is a sincerely reflective response to women's image of themselves and to the society in which they live.

Beene shows a solid understanding of the principle that if clothes make a psychological and sociological statement about their wearer, no woman of intelligence and complexity would wish that message to be a monolithic, single-minded one—particularly if it was drafted on her behalf by a designer who had assembled the same package of self-expression for a thousand other customers. Beene is a master of contrasts and contradictions within a single outfit. In his new collection, he used

an infinity of contradicting textures and colors of fabrics—
silk under corduroy, bulky hand-knitting over fragile sprigged
cotton, shearling jackets over flimsy evening clothes, quilted
cotton over velvet, to name a few. Most of his skirts floated
wide and full to the graceful low-calf length. But then he slid
away from the romantic effect of such skirts (which are also
styled for comfort, since one may sprawl or sit cross-legged in
them as readily as in pants) by combining them with touches
of clumsiness. These touches of self-parodying buffoonery—
whose presence always conveys an essentially youthful message—included funny brimmed hats jammed low on the brow,
dumpy flat-heeled boots, and pink ballet slippers worn with
cream-colored hand-knitted legwarmers that rippled into
wrinkles round the ankles. (Beene is one of many designers to
have been influenced this season by dancers and the dance.)
His standard of workmanship is high, and he uses superb and
exclusive fabrics. Prices—at least in his couture collection—
are considerable. (Those of Beene Bag, his sportswear department, are more moderate.) But the customer who would wear
the clothes from his fall collection is not the sort to flaunt
her ability to pay for them, and they are pregnant with ironic
mixed messages about their value, besides being combined
contradictions of style. Other designers showed flashy furs and
metallic fabrics that throbbed like Times Square neon with
information about their cost. But when Beene showed a lux-
urious-looking coat with deep sable cuffs (there was something of the Balenciaga years in the generosity of its cut) the
coat itself was made of a relatively humble chocolate-colored
corduroy. The collection was distinctive, too, for its abundance
of interesting details and playful accessories: a sausage of
trapunto trimming the armhole of a jerkin; gloves and stockings in homespun-wool knit; and belts that were a study of
textural contrast within themselves. One belt was a twisted
combination of fat noodles of hessian and turquoise silk
wound with strings of glitter. Some of the belts were further
enlivened by a sprig of eucalyptus or a jaunty teasel.

. . .

Harriet Winter's clothes have a style different again from either Beene's or Klein's, but, like theirs, they are bathed in an imaginative atmosphere that feels just right. Her designs for Yesterday's News have a self-contained, almost introspective tone, and a sense of secure, unfrilly femaleness. They have a palpable aura of peace. Skirts in the collection fell gently to boot length and were made of fluid crêpes and jerseys. Her colors were well chosen and well combined, and detailing was interesting without seeming gratuitous. Many of the details, in fact—wrapped and gathered waists; loops of fabric forming ties on jackets; knots at the back of the ankles of loose-limbed pants; and seams that were exposed on the outside of the garment—also performed a function and were an integral part of the structure. (Only in the case of the drawstrings that she used in several styles did Mrs. Winter's tireless investigation of the possibilities of this structural detailing come close to running amok and marring the simplicity of the whole effect.) She also used details with no particular purpose beyond their allure—the superposed double and triple Peter Pan collars she has long favored, and handkerchief schemes of self-fabric falling softly around the throat. Mrs. Winter has said, with a more sincere understanding than many men designers who express similar opinions, that all clothing is an extension of a woman's psyche. She has also described her own designs and techniques as being "machine couture." Between them, these two observations encompass the essence of her style. Her clothes are ladylike without being pompous, and they represent a misty, streamlined dream.

The most compelling new fashions often incorporate the principle of mixed messages, and the new hair styles and accessories are instrumental in the expression of these contradictions. Although clothes have eased and softened from the rigidly classic sportswear that was around a few seasons back, many of the new clothes can still look "straight" and fairly boring if they are worn with hair and shoes that match their style exactly. But if they are worn with the new crazily sprouting hair styles or with the eccentric foot and leg gear that is around, the effect, though somewhat schizophrenic, is more satisfying. For the most fashionable young women, heads and feet have become prime vehicles for the expression of fantasy. The most interesting styles for these extremities set out not to look flattering but to look witty. One still saw, in some of the shows, hair that had been set on rollers or else blown-dry into Waspy-looking pageboys, and nice little flat-heeled pumps or sexy high-heeled evening sandals worn with natural nylons. But all these looked tired and timid beside the freewheeling notions that other designers explored—hair that had been rumpled with the fingers and left to dry naturally under heat lamps; hair set into intricate braids when wet and either left that way or unleashed into a fluffy thatch of Botticelli frizziness; strange-colored combinations of hose and boots, worn in layers over each other; and rumpled, old-mannish socks over hightop sneakers, medieval sandals, or Chinese cotton Mary Janes.

Giorgio Sant'Angelo's show—although badly in need of editing, one of the season's most imaginative—explored to the utmost the contradicting possibilities of styles for heads and feet. His shoes were uniformly well chosen (credit for them was given to Judie Buie, Sasha, Maud Frizon, Charles Jourdan, and Reed Jay Evins), and they often deflected or scrambled the message of the outfit they accompanied. The lacy refinement of an embroidered Ultrasuede skirt was combined with dark stockings and ankle-high boots with hippie-style Indian fringes at their cuffs. A fringed blanket coat of fire engine–red mohair, with overtones of wintry, log-fire coziness, appeared with opaque red stockings and matching but distinctly summery sandals. A wispily glamorous evening dress was worn with high heels and thick purple stockings. The hair styles in the show were equally original. (Credit for these was given to a hairdressing firm called Christiaan Laboratory.) They often involved very intricate braiding that began at the roots of each section of hair and then wound itself close to the scalp to give the effect of a small head. Hairdos like these, when created for the fine and very often blond hair of white models, not only embody a witty contradiction between themselves and the more formal outfits they accompany but also play on the styles of different races. The effect of braids close to a small, neat skull obviously derives from the often exquisite patterns of cornrowing that are seen on the heads of young black women—and on young black men, too.

The most interesting new fashions in hair—and probably in clothes as well—owe much to the coming together of black and white styles. Where five years ago black designers and fashionable young black women had their own quite distinctive and separate brand of élan, they have now brought it into something more like the mainstream, and often give to fairly classic, conservative, and expensive styles their own special flair. It is significant that the new hair styles—whether braiding or unleashed Pre-Raphaelite fullness—may be practicably effected on the very different textures of white and black women's hair. The effect is somewhat different in the two cases, but it is equally spectacular. If the new frizz is perhaps some distant descendant of the Afro, it is a gesture of stylishness rather than politics, and its shape—with fullness in the back and sides below the ears rather than on top of the head—is radically different. But the simple unraveling of wet-braided hair into a downy isosceles-triangle shape is not the end of the tale. The locks that come foaming forth like a bush of spirea are then sometimes partly recaptured in a braid that hangs down over one eye, or wholly caught up in a lunatic tuft, sprout, or ponytail set off-center on top of the head or at any other place that takes the wearer's fancy. And then these caught-up sprouts (or the whole bush) are taken a stage further and decorated with what might look to an unsympathetic observer like bits of rubbish. (Although sprout decoration was seen in various places and on many white women, it is true that it was seen at its most stylized in the show given by Scott Barrie, a black designer, who employed a greater proportion of black models than did most of his colleagues on Seventh Avenue.) Flowers and combs in the hair have now been so widely adopted and have such uncompromising, uncontradictory messages of sugary femininity that they are beginning to look passé. Instead of these, the new hair ornaments are dime-store barrettes; fishing flies; strings, loops, and streamers of metallic ribbons, beads, or pearls; funny bits of feather and fur; and sets of bows made out of twisted candy wrappers. The image the new hair styles bring most readily to mind is of Christmas trees lying in the streets at the end of the festive season and strewn with windblown, rain-tangled remnants of tinselly trimmings.

British Genius

I n London this year, a somewhat shabby-looking exhibition dedicated to "British Genius" told the world that the electric light bulb was invented by an Englishman named Joseph Wilson Swan, who while experimenting with filaments discovered a way of making rayon. Authorities in Victorian Britain were obdurately convinced that the building of a power network would prove too costly, and so the first large power station in England was designed by Thomas Alva Edison, who—unlike his transatlantic rival—had had the foresight to patent his ideas. As for rayon, it came to be associated in the public mind far more with the French, because it was employed by the flamboyant Count Hilaire de Chardonnet for objects more appealing to the waggish imagination than practical old light bulbs—ladies' negligees and panties. A syndrome of unexploited opportunities, evident a century ago, afflicts Britain—in its fashion industry no less than in scientific and technical fields—to this day. British talents come up with extraordinarily free and inventive ideas that all too often suffer from bad management, uninspired salesmanship, and the timidity of public authorities or large and bureaucratic companies. It is frequently left to better organized and more aggressive outsiders to promote and capitalize on British ideas. Yet it was the spontaneous and sometimes unbusinesslike inventions of fashion-minded young people in Britain which set in motion a cycle of fashion that persists—often in French,

Italian, Japanese, or American versions—some ten years after it first showed up on the streets of London.

What are these proved trendsetters up to now, and why do they not get wider international recognition? The answer to the first question is work that is often brilliantly innovative and fastidious. The answer to the next is more complex. There is a temptation to think of fashion as a purely private impulse connected to the future—an individual's enthusiasm for the next shape or for the up-and-coming name. But before fashion can reach the public it must contend with the meshes of an elaborate industry that is profoundly wedded to its past. Like any other original idea or design in Britain (any tangible one, at least; the arts, where no manufacturing process is called for, fare better), high-fashion design must live within a complicated industrial society that has generally failed to support originality or has actually been hostile to it. Britain spawns designers, prolifically, and in many cases at state expense, from long and sophisticated fashion training in such art schools as St. Martin's, Kingston, Harrow, Ravensbourne, and the Royal College of Art. Where in America there is still only a handful of full-blown designers of the younger generation, in Britain they are produced in the hundreds each year. (It is true of Britain in general that educational institutions produce more people who are ambitious and able than a country of its size can conceivably absorb. Indeed, much of Britain's articulate and anxious dissatisfaction of the past few years may stem from a population overqualified for the only roles that society can conceivably offer.) But the British fashion industry has been singularly remiss in its treatment of the young designers that the state and the education system has fed to it.

From the moment of the young designers' emergence from the colleges, there appears to be no shortage of possibilities open to them. Many, indeed, are given dramatic breaks as a result of the graduation fashion shows, where they present their college work, and which are attended by talent-spotting members of the industry and the fashion press. Some of the fledglings are siphoned off into the huge textile companies, such as Courtaulds, Imperial Chemical Industries, and Tootal. But the demand for original fashion or textile design within such giants has, in the past, been limited, and the collaboration has rarely proved a happy one. Other graduates are snapped up by British clothing manufacturers, but this encounter between art and commerce, like any other, has been known to lead to painful disillusionment for the designers. As a result, some young British fashion designers do not even risk contact with British manufacturers; instead, as soon as they are trained, they are wooed away by offers from Continental Europe. This "brain drain" has been steadily increasing in recent years, until, by some estimates, as many as 25 percent of the best of British fashion and textile graduates now leave immediately to take jobs abroad. Behind some of the most successful names of European ready-to-wear—among them Daniel Hechter and Dorothée Bis, in France, and Fiorucci and Missoni, in Italy—lie stables of designers in which young British talent plays an important part. Still other young people, either without venturing into employment with manufacturers or after having their fingers burnt by such an experience, have chosen to set up in business on their own.

It is with small, scattered, designer-based independent companies that the verve and refinement of British fashion now reside. Independent and original designers exist in great numbers in Britain—often beginning on a shoestring, with one sewing or knitting machine, and then deliberately choosing to remain small, in order to retain control of ideas, quality, and "image." It isn't easy for such minute, often undercapitalized outfits to survive the economic trauma that Britain has known in the present decade, or for them to get supplies in the midst of an industry geared chiefly to mass production. The choice of long-term fulfillment outside the main fashion system over the possibility of quick enrichment within it involves considerable self-sacrifice. And high fashion must involve a kind of artistic élitism that may prick the conscience of its exponents —many of Britain's most determined new talents are the state-educated products of working-class backgrounds—in a welfare state whose commitment to egalitarian leveling-down extends from the government's policy of nondiscriminatory education and health care to the fashion industry's traditional goal of cheap, if undistinguished, clothing for the masses.

It is encouraging that independent and original designers manage to keep themselves bobbing along through the buffetings of a rocky economy and the constraints of a mass-production industry. Somehow, Janice Wainwright can go on producing her designs in hand-painted French velvets; Bruce Oldfield gets national publicity for his small range of streamlined evening separates; Janet Reger successfully runs two shops filled with her exquisitely sensual lingerie; Clive Shilton makes a decent living by creating painstakingly crafted handbags shaped like flowers or scallop shells; Esther Pearson's workshop goes on performing magic in hand-knitted wisps of pastel mohair; and a team like Sheridan Barnett and Sheilagh Brown still retains the courage and the gaiety to scheme up inventions like a pair of jodhpurs made of sugar-pink moiré. Small firms fare best when they involve united and devoted teams—some part artistic, the other more practical and businesslike—that are members of a family, or husband and wife, or the like. One great advantage enjoyed by small design firms in London is a supporting network of boutiques that respect and depend on original work. Shops such as Elle, Chic, Parker's, Gibbs, Crocodile, Roxy, Mrs. Howie, and Browns will, to varying degrees, encourage impoverished designers at the outset of their careers by helping them invest in fabrics and by guaranteeing them an audience for their finished clothes. (True, the relationship between fledgling designers and such stores can turn as sour as that between designers and manufacturers or between designers and entrepreneurs— more so, even, because, being more intensely personal, it carries echoes of the strains between parent and child. Designers complain of exclusive, binding arrangements—sometimes without credit to the rising name—in spite of the security these provide; stores complain of ingratitude and inconstancy.) Inevitably, a hundred different designers succeed or fail for a hundred different reasons. The weakest fall by the wayside through lack of talent or lack of commitment to their aim. Others fail through sheer bad luck when they are marketing a volatile product in an uncertain economic and psychological climate—getting either too few orders or so many that their little production system is overtaxed, goes haywire, and collapses in disarray. Some go through troubled times or fall foul of the system—Jeff Banks and Ulla Heathcote spring to mind—then pick themselves up and start again from scratch. The lucky ones are able to press on steadily, with student dreams perhaps a little dented by contact with the real world, but with their talents fundamentally intact. Something in the atmosphere of Britain has permitted them to survive against apparent odds. And, these days, new conditions in the fashion industry may be starting to work in their favor.

Ten years ago in Britain, there were Twiggy, the Beatles, and a spontaneous eruption of miniskirted street fashion that was the instantaneous reflection of a revolution. British fashion of the sixties was a joke and a lark, and when it cost anything at all it was ludicrously cheap. You could shear off your skirts for nothing, or else go to Mr. Freedom and get a Mickey Mouse T-shirt for a quid, or capture the murky, Pre-Raphaelite mood of Biba in a dress that set you back a fiver. Tommy Roberts, who ran Mr. Freedom, and was once the wacky genie of "Swinging London," is now collaborating on a pop musical with Justin de Villeneuve. Biba, which grew in the space of ten years from a tiny boutique into a huge department store that was probably the world's boldest experiment in selling fashion as a mood and a form of theatre, has closed its doors, and its designer is living and working quietly in South America. The Art Deco building in Kensington High Street which was the last shrine of the extraordinary Biba vision fell victim to the wheeling and dealing of property speculators, who have yielded up the premises for occupancy half by Marks & Spencer, half by British Home Stores—two pragmatic, value-minded chains. Biba's fantastical world is gutted now. Gone are the peach-colored Art Deco sofas and the acres of peach-colored glass, the ostrich feathers and the hair pomades, the funny hats and the monocles, the tea dances softly lit by neon rainbows. All this highly personal kitsch and taste, this distinctly British life and wit, have been swept aside to make way for the hygienic, sensibly air-conditioned, coolly fluorescent decorating formula common to every branch of Marks & Spencer from Darlington to Paris, from Glasgow to Plymouth —a style of décor that has about as much romance to it as a giant, automated poultry-dressing factory. The big-business Monopoly game to which Biba fell victim and the symbolic fate of the store's premises still rankle with fashion-minded people concerned about the nation's fund of design inspiration.

In its way, Marks & Spencer has done a fine service, by providing reasonably priced and durable clothing, household goods, and cellophane-packaged foods to the common Englishman—and, to judge by the babel in its London branches, to hosts of common Frenchmen, Germans, and Arabs as well. In a nation that often, in spite of internal irritations, seems like a single family, "Marks & Sparks" has established itself as a part of social mythology—a family joke—in a way that no Sears or J. C. Penney, no Levi Strauss or Bloomingdale's could ever do in this more diverse land. The store gained a place in the British heart, but its example also gained a stranglehold on the British fashion industry. In the short term, monolithic retailing companies may have served Britain's population by offering what it knew it wanted already; in the long term, by failing to foster original design, they jeopardized the fiber, textile, and fashion industries, which are the third-largest employer of that population. Mills and manufacturers, geared to producing billions of yards and millions of examples of stereotyped styles for giant outlets, grew reluctant to bother with small and innovative orders or to invest in machinery to make up different shapes. As long as the fashion industry's horizon was limited by underpants and football socks that sold effortlessly, through the word of mouth of a nation's harassed mums, the industry saw no need to raise the level of public taste or to bestir itself to promote its products in the international market.

There are signs, though, that the established patterns and structures of the British fashion industry are giving way, and that original and independent designers are starting to benefit. Inflation has done it, to a great extent. The faith in endless growth and in making more and more of the same things, ad infinitum, has been sorely shaken by the economic crisis. Clothing has traditionally been relatively cheap in Britain, because of a long-established mass-production structure and because of the underlying puritanism in the British character, which made for reluctance to spend money on fancy clothes. But inflation has meant that people cannot afford to spend as much on clothing, however cheap, as they could when times were good. Fashion, meanwhile, has been bubbling away underground, outside the system, and becoming more and more expensive. British fashion designers, like their colleagues around the world, have during the nineteen-seventies been increasingly drawn to artisanship, exclusiveness, and fine fabrics. Ten years ago, fashion was as cheap as any other clothing, because it was still tied in with the mass-production scheme. In opposition to mass-produced dowdiness, the fashion explosion poured out a code of mass-produced gaiety—Mary Quant–styled miniskirts and the newly invented pantyhose to wear with them, and Union Jack–patterned shopping bags that were turned out by the million. In time, though, that code outlived its original iconoclastic exuberance. Designers who were at first content to express a generation's restlessness by working for manufacturers discovered that, however enlightened or trendy these seemed, they were only businessmen after all. Designers yearned to express their own uniqueness more than that of their age group. They began to set up on their own, and to make more expensive clothes. The center of fashion has now shifted from amateur street fashion and mass production to designers—who, with their professionalized individualism, bridge the gulf between the two. Clothing may remain cheap for the British, but fashion is expensive now. People concerned with the over-all health of the British fashion industry are much concerned, these days, with helping exports and therefore with the process professionals refer to as "upgrading." This involves teaching and encouraging manufacturers to produce fewer things of better quality—to the standard that is in demand abroad. Stores and shoppers at home either will adjust to this internal change in the industry by buying better British clothes less often or will continue to buy cheap clothing, but discover that it has been imported from the sweatshops of Korea or Taiwan. Original fashion designers, stronger and more mature than they were five or ten years back, and with a product of high quality which they are very sure they want to make, are beginning to be courted again, on different terms, by clothing manufacturers, whose confidence in cheapness and sameness has been shaken by a depressed domestic market. Faced with reduced orders from the giant stores, the owners of small factories that once hummed with the production of a single style of inexpensive pajamas now look with renewed respect on the breakaway design talents. For all their defiant "artiness," these look enviably self-confident, and they are manifestly onto something. If their inventions are too odd and too costly for the provinces, they still find customers in London. More important yet, the designers hold the key to a product that is in demand abroad. In response to the discovery that quality can be profitable, the cycle of an industry begins to change.

Current British fashion has grown out of the country's history and maintains an ineffably British character, but it thrives by turning its back on Britain and selling only to cosmopolitan London—which is like a separate nation—and by looking out to the rest of the world. In this respect as well as in price, British fashion of the seventies is distinct from that of the sixties, which was a celebration of provincialism as well as of youth. London has never ceased to show signs of lively prosperity—not even in the depths of the country's economic gloom some years back, before North Sea oil seemed a totally credible hope, and before London was invaded, like Rome by the Visigoths, by wave after wave of free-spending foreign visitors. Restaurants boomed, the price of fashion soared, and a good proportion of the customers for both continued to be British. Porsches, Jaguars, and Maseratis stood gleaming at London curbsides before beautiful houses whose drawing-room curtains, left open at the hour of dusk, framed visions of exquisite antiques or priceless Milanese modernity for the benefit of the curious passers-by. (The display of wealth in any European capital is, admittedly, particularly striking by contrast with Manhattan, where stupendous fortunes hide far away from street crime in towers above Fifth Avenue, and few men in their sane senses will bump across the city's pot-holes in a thirty-thousand-dollar car.) Satisfactory explanations of persistent individual wealth are scarcely ever offered in England. Its source and nature must probably remain one of the many mysteries of the British economy, which has for so long frustrated the people who have to live with it and the governments that try to tinker with it. How did the crisis creep up on Britain, and what was the nature of the beast? Was it unique, or something that could happen to us all? Were in-exorable economic forces to blame, or was it something more personal and psychological—the prejudices of managers, the blindness of politicians, or the aspirations of the working man? It has been said that all the important stories of the modern world become incomprehensible in time, and that of Britain over the past ten years will doubtless prove no exception. Mean-while, there are signs of national hope and change.

The notion that "small is beautiful" has had a powerful hold on the imagination of the British from the start of the Industrial Revolution, whose effects they have experienced longer and more intimately than any other nation in the world. E. F. Schumacher's examination of "economics as if people mattered" holds great appeal for the homespun and individualistic streak in the British character. William Morris set forth his vision of a utopian reversal of monstrous industrialism in *News from Nowhere*, which was published in the eighteen-nineties. Life was to be simple, artifacts beautiful, and work fulfilling without the need for cash rewards. Faith in industrial, technological, economic, and even social progress has been still more severely tested in Britain than at the time of Morris's pipe dream, and more and more of its people are thinking of dismantling the machinery of progress. Every part of modern British society is under examination and challenge. Doctors complain of the unresponsive bureaucracy of the National Health Service; teachers and parents question the state educational system; workers are starting to wonder whether the giant trade unions are serving their best interests. The British have taken their doubts about the government in Westminster so far along the line that they are close to Devolution—the dramatic proposition that a country as small and as isolated as Britain should split itself up into even smaller and more isolated self-governing units.

If the liveliest members of the British fashion industry are leaning toward smallness not merely as an abstract artistic ideal but as a means of economic viability, it may well be that this tendency is symptomatic of change in the society as a whole. The textile trades have played a central part in the history of industrial and post-industrial Britain. When the cotton and woollen towns filled the valleys of Lancashire and Yorkshire, they marked England's move from an agrarian age to a mechanized one. The explosion of the industrial North, with the bustling philistinism of the "rags-to-riches" manufacturers and the fierce, proud neighborliness of ill-housed laborers, created something like a separate psychological nation within England, and a lack of sympathy between North and South which persists to this day. The failure of communication between, on the one hand, the weaving and spinning North and manufacturing Midlands (where the knitwear industry is largely based) and, on the other, London, where fashion ideas are chiefly generated, has undoubtedly hampered the development of the modern British fashion industry. The gap between the defiantly suspicious North and the effete and snobbish South is a class-ridden, peculiarly English divisiveness, which runs deeper than that between Paris and the manufacturing centers, like Lyons, that feed the French fashion industry from a provincial distance. In the early days of the textile industry in Britain, hand-weavers smashed the new power looms with a desperation that linked them to Chartism and the birth of the trade union movement. Their trauma carries on, generations later, as a profound suspicion of new technology among workers in the contemporary British fashion industry. Out of the hardship shared by early workers in what William Blake called "dark Satanic mills" came the sense of community that gave rise to the Co-operative Societies—whose stores, offering reliable goods at unexploitative prices, were the philosophical forerunners of Marks & Spencer. As long as England boomed and the Empire provided a ready export market for its products, the British fashion industry boomed, too. The nineteen-sixties were a historical fluke, whose windfall benefits masked the faltering of the industry's cycle of endless growth. In the present decade, until the decline began to ease a year ago, the industry has been in a most appalling slump.

Some aspects of the clothing industry distinguish it from any other large industry in Britain, and may make the possibility of reform from within—an industrial version of Devolution—more genuinely feasible. Even as a mass-manufactured product, clothing has psychological significance for the person who wears it, and can speedily reflect his changing attitudes. And because the clothing industry has retained, despite centuries of mechanization and increasing shoddiness, a respect for craftsmanship, if not always the craftsmanship itself, it is possible to envisage a form of that industry in which job satisfaction takes precedence over faceless industrialism. One often wonders, in contemplating the tinniness of the ordinary new car in Britain, the tackiness of the average new house, the hideously tasteless flimflam of a new hotel, whatever happened to legendary British craftsmanship. It still exists, but its practitioners are getting older all the time, and are not yet being replaced in sufficient numbers by a younger generation seeking out its values after a generation of neglect.

When a young British designer looks for outworkers to make up her beautiful hand knits, she is likely to find a group of rather elderly women; when a graduate of the Royal College has need of a splendid tweed, it will probably be an old man who will reach into his memory, dust off some ancient machine, and have a go. But craftsmanship is still alive to teach, and still, on occasion, capable of fire and pride. If the new designers are quick off the mark, they are just in time to benefit.

That Missing
Button

D istance lends enchantment to the view," a cliché
beloved of Victorians contemplating nature from a
cozy vantage point near the picnic basket, is a pre-
cept as fundamental to the history of modern fashion as to
that of art and design. Ideas from other countries strike
fashion-minded people with greater force than ideas that are
indigenous. (Temporal distance—the nostalgic rediscovery of
long-despised styles—has played a key part in modern fashion,
too.) Among both amateur and professional exponents,
fashion communicates itself rapidly and on a thoroughly
international plane. For people who care enough about dress
to generate, or to be the first of their friends to adopt,
a new idea—a small group indeed, perhaps numbering in
the hundreds in each of a few cosmopolitan cities in the
world—magpie gleanings from abroad must rank especially
high. Members of this community travel freely to different
points of their own distinct universe, breathing a common
air, sensing and exchanging enthusiasms for novelty or re-
jections of whatever seems passé. They might at any time be
struck by the way French girls fix their hair, English school-
boys carry their homework, New York housepainters dress,
or California ballplayers wear their caps. They carry back their
scraps of alien quaintness to be admired and absorbed at home

and often sent winging out again, as full-blown international fashion, to the country they came from in the first place.

At a broader fashion level, a rung below the trendsetters, people are drawn to the styles of alien countries not for their exhilarating novelty but out of an unconscious feeling of familiarity and because the styles have a vaguely sympathetic "mood." At street level, the most potent expression of this form of fashion internationalism goes on and on being denim. Throughout the world, the young and their allies are drawn hypnotically to denim's code of hope and solidarity—to an undefined vision of the energetic and fraternal Americanness inherent in them all. London is full of locals and Continental tourists who sport the pants, shoes, and shirts of blue-collar America or sweatshirts that spell out "Cornell," "Dodgers," or "Alcatraz." And at a slightly more self-conscious fashion level the blue jean idea of Americanness is often combined these days with a top half involving tweedy, landed-gentry haberdashery and summing up the idea of Englishness. The great appeal of these common international ideas is that they have a fuzzily romantic socio-historical aura and that, although they sometimes overlap with fashion, they are primarily practical, neutral clothing. Englishness or Americanness is as accessible to the French, the Italians, or the Japanese as it is to the fashion designers or the inhabitants of its country of origin. Fashionable British young people approach the idea of generalized and international Englishness with almost as much detachment as if it had grown out of some country other than their own, which in a way it has. This Englishness is once removed from the modern, postwar Britain they grew up in. It is a confident, insular, countrified style filtered down through nostalgic films, television programs, and advertisements. It is only one of the styles that British fashion designers work in, and it is not necessarily their most colloquial or their most authentic. They examine Englishness partly in response to foreign enthusiasm for it. Just as the French or the Italians give Anglophilia their particular signature, the British regard it in their own way, with an attitude that is inevitably tinged with irony. Sometimes fashionable young British people see Englishness as a purely foreign idea and prefer to buy it in a French or Italian version.

In London, there is no clearer demonstration of the way fashionable design ideas and fashion-minded people bat about the world than the development of the Covent Garden area. Like the old Paris market Les Halles, the flower, fruit, and vegetable market of London has now moved to a more logical site on the city's outskirts, leaving behind an ancient neighborhood with interesting spaces, and these are being filled by newcomers concerned with the arts, crafts, and design. The streets are steeped in a uniquely British past, with memories of greasepaint, applause, and bouquets from centuries of opera, ballet, and theatre. Thomas De Quincey once lived there, and so did Henry Fielding. But this past is appreciated by new residents with a self-consciousness that is more like the response of experienced international tourists than the careless affection (or even indifference) with which the British habitually regard their surroundings and the evidence of the nation's past. Like the conversations in any fashionable restaurant in London, the new Covent Garden is full of international echoes, and references to Paris, California, and New York. Lynne Franks and her designer husband, Paul Howie, run a shop in the area's Long Acre stocked with the designs of a select group of young compatriots. The tone of the shop seems to be shifting from a slightly campy razzle-dazzle, inspired by nineteen-fifties America, to a scrutiny—high-principled, and as minute as any lepidopterist's—of the idea of Englishness. But the Aran sweaters, the gaiters and hand-lasted walking shoes, the purses shaped like fishing creels or game bags, are displayed within a décor whose industrial-functional style is redolent of the new Paris boutiques around Les Halles and also of the new Beauborg art center that was built near that market's old site. Pat Gibb runs a boutique in nearby Floral Street with a stock of one-of-a-kind British designs that have more consistent delicacy and drama than anything else in town. She is also the proprietor of a ballet school and of The Sanctuary—a women's health club, housed in what was formerly a banana warehouse. As well as the predictable gymnasium, swimming pool, and health-food bar, this establishment has an astonishing indoor lake, dotted with water lilies and crossed by a winding wooden causeway, where the visitor half expects a file of native bearers to pad by in the wake of some exploratory expedition. A canopy of jungle plants is brightened by the splash of orchids, and echoes to the squawk of parrots. Outside London and what Pat Gibb cheerfully characterizes as her "dreamworld," the impulse to carry through such a fanciful project dedicated to the perfection of the body could exist only in California. And a newly opened restaurant called Friends, in the neighborhood's Wellington Street, has the international rock star Elton John for a backer; a stylized, California-springtime décor of latticework, greenery, and kitschy knickknacks; and a menu whose reckless combinations of health-food textures and liberal use of limes one might expect of an ambitious, Vivaldi-playing spot in the West Village.

In the form of fashion that communicates itself on a private or an only incidentally professional level—the germ of fashion, at its most volatile and its most compelling—the British are masterly. It is because many fashionable Londoners have antennae finely attuned to the vibrations and crosscurrents of trend in all its guises that individual British designers often succeed in capturing it so joyously and with such authority. But today's international fashion is not limited merely to the free flow of private ideas and personal impulses. It is also a public marketplace, involving large-scale importing and exporting and the professionalized communication known as promotion. In selling and in promoting its products abroad, the British fashion industry is somewhat feeble.

Although, in their attempts to stay ahead, exclusive fashion shops throughout the world are likely to have scouts reporting back from Europe all year round, the greatest share of buying and selling goes on at semi-annual showings. These send store buyers and fashion journalists zipping from America, Japan, and all corners of Europe to Rome, Florence, Milan, Paris, and London. A shifting emphasis—which city is up or down at the moment—leads participants to skip some stops and stay longer at others, but for the present the order of the round seems to be firmly fixed. (Americans have to visit showings in New York, as well.) The form that the different countries adopt to ply their wares varies. France, with an instinct for centralization which dates back at least to Louis XIV and Napoleon, has an efficient modern exhibition center at the Porte de Versailles, with the capacity for showing all its native talents, should they wish it, beneath a single roof. Increasingly, though, Paris ready-to-wear designers show their collections, on models, at "interesting" spots scattered all over town, and with a frequently raucous theatricality. Indeed, the French picked up the trick of dramatic fashion shows from New York designers, who have never had a centralized showcase.

London has bumbled into a system all its own. Only a few British designers are rich enough to stage fashion shows. (Among these are John Bates, Zandra Rhodes, Bruce Oldfield, Janice Wainwright, and Bill Gibb—who is about to fill the Albert Hall's eight thousand seats with a spectacular retrospective of his work.) There still exists the possibility of fairy-tale discoveries by visiting buyers working off their own bat to find new names in little shops and studios. It was legendary unearthings of obscure talent by initiative buyer power—on the lines of "In the beginning, Geraldine Stutz found a little Left Bank shop called Sonia Rykiel"—which launched the current scramble to import and export exclusive international fashion, and they continue to fuel the process. But some talented British designers (Kay Cosserat, for instance) do not even have showrooms in London for buyers to visit. And by the time the fashion circus gets that far, buyers are weary and jaded, and need to be cossetted by seeing a lot of clothes in one place. When we read reports of the international collections in our newspapers, contemplate the European fashions that are sold and promoted by the stores, or from general impressions of each nation's fashion status, we can never underestimate the part played by the fatigue of those whose task it is to go over to Europe and bring back the news. If some of the prettiest clothes in New York stores at the moment are Italian, and the Italian fashion reputation is riding high, it can be no coincidence that the Italians are first in line to show their clothes, so buyers see them when they are calm enough to make decisions with a fresh, enthusiastic eye. The British fashion industry tends to have a mental block about the number of venues where designers may display their clothes for international buyers, but there appeared at recent count to be five. Styles of the shows range from Mayfair-grand, through exclusive-artistic and shoestring-artistic, to Earl's Court–shabby. And then there is Birmingham. This last, the only show to have anything like a government seal of approval, takes place at the new National Exhibition Centre, which is Britain's answer to the Porte de Versailles. There isn't a chance in the world that the international fashion brigade, accustomed to junketing in the night clubs and restaurants of Italy and Paris, and feeling at home and at ease in the West End of London, will trail up to a dreary provincial city a few hours to the north.

"God help the Minister who meddles with art," Lord Melbourne once remarked. The relationship between government and fashion designers is quite as prickly as that between government and artists. Some fashion designers in Britain, when they compare the way they are sold and promoted with the style of their rivals in France and Italy, mutter darkly that those countries have the edge because "their governments back their fashion industries like mad." Certainly successive French governments have long been fiercely chauvinistic about their fashion industry, and fiercely protective of it. (The suspicion that Britain—"perfidious Albion"—would prove her most aggressive commercial rival may have been the hidden reason that France blocked Britain's entry to the Common Market for so long.) British designers point out that when the Italians show their most important fashions in New York, it is as part of a whole Italian Week, with national flags along Fifth Avenue and a gala ball attended by Italian diplomats and local celebrities. The British are determined to change the pattern of their own recent sorties to New York, in ragtag, unpublicized groups, with government participation limited to getting some junior attaché to make a few last-minute calls. (The last time British designers made a significant mark here was in the wake of the Beatles' first, triumphant tour, when the promotional work was all done naturally.) But laments about the government role in fashion are usually followed instantly by the observation that if British officialdom ever did set out to back the fashion industry, it would be sure, as with the Birmingham debacle, to get things wrong. British designers may grumble about being left to stand on their own feet, but they are secretly addicted to their independence.

At all levels, fashion spreads through talk and feelings. What visiting professionals say to each other and hear said, together with the amount of extramural fun they have in the various fashion countries, is as great a part of the international fashion story as the clothes they see or buy. It is this talk that promotion is intended to affect. To some extent, American fashion visitors have lately had the impression that among the fashion-originating nations of Europe—Britain, France, and Italy—the British are the stepchildren. (The only other serious contenders for membership in the world's club of fashion-inventing nations are America and Japan. Both countries have increasing numbers of confident and original designers, but they are still principally imitative of Europe's lead. Individual Japanese designers, when transplanted to Paris or London, have had tremendous influence on recent European fashion. The way American fashion might compare in originality when it is seen side by side with a wide range of European fashion—in inverse ratio to the way the shops look here—has barely been tested as yet. The American designer Geoffrey Beene is making the apparently fruitful experiment of producing some of his designs in Turin and selling them in Europe. But American high fashion made in America is usually too costly to compete with European high fashion made in Europe.) International fashion rumor has it that British designers are disunited, hopelessly cranky about the company in which they deign to show their clothes, and too individualistic to pull together for the common good. But the real explanation for their image abroad is more flattering to British designers. Perhaps, in a society keenly aware of the finest distinctions of class and style (if it is no longer true that every time an Englishman speaks another Englishman condemns him for his accent, relics of past attitudes remain), British designers are especially sensitive about what type of designer is assigned to the neighboring stand at a trade fair. But the need to protect the "image" that, as much as his ideas, represents a designer's livelihood is common to all good designers in the world. It is true that the French fashion industry has a strong tradition of uniting proudly against any threat from the outside world, but beneath this patriotic umbrella and on a personal level there is probably more rivalry and backbiting among French designers than among their British competitors. Without the uniquely powerful organ *Women's Wear Daily* to give the impression of a common cause, American fashion designers might turn out to have scant unity, too. The problem of the image of British fashion designers—if it really is a problem—begins with what they themselves say. "The British love to moan," said one of the number recently, in a perfect example of the self-deprecating honesty that has been described as commercial masochism. This baffles visitors from France and America, where fashion is inextricably entwined with loyal, mechanized enthusiasm and professional propaganda. Part of Britain's image in America certainly depends on the British designers' habit of talking unguardedly and in a tongue that Americans can understand.

The British are not particularly modest at heart, but they are not naturally boosterish, either. Painfully aware of their inability to blow their own horn, they gaze with envy at the sight of the united French fashion industry capturing the dollar and with awe at the great, gleaming machinery of American promotion. They worry away about sounding too much like a chorus of disparate voices, and they bone up on promotion. The cycle of design empires based on the promotion of a name is lamentably under way in Britain already. Zandra Rhodes and Bill Gibb, two of the most brilliant designers that the postwar generation has produced, are already one step removed from their prime artistry, and on the way to being submerged in the image of themselves. She lends her name to sheets and machine-made polyester lingerie, he to machine-made knitwear—all respectable enough when considered in isolation, but a travesty when compared with the opulent, highly wrought, imaginative evening gowns that were the original statement of the artists' vision. The world has enough fashion businesses in which the promotion of a name and the idea of "status" design takes precedence over good design inself. British fashion designers have something more valuable to offer the world than this sort of promotional sleight of hand: fashion that is receptive, spontaneous, and unblinkered by the habit of self-aggrandizement. The British can still come up with fashion on a human scale.

When British designers talk vaguely about improving their promotional skills, they ignore the way many of them have instinctively evolved into small, individual units producing clothes of high quality and originality—characteristics that survive well without aggressive promotion, and are often irreparably damaged by it. The designers are so mesmerized by the example of the American fashion industry—which developed its superb, unparalleled promotional expertise initially as a way of compensating for a lack of original design talent—that they ignore the lessons of the Italians' current success. The orchestrated enthusiasm of promotion grew up as a method of getting masses of products out into huge domestic markets, but it is not necessarily relevant or helpful to the business of importing and exporting exclusive fashions. The exchange of international fashion is a mammoth process, involving hundreds of thousands of professionals and billions of dollars. But it has grown up in reaction against the greater vastness of each country's more predictable, more stereotyped, and more readily manipulated domestic market. International fashion is far more personal than ordinary domestic fashion. It is illogical, perverse, fanatic, passionately loyal and disloyal —and thus approaches the intuitive international fashion pursued by traveled amateurs. The more personal form of buying and selling that goes on at the European shows involves many aspects of private trend setting, including confidence in offbeat instincts; boredom with what is established as successful; and resistance to the hard sell.

In spite of their Italian Week, the Italians have not known any striking promotional genius since the heyday of Emilio Pucci—who, incidentally, fell on the fertile ground of an America just beginning to travel widely to Europe and fall in love with Italy. The Italian designers are certainly quite as disorganized and disunited as the British. But the Italians are riding the crest of a wave at the moment, while the united and well-promoted French seem to be temporarily played out. The French have settled into a more fixed and more "salable" style, presented with such violent ballyhoo that visitors are beginning to wonder whether such fashion merits the discomfort entailed in viewing it. In place of the Paris drum banging, the Italians offer a sympathetic atmosphere, a creative and enthusiastic temperament that generates its own publicity, and the right fashion product—intimate, craftsmanlike, effortlessly luxurious—for the mood of the time. Fashion now goes in cycles not only of theme and silhouette but also of national influence. At a given moment, one or another of the fashion-producing nations will have fashion whose tone will appeal throughout the fashion-minded world. This depends on the national character and the way each country's fashion industry has evolved. The Italian tone is particularly appealing now because Italy's fashion business is the least mass-minded of any among the fashion-producing countries. It depends not on chain stores but on a host of small shops; not on giant textile firms but on flexible little companies that can run up beautiful and unique prints or knits in tiny amounts. But already, in response to international demand, the Italians are beginning to make their highly personal product in greater quantities and are thereby turning it into something else. It may well be that in the cycle of international fashion Britain's turn is next. As Italy moves toward mass manufacturing, it may be superseded by those British designers who are so excitedly throwing off the shackles of growth. They already have, in London, an ambience that foreign visitors enjoy. And they have a product with an increasingly influential national tone.

British designers were the first to latch on to what has become one of the first principles of style today: that however much the wearer cares or spends, the clothes should never look entirely *serious*. Funny, droopy shapes, irrational lengths, and ironic combinations of ideas and messages all sprang from a youthful British appetite for comedy and eccentricity in dress. The "Annie Hall" look is supremely British. British fashion today isn't the costume it came close to being in the late nineteen-sixties. On the contrary, it is often extraordinarily and meticulously refined. But it always retains a touch of affectionate humor. Fashion played a particularly important part in Britain's version of the revolution in tastes and attitudes that took place in the nineteen-sixties, when the bulge of war babies set out to teach the world what it meant to be young. Young people in Britain continued to be preoccupied with dressing up when parallel movements in France and America turned their energies either to political philosophies or to explorations of consciousness and alternate life styles. Late-sixties British dandyism was a weird form of fashion, intentionally incomprehensible to earlier generations, but it was fashion just the same. When young people in America and Britain discovered eclecticism in dress, Haight-Ashbury went for beads and headbands as symbols of its state of mind and as a form of anti-fashion, while London went for nostalgia—an exuberant exploration of the history of fashion itself. Costume continues to play a uniquely important part in any feelings of youthful rebellion in Britain—feelings that are now most intense among the working class. All the successive waves of youthful working-class dissatisfaction and solidarity in the past fifteen years— mods and rockers; skinheads; and now punks and Teds—have had their distinct and elaborately stylized fashion uniform. (Just as the punk-rock movement has sinister aspects of perversity and violence as well as endearing aspects of innocent, amateurish, three-chord-rock self-sufficiency, its official attire is both frightening and touching. The young salesgirls in the King's Road punk boutiques called Boy and Seditionaries— the latter has only recently intellectualized itself by changing from its former name, Sex—may be wearing army fatigue pants with the legs strapped together, and a safety pin through the nose, but their spiky crewcuts, dyed lettuce green on one side and fuchsia on the other, are irrepressibly jovial.) When a generation of potential designers dropped out of fashion in other countries, their counterparts in Britain went on honing their shades of meaning, refining their jokes into layer upon layer of gentle irony, and steadily learning their skills, and their trade. Perhaps surprisingly to an outside observer with a preconceived notion of "typical" British style, these designers made a name for themselves commercially with what their international buyers dubbed "fantasy evening wear." In the early seventies, at a time when most high fashion seemed to be turning away from evening clothes altogether, there were enough young people in England dressing for occasions, and enough of their contemporaries designing for them, to keep the form vital and developing. Young people in Britain were the first to detach themselves from the preconception that the prime function of evening wear was to look expensive, and they took out its stuffiness and replaced it with wit. With their evening dresses, designers found a way of combining modesty with outrageousness to make a lightly comic femininity. At the same time, they were exploring a daytime style that united elements of that fragile and comic femininity with the tongue-in-cheek masculinity of landed-gentry Englishness. And all the while they were perfecting a distinctive and internationally marketable fashion of mood and play.

A fashion-minded community, closely attentive to the significance of dress, persists in Britain in the midst of a society that seems, on average, to pay less heed to fashion than most. Although increased British experience of holidays abroad has meant that family beaches at home are now as likely to be dotted with trim shapes in tiny bathing suits as with traditional cloth caps and shapeless cardigans, the British citizen is still far from possessing the vanity of the Latin temperament. But it is precisely because of the indifference of the majority that the fashion-minded minority in Britain has developed its marked sense of self, and is so influential in a fashion era when even those in the world who care passionately about clothes want terribly to look as though they didn't. British fashion rebelled against national indifference and incorporated that indifference into a special, tossed-off style. Jeff Banks, a talented young British designer, recently talked about the particularly human quality present in even the most sophisticated examples of the British style. "British fashion isn't heavy and intense, like fashion in France and Italy," he said. "It's got a bit of cuddliness, a bit of lumpiness and bumpiness that laughs at you. It's the slight tractoriness of an Aston Martin instead of the slickness of a Lamborghini. It's all the funny street parties of the Jubilee. There's something warm and friendly about it—like a button missing off your favorite cardigan."

Strange as it may seem, the restless, high-powered world of international fashion just may be ready for that missing button.

1978

"Women of Style"

When the fashion designer John Anthony presented his fall collection recently in New York, he announced portentously to the world that he was dedicating his new styles to the spirit of the illustrious French literary character Colette. Oscar de la Renta was even more extravagant, dedicating his collection to the "many fabulously articulate women of style and individuality who, through time, have summed up the mystique of clothes." Jane Austen, George Sand, Emily Brontë, Edith Wharton, Gertrude Stein, Vita Sackville-West, Lesley Blanche, and Lillian Hellman were singled out in particular as his sources of inspiration. Giorgio Sant'Angelo's latest creations were launched together with a press release which stated firmly that "the American woman has gone far beyond caring what's 'the latest.'" In Paris, the milliner who supplied hats for the supremely fashionable Karl Lagerfeld collection gave an interview to *Women's Wear Daily* in which she stated flatly that fashion simply does not exist. "An out-of-date woman can look superb," the milliner said. "I don't like people who are fashionable. No, it's worse than that: I detest being able to put a label on clothes. Frankly, it makes me sick." The Big New Looks—to call upon the parlance that a confused and confusing fashion industry still clings to—include padded shoulders, tailored coats and suits, flat-heeled shoes, and zoot-suit or peg-leg pants. Most of these new looks have been seen before in fairly recent history. For the fashion sensibility that thrives on "The Late Show" and thrift shop glamour, they have never disappeared.

All this might suggest that designers are trying to tell us something. Clearly, there finally is an erosion of faith in novel and dynamic clothing fashions among the very people whose livelihood depends on producing and promoting them. Many designers might well agree, in private, with the Parisian milliner and admit that there are few more dispiriting sights than that of women trekking loyally to the stores each season to get themselves all rigged out in the designers' latest schemes. Although the industry still feels obliged to make a pretense of movement and indispensable novelty, there exists among its more thoughtful members a widespread feeling that novelty has nothing to do with the real style they profess to admire. Strangers to the demented rituals of the fashion show season might be forgiven for believing that they were indeed witnessing the birth of novelties and for failing to notice that the shapes, lengths, and details of the clothes on parade—the clothes themselves, in short—were really insignificant. Outsiders who visit only one sardine-packed fashion show, with its dramatic music, lighting, and décor, might even be as fully excited as they are primed to be. But professional fashion-watchers, who may attend hundreds of such shows here and in Europe in the course of a year, are by now largely unmoved by the mechanism of stimulation. Like people who live near an airport, they learn, for the sake of their nervous system, to tune out all the racket and attend as comfortably as they can to what is really going on.

What goes on, in ways that vary from the very crude to the very subtle according to the designer, is communication by way of symbol. It is as though the content of fashion has dissolved before our eyes, leaving us only with its language, its code, and its style. As faith in the authority and significance of new clothing fashion declined, the vacuum was filled by another form of fashion, in which clothing was not an end in itself but a vehicle for meaning. Increasingly, audiences at fashion shows see clear through the clothes to a network of messages as complex, as contradictory, as perplexing, as dispiriting, and occasionally as exhilarating as modern life itself. Designers are not always the best communicators of meanings. Sometimes they project them cynically, just to get the audience talking or keep it awake. There have been some gross examples of perfectly ordinary clothes for perfectly ordinary women being presented in fashion shows accessorized by the whips-and-leather symbols of sadomasochism, presumably on the principle that it is better to see the audience titillated or indignant than bored to tears. Sometimes designers' passion for purely visual effects leads them to project meanings they might not have intended either emotionally or intellectually. It is said that Lagerfeld, in Paris, was stunned to find his audience disturbed by overtones in his show of admiration for Nazi authoritarianism and by a prison-bar décor reminiscent of the concentration camps. It was just that he fancied the way the idea *looked*, he is reported to have remarked plaintively. Sometimes meanings presented in shows are completely spurious. Sometimes, as in the not infrequent hints of militant homosexuality one sees these days, meanings and messages begin and end with the designer himself, and are more or less extraneous to the women's clothing he designs. But for the most part the meanings and messages communicated by designers who really know their business are reflections of attitudes they know their customers already hold.

Undoubtedly the most distinctive and disquieting theme running through the collections both here and in Europe was the troubled relations between the sexes, along with the image of the aggressive new woman. In Europe, the image of woman clad in black leather or with the gloves-in-belt, bemedaled, military-capped trappings of the prewar officer class was far more closely mingled with political ideology than it was by the time it showed up in a modified version here. The European designers were flirting with a stylistic totalitarianism in what were for them very anxious political times. The French were working on their collections at a period when it seemed possible that the country might move radically to the left, the

Italians under the continuing trauma of terrorism and with their nation in appalling crisis. The same silhouettes and accessories of aggression were employed in New York to symbolize politics that were less national than sexual. The image of woman as it emerges in its broadest outlines from the fall collections is of her marching forbiddingly through her days with squared shoulders and a traveling greatcoat, in practical shoes and army surplus socks, taking the business world for all she can get. By night, she strips down to something minimal and satiny and takes the unfortunate men in her social life for all she can get. Happily, this is the picture in its broadest and crudest outlines. There were many encouraging exceptions—designers whose image of woman is more consistently human and feminine, with no schizophrenic divisions between the moods of day and night. Gil Aimbez, Willi Smith, and Geoffrey Beene were among those who, in different ways, effected a comforting balance here. Even the very skimpy disco clothes of Stephen Burrows and the wispy evening styles of Sant'Angelo—which would look better on Cher Bono Allman than on most of the rest of us—had their own integrity and a kind of innocent exuberance. Nor is there anything intrinsically sinister about padded shoulders: handled with taste, and on the right frame, they can be profoundly flattering.

But the haunting and worrisome image of "the new woman" remains. Many of the new clothes, for day and night, suggest a throwing down of the sexual gauntlet. (Gauntlets, incidentally, were a favored accessory in the shows.) Essentially, this new woman does not need the love or companionship of men. She seems determined, rather, to provoke their fear. The whole idea of those "fabulously articulate women of style" which has dragged poor Jane Austen and Emily Brontë from their fancywork and their parsonages to the jungle of Seventh Avenue rests on admiration less for their delicacy and sensitivity than for their independence. Being dead, moreover, they are securely *hors de combat,* sexually. It is good for a "woman of style" to demonstrate some worldly knowledge of the forces of sex, but she is not supposed to be actively and straightforwardly trying to balance them with her day-to-day life. Instead, she dresses with flair and expresses herself through her work. The idea of women of style is one with particular appeal to homosexual men, to whom they pose no threat. But apparently it also appeals to the new woman, who has either dropped out of the sexual contest or evolved far beyond being merely contentedly heterosexual. Two shows in particular—a self-indulgent, badly edited one put on by Richard Assatly and a totally consistent, slickly professional one by Donna Karan and Louis dell'Olio for Anne Klein—projected the image of the new woman to perfection. Models (the same women we have seen in other clothes looking meltingly feminine) looked hugely tall and frightening, striding along with angry glances to military music. The Klein firm's press release came right out and said that its clothes were aimed at the aggressive new woman, and anxiously disclaimed the notion that there might appear to be anything "butch" about their tone. There were high-heeled boots and leather skirts slit to the thigh, rolled hair and Garboesque masculinity by day. (The designers had obviously been influenced by costumes for the movie *Julia*.) For evening, there were slithery little satin dresses, with even higher slits and very revealing tops, worn with stiletto-heeled sandals. All this, like many other evening styles on Seventh Avenue this year, shrieks out the official message of "sexiness." Sexy such clothes may or may not be, for one-night stands— although even in those circumstances all but a handful of the most intrepid men might well run a mile. They are clothes to make assertive passes in, perhaps. But they are certainly not fit for starting or sustaining those "lasting relationships" that people, in spite of themselves, persist in craving. In the end, most of the sexy new clothes look like costumes to caricature sexuality. For beneath the clothing that symbolizes the new woman lies the new body. This is jogged, Jacuzzi-bathed, exercised, and dieted to the point of looking androgynous. It needs sex the way it needs kelp or B_{15} vitamins, but it is fundamentally self-sufficient.

Symphony in Lilac

American high fashion either has been rendered thoroughly cosmopolitan and European by now or has come of age in its own right. But fashion keeps moving forward—not because of people who are satisfied with what the stores are offering at the moment, of course, but because of people with vague feelings for what they might like to wear or see in some unspecified future. The cut of a collar from history, a particular color from a work of art, the atmosphere of a movie or a book—all these float up unbidden, for some, to become images and hankerings, certain little ideas. There are no "how-to" guides to this hypothetical fashion, and intuition can't be institutionalized or massproduced. I've noticed lately that many people in the instinctive-fashion school have been having fairly specific fancies—for six perfect so-and-sos, in half a dozen colors, or several basic such-and-suches in different kinds of fabric. It might seem at first that they are anxious to put the whole idea of fashionable dress behind them. But in fact they are moving beyond the idea of mere "style"—at a time when good taste and flair are within the reach of many—and thinking in terms of creating an impeccable, highly personal "uniform."

In one of the European glossy magazines a while back, there was an article—an ecstatically celebratory obituary, actually—about a Parisienne named Mizza Bricard. This woman's outfit at a luncheon she gave at the Plaza-Athénée some two decades ago is recalled in the greatest detail. She was on that occasion a symphony in lilac: coat and pleated skirt of fragile wool, blouse of textured chiffon, and a chip-straw hat anchored with a huge baroque pearl. "Men always notice details" is one of the maxims attributed to Mme. Bricard. "Always dress in only one color" is another. By night, she wore extravagant *tenues*, exotic headdresses, flowers in her hair. She had a spectacular collection of jewels—which she sported only in the daytime— having followed the advice once given to her by the couturier Jacques Doucet: "When a man wants to send you some flowers, tell him 'My florist is Cartier.'" By day, she wore romantic hats she had designed herself, inspired by memories of the great *fin-de-siècle* beauties and *demimondaines* she had seen in the Bois de Boulogne and at Auteuil as a child. But all of these put together were not as memorable as the luxurious simplicity of her everyday uniform, which consisted of variations on that outfit first seen at luncheon—"a collarless jacket, a pleated or A-line skirt, made from a silk or tweed as airy as lace, a chiffon blouse . . . with shoulder straps made from bows." These pieces were all in one or another of the only colors she considered acceptable—black, navy blue, cream, and lilac.

There is little question that uniform wearers of Mme. Bricard's kind are often more appealing in the abstract than on direct acquaintance. The pursuit of such perfection involves a strict self-discipline and a sometimes intolerant dismissal of the sloppiness of others. In a tasteful world of one's own creation, with rigid rules of one's own concocting, one might well be prey to loneliness and prone to crabbiness. Coco Chanel, one of the most famous uniformed women ever, was notoriously difficult. Uniform wearers are more likely to converse in maxims and dicta than in gentle empathizings. The redoubtable Diana Vreeland—with her black Saint Laurent pants and turtlenecks and her birdlike evening outfits in lacquer red—is in the long tradition of uniformed and cosmopolitan *grandes dames*, and has been known, on occasion, to prove intimidating.

But anyone who loves clothes for their own sake might find herself drawn to fashion uniforms just the same. Such a uniform has its greatest impact on the imagination of observers when it is worn by a strong character who either designed it herself or cooperated closely in its inception. But sometimes two relatively delicate elements can combine to create a single, powerfully evocative uniform. The couturier Givenchy and the actress Audrey Hepburn came together to create such a vision at one period, and neither party has been quite so memorable since. The actress Joan Crawford was dressed by Adrian, the Hollywood costumier, but her personality was so forceful that her uniform became "the Joan Crawford look" and barely seems, in retrospect, like the result of teamwork at all. At second hand, a fashion uniform becomes a very different matter. The Chanel uniform on Mademoiselle herself is impressive even from the distance of old photographs. But when it was adopted as a mass fashion it degenerated into a uniform of quite another sort—that of social suitability alone. Instead of accentuating a unique self, it denoted the abdication of self in millions of women. The connection between an individual fashion uniform and mass fashion has always been extremely tenuous. Uniforms become more or less fixed at a certain point in the wearers' relations to the world. Thereafter, they deliberately allow broad fashion movements to overtake them, and gain strength from flouting other people's rules.

Nowhere is this more or less conscious holding back from ordinary fashion more striking than with those singular uniforms—the wardrobes of the British royal family. Prudence Glynn, the fashion editor of the London *Times*, devotes an absorbing chapter of her new book, *In Fashion,* to the clothing styles adopted by the royal ladies. In the case of the two uniforms that are most consistently sui generis—those of Queen Elizabeth II and Queen Elizabeth the Queen Mother—a framework was established decades ago. The Queen favors a certain boxy, semi-fitted silhouette, which her dressmaker, Sir Norman Hartnell, devised for her sometime in the nineteen-fifties. Her mother is loyal to a style of fullskirted, exuberantly feminine floatiness, often with feathery width around the shoulders. This goes back to the style, inspired by Winterhalter crinolines, that her husband encouraged her to adopt in the nineteen-thirties. (Queen Mary, the present Queen's grandmother, remained steadfast until her death, in 1953, in her allegiance to the hats and floor-length hems she was wearing during the First World War.) Royal wardrobes keep themselves aloof from styles that might be carried off by any merely fashionable, social, and wealthy woman of the world. Miss Glynn advances the interesting hypothesis that, in history, ruling ladies who took a passionate interest in dress (Queen Marie Antoinette and the empresses Joséphine and Eugénie, to name but the fashion-susceptible French) were likely to come to grief. The author suspects that Mrs. Simpson, elegant in her Mainbochers and Schiaparellis, might have been rendered unfit to rule simply by her obsessive interest in chic.

Of course, the women in the British royal family are not autocrats by temperament—not self-created aristocrats, like some of the women who have devised noteworthy fashion uniforms. Proust described his Odette, and friends described Mme. Bricard, as being a queen of dress—regal by virtue of exquisite taste and utter disregard for popular predilections. But the Queen of England actually *is* a queen, and it would be foolish to pretend that some of the significance of her wardrobe of sometimes quite homely looking clothes does not derive from her position. One scrutinizes the Queen's hat, handbag, and color scheme partly because they are expected to be scrutinized. The pillbox hats and little white gloves worn by Mrs. Kennedy as First Lady would have been considerably less riveting if she had not played a central role in a dramatic administration that lives indelibly in the public imagination. Privilege, stardom, a life lived in the public eye—all these undoubtedly add to the power of personal fashion uniforms.

But some of the compelling quality of all distinctive wardrobes relates not to fame or high office but to the clothes themselves. Such wardrobes have a consistent, self-contained vocabulary. They are usually simple, beautifully made, and scrupulously accessorized. They evolve in response to specific practical needs and enable the wearer to feel confidently at ease at all times. (In the case of the Queen, these practical needs are, admittedly, quite unusual: hats that permit her loyal subjects to see her face, and evening gowns with bodices that set off the Order of the Garter and magnificent, historic jewels.) By selecting a restricted style and retaining it for years, a woman is freed to concentrate on quality and pursue perfection. For many ordinary women, the formal bridal gown provides the only opportunity to follow the principle of dressing in a form of uniform. The gown is of interest to spectators partly because, for one day, the wearer has a public role to play; partly because differences between one example and another are vital, since convention sketches out the basic rules beforehand; and partly because a bride leaves no detail of the whole effect to chance but is aiming for perfection.

A simplicity of cut bordering on austerity has characterized some of the most famous fashion uniforms in recent history. Mme. Bricard is said to have envied nuns for the simple dignity of their habits. The remark may seem shocking, coming from a woman admired by such hosts of obedient gentleman patrons of Cartier. But behind any striving for perfection in dress there lies a quest for harmony and serenity, for a quasi-artistic integrity and purity. Trade has flooded the world of late with clothes that bring all varieties of "style" to a wide audience. But it may turn out that restricted, tightly edited personal uniforms will emerge to stand out above ordinary fashion in our time, as they have done in the past. You have to know and then ignore all the rules and possibilities of the common language in order to write memorable poetry. And the limited message of the individual uniform may prove to be the sharpest possible clarion call of authoritative and imaginative fashion taste.

1979

The Executive
Woman

L ong before this fall's designs were sketched or cut,
Seventh Avenue was peering into the murky crystal
ball of fashion in the nineteen-eighties. What lives
would women be leading in the next decade and what clothes
would they need, to match? One clue presented itself in
statistics. By 1980, for the first time in American history, more
women would be working outside the home than staying in it.
Behind this fact lie great changes—some actual, some still
potential—in the way the sexes relate to each other and in
the way society functions. To the alert businessman and designer, this fact indicates a market, too.

Working women of interest to the sort of designers who
put on fancy shows and describe their ideal customer in program notes are not exactly average working women—not
those who simply *have* to work, to support their families or
to make ends meet. Customers for the designers who talk
enough about their goals to generate publicity are well-heeled
middle-class women who very likely work out of choice and
for their own satisfaction. In addition to pursuing a career,
they have the time and the inclination to look up-to-date.
Designers are banking not merely on such working women's
need for clothes but on their taste for fashion—for a fashion
differing from the fashion they would choose if they simply
stayed at home. A form of women's fashion is evolving which

is deliberately designed to fit into the world of men. It is fashion intended to project a particular image—an aura of competence, of self-confidence, of a sexuality that can be drawn on at moments when it seems useful and flatly denied at inappropriate ones. This is feminine fashion that prides itself on having the look of "power." Many designers are seeking the costume formula for this image at the moment. One designer summed up the image for many of his colleagues when he described the customer for his fall clothes as "the emerging Executive Woman."

Catch phrases are not always the most accurate reflections of confused reality, and styles of dress are only hints or sketches of people's lives. The phenomenon of women in business is in a transitional, if no longer a completely germinal, stage. Even if designers succeed in selling all the outfits for executive womanhood which they could possibly wish, it is clear that there will not be enough executive-level jobs to match. Some designers and some customers are apparently going to go for the costume of success and power first, trusting that those attributes will follow. If one had to sum up the current vision of executive womanhood—it is a simplification, because designers have widely differing interpretations of the theme— one would have to begin with a fairly strictly tailored suit. This prototypical tailored suit has a straightish skirt, with a hemline ending around the knees. The jacket has shoulders that are often padded or otherwise enlarged. But, as if pulling back from any austerity or masculinity inherent in this silhouette, designers add to it exaggeratedly feminine accessories: frivolous and impractical hats; shoes with recklessly high, thin heels; and unusual gloves. People attending the fall collections often had cause to wonder what the clothes would look like if they were shown straight, without the support and distraction of stylized accessories. In many cases, they might look quite tedious. The prize for the most obvious hedging between whimsy and rigidity must go to the presentation of the new coat collection designed by Zandra Rhodes. The styles had dignity, and even beauty, but were of a conventionality surprising for Miss Rhodes, who is known for her strikingly avant-garde imagination. The coats themselves looked like something paraded in any expensive suburban coat department in the early nineteen-sixties. But the models' heads erupted in surreal décor: mysterious, boxlike face masks of scarlet satin; curly, wildly sprouting hairpinnings, like electrified pigs' tails; and wiggly lines of jeweled beading glued to the cheeks.

The tremulous balance between the utterly nonsensical and the strictly pedestrian which characterized so many of the fall collections—not only those directly aimed at the emerging executive woman—has many origins, including internal commercial factors of the fashion industry and the twists and turns in the sensibility of designers. Manufacturers of tailored coats and suits, who have for a long time been faced with a declining market and a shrinking force of labor skilled in tailoring techniques, have found at least temporary resurgence through reactions against ample and unconstructed silhouettes and in the current flirtation—the latest in a series—with nostalgia for earlier fashions, especially those of the nineteen-forties. For years, customers have been leaning toward the comfort of knitted fabrics, the versatility of separates, the freedom from the obligation to put together complicated accessories. In the long run, they will probably continue to do so. But there is currently an appetite for a more formal-looking fashion that will provide an alternative to easygoing styles without necessarily supplanting them entirely. Revolutions of the eye and a taste for change from what a lot of women have been wearing for a long time are not the exclusive prerogative of a fashion industry that hopes to cash in on them. Even ordinary women occasionally get bored with last year's styles.

As for American designers' allusions to the archives of fashion, they are to some extent re-echoing themes that have been preoccupying designers in Europe for a year or two. But the universe of fashion is too cosmopolitan and unified these days, the crosscurrents of inspiration too complex, for talk of Europeans' inventing fashions and Americans' copying them. One has only to review the transatlantic tennis game of fashions in denim, army uniforms, and active sportswear to be reminded that fashion is no longer a one-way passage from Europe to the States. One would be hard pressed to say that five or ten years ago there were more trendsetters in Paris than in New York who were searching in flea markets for padded shoulders and amusing hats. Nostalgic fashion—now referred to in America as "retro," a name bestowed on it by the French—has been bouncing around in fashion-minded circles of the world for ages.

What is new about the modified retro pervading the fall collections here is that it is provided by mainstream designers for mainstream customers. The people who prefer to follow fashion rather than lead it are being given the chance to experiment with shapes and moods that the "innovators" who first recycled them from thrift shops have begun to tire of. We may be witnessing a final paroxysm—a last fling—of historicism in fashion, and anyone who hasn't got around to playing with it all had better try now, before it is too late. For it is clear by now that the age of highly individualistic and eccentric "style" is really past. Style is on the wane because too many fundamentally unstylish people are wearing the symbols of it. Trendsetters are not and never will be democrats, and they'll change the rules of the game sooner than compete with imitators. The high-spirited, often deliberately provocative panache of the sixties and early seventies was a spontaneous emotional reaction by a few people to a set of historical circumstances that no longer prevail. There were still rules, upheld by the majority, for the minority to rebel against or break. The fashion industry was more monolithic and structured than it is today, and obvious conformism more prevalent. The change that earlier trendsetters sought to hasten by example—people's right to wear what they felt like on any occasion—has been largely accomplished in private social life, if not yet in the business world.

Much of today's retro feels harmlessly derivative, and it doesn't pack enough punch to justify annoyance with it. Fashion-minded people, who used to get quite exasperated with other styles at the height of the battle for freedom of self-expression, tend to be more tolerant these days. One designer, who used to get very intense about the need for innovation, said to me recently, with a benevolent shrug, that there was room in the world for all sorts of people and all varieties of style. I certainly see no point in castigating Oscar de la Renta or Bill Blass, for example, because he was in the mood to design nostalgic, flamboyantly let-'em-eat-cake fall collections. What does it matter if de la Renta's Balenciaga- or Lillie Langtry-style ball gowns won't fit into cabs or closets, or if Blass's Adrian-style *numéros* cost several thousand dollars and are not relevant to struggling working girls? These two designers went on producing sensible enough collections in past seasons, when younger and sometimes less competent colleagues were fooling passionately with nostalgia. It is scarcely surprising that the two men—each with the security blanket of an affluent and loyal following, and with grounding in the techniques of the grand couture—could not resist showing off in the late flowering of retro and demonstrating how spectacular the old élitist styles could be in the hands of an experienced pro. And if fashion continued to be created from ivory towers by designers going to museums for inspiration instead of to the lives of customers, one might be justified in taking issue with the pretentious and campy notes that the designer Mary McFadden launched with her latest collection. ("For more than three thousand years they had moved back and forth across the boundaries of Asia . . . Goat leather drums throbbed in slow rhythmic steps. Black tents were struck and folded. The Horde has been the inspiration for the 'Nomads Then' Collection '79.") But Miss McFadden's clothes are pretty, and a lot of women like them. Who, at this point, is to deny her her right to celebrate an aspect of fashion which will never be entirely submerged—the purely decorative, evocative, and utterly irrational?

Some observers—including some who identify with the interests of designers and some who identify with the interests of consumers—have run counter to this tolerance of different

styles, and suggested that designers are in the midst of a re-
prehensible bout of hermetic self-indulgence. If this should
prove true, the designers alone will suffer, for women will
ignore their work. It is a designer's concern if he is commercially reckless enough to produce clothes that women do
not want to wear, at this particular season or at any in the
future. I cannot give credence to the persistent myth that the
fashion industry is coercive and retains the power to impose
styles on an unwilling audience, because I do not believe that
women are so stupid, as a group. It happens that the notion
of emerging executive womanhood strikes Seventh Avenue
at the same time as a taste for retro. Indeed, it would seem
that in groping for clothes appropriate for the contemporary
career woman, designers are irresistibly drawn to the co-
herently packaged vision of her celluloid precursor—the look
of Joan Crawford in the boardroom. But if—and it is an if—
women go for the overlapping fashions of retrospection and
executive womanhood which they are being offered for fall,
it will be because those fashions correspond in some way to
real-life feelings and needs.

It would not be so surprising if the besuited, carefully accessorized, high-heeled, and vaguely retrospective look attracted
a following among women who aspire to being executives.
Women have not been in the business world long enough to
take themselves for granted. They still have to be slightly
more than men in equivalent positions—slightly harder-
working, slightly brighter, slightly more self-protective, perhaps even slightly more aggressive. And they feel impelled to
give far more attention to looking well dressed. The suggested
fashions for women in business begin with the uniform of men
in business—the suit—and then add touches of self-consciousness, or even of self-parody. The female version may take
itself more lightheartedly, or perhaps more seriously, than the
male, but it doesn't simply take itself for granted. The traditional business uniform of men—matching jacket and pants
in a neutral color, an easily laundered, simply styled shirt, a
pair of comfortable shoes, even the necktie that adds a touch

of color and the means of transmitting minor social messages—
continues in favor not only because of conservatism but because it is eminently practical. It is a style of dress that can
be forgotten about while the people wearing it devote their
attention to the job in hand.

How is the forgettable masculine uniform modified when it
becomes a woman's fashion? In the first place, by looking like a
fashion at all it gains triviality and becomes something like
the costume for a role. The designer Gloria Sachs, in acting
as commentator at her fall collection, touched on this. "Remember the man in the gray flannel suit in the nineteen-
fifties?" she asked her audience. "I see women being something like that in the eighties. My daughter and her friends
are all in law school, and they are playing at being very professional." The remark may have seemed like a put-down, and
not only for the daughter and her friends, but it may also
have contained a grain of widely applicable truth. Many of the
new fashions for young executive women somehow imply a
playing at careerism. And where they are combined with
retrospective detailing they further distance wearers from
total commitment to the here and now by veiling them in
complex historical and visual ironies.

Inherent in such fashions, too, are confusions and conflicts
about how to be a woman in a world of men. Femininity does
not reside in symbolic wisps of net on a hat or in spindly heels.
No woman is going to find the key to a harmonious personality
by tacking such touches on to a sternly masculine tailored suit,
any more than she can become a great lover by buying a red
silk dress with a plunging décolletage. It was probably inevitable at this stage of fashion history that some women
would want slimmer skirts again. But some skirts for suits are
now so tight that designers have to employ devices such as
slits to make walking possible at all. (For the benefit of any
who are curious or hopeful, I may add that some designers
now show some miniskirts and that some young women may
sometimes wear them. But at this distance from the era of
liberation which spawned the length, it is really no big deal.)

In spite of severity of tailoring, there is in many of the coming fashions a great emphasis on legs and bottoms. If half of executive womanhood is swinging down the office halls inciting low whistles, if not pinches, while the other half is busy taking the boss to court for sexual harassment, we must indeed be living in transitional times.

1980

Retro: A Reprise

Fashion appears to have reached an impasse. The curious impression that everything is withering cannot be entirely explained by the fact that the collections that designers have recently unveiled are for spring, and therefore by tradition are less ambitious and less innovative than those for fall. Nor does the current economic climate—a time of anxiously watched inventories and tightened credit—really account for the inhibition of experiment and progress. In truth, fashion has been atrophying for a decade or more. It may now simply have achieved the end toward which it has been tending: to short-circuit or completely foil spontaneity in its creators and its followers. The snag is that spontaneity is the whole point of fashion. It's the golden egg, the jewel in the crown, the mainspring at the center of a mechanism of otherwise unworkable and irreconcilable contradictions—between commercial dissemination and amateur self-expression, between fashion and anti-fashion, between conservation and progress. If you take away the light in the individual eye, can there be fashion at all?

The process began when it became clear that the way clothes *looked* was essentially unimportant; what counted was who looked at them or wore them and therefore what they *meant*. This surprising and apparently self-destructive shift in emphasis may in fact have been based on the valuable perception that the people who looked best were not those in the latest or most expensive fashions but those with the most vitality. For whatever reason, changes in shapes and hemlines really don't seem to matter anymore. Such purely visual significance was banished years ago, when the era of meaning was ushered in. Yet even in this new age, there remained the nagging problem of the tangible, visible existence of clothes. Of course, anyone with any fashionable instinct knew that this didn't count. But there the clothes still were—public statements that some people might perversely persist in seeing, judging, or misinterpreting. So, hard upon the era of meaning, there came the era of protective intellectual coloration and of obfuscation. Clothes came to be worn and seen as an assemblage of thought-out paradoxes, as irony, whimsy, or deliberate disguise. Thrift shop dressing carried it all to its ultimate. We took to clothes for which we had spent little money, which didn't necessarily fit us, and which had belonged in the past to some dead stranger's life. Behind the bravado of what came to be known as "style," there may have lurked a fear of being part of our time, of being locked into our own personalities, and of revealing too much about our own lives.

Above all, what ultimately characterized the fashion of the past decade was detachment. People went out of their way to dissociate themselves from what their clothes might say about them. Observers of other people's clothes were at the last baffled by all their contradictory reactions and too discouraged and exhausted to figure out anything at all. Clothes were set free to float in limbo, with no one to take any particular responsibility for them. Designers discovered that their work could coast in a no man's land between vision and meaning. If anyone seeing their styles detected a meaning that seemed undesirable, creators could simply say there wasn't supposed to be a meaning there, that they were just plain visual folk, expressing themselves intuitively and casually pulling ideas from an "atmosphere" they were not in the business of philosophizing about. In the main, these evasive tactics worked quite well. If, for example, one wonders out loud about the moral implications of the cold and brutal sadomasochistic fantasies in the fashion photography of Helmut Newton, one is made to feel—and really does seem—visually insensitive, old-fashioned, and gauche. Or take the absurd headgear shown with some of the recent Paris prêt-à-porter—hats like windmills, brioches, or First World War biplanes. If anyone was reminded of the desperate gaiety of Schiaparelli's lamb-chop hats or the wood-shaving confections of women in Nazi-occupied Paris, it seemed too tediously pedantic to point it out. If styles look right for the moment, art for art's sake is the spirit that prevails. If they don't look right, it must be the fault of the observer, who has missed their meaning and their point. By now, obfuscatory style is deeply ingrained in even the most derivative and commercial dress designers. The job of deadening direct visual response and baffling interpretation is virtually complete. One can sit through a fashion show in a peculiar state of seeing and yet instantly discounting the thing seen—with eyes fixed unnaturally wide before a panoply of color and movement and shape but also with an odd sensation of suffocating for lack of life. The whole dream is dismissed with a blink; the image of the show has faded from the retina before the spectators have left their seats. And no one, least of all the creators themselves, seems to have much idea of what fashion means or how it is supposed to look.

Small wonder, in this perplexing environment, that fashion designers should so often have been drawn of late to "bold" designs in black and white that take their tone, if not their entire shape, from fashions of the past. Many fashion shows open, these days, with stark, static tableaux that have been repeated often enough to have become a cliché. Groups of models in angular poses are lit to appear only as giant silhouetted shadows—faceless beings in dramatic hats, gloves, and hard-edged "chic." The intention behind such introductions— which often resemble old fashion photographs—seems to be to instill in creator and audience alike the confidence that here, at least, in this protected world, everyone is in the presence of something that may still be called fashion. Such friezes are a visual incantation, a hopeful ritual summoned up to keep a crippled, schism-riddled faith. The fashions of the past continue to recur not so much for love of their details and lines as for the security blanket they provide in these times of terrible confusion. The past offers a vision of measurable, wrapped-up order. Fashion had its place, once upon a time, and its own clear rules. It could put one elegant foot in front of the other from one season to the next, and quite unselfconsciously. Many fashion designers today—at least, many of those who attempt anything more artistically ambitious than the merchandising of blue jeans—are drawn time and again to the past as to a world of paradisal certainties.

It is a measure of how inextricably the visual language of the past is tangled with that of the present that you don't hear much mention of historicism in fashion this season. You'd think that "retro" was a cloud that passed, some five years back, leaving us with a brilliant expanse of purely contemporary style. That most collections both here and in Europe continue to be absolutely saturated with more or less direct borrowings from the twenties, the thirties, the forties, the fifties—and now the sixties as well—is often passed over in silence. In some part, this is a conspiracy among those whose business is the promotion and sale of new clothes. Too many potential customers are either bored by the idea of retrospection or still made nervous by the untried prospect of it. If a brand-new fashion is really blatantly retrospective, some expert is called in to wave a magic wand and pronounce that, this time around, it has been done "in a contemporary way." Often, though, it's not even a question of denying the presence of retrospection. In all sincerity, we simply don't see it, so successfully has our eye assimilated it and our mind forgotten how to distinguish it from innovation.

Who could possibly have foreseen in the spring of 1970 what some of the world's most respected, well-established designers would deem appropriate for that of 1980? Here is Bill Blass, giving his wealthy customers a lavish show of styles with a marked resemblance to what those customers were wearing in 1960. As if to wryly underscore the mad evanescence of it all, Oscar de la Renta has come up with Balenciaga-style balloon skirts that are printed with a design of carnival balloons. When they started on this tack, it was all supposed to be fun, a glittering and gorgeous charade, but by now it has an uncanny, Fellini-like unreality. Instead of lifting the spirits, it somehow oppresses them. There's an edge-of-the-precipice defiance to it, a sterile irony that amounts to cynicism.

Now that fashion has started reviving the nineteen-sixties, it seems clear that we've reached the end of some sort of line. Dislocation, mystification, revival—these, more than anything else, were the hallmark of fashion in the seventies. You can't fake innovation indefinitely, any more than you can revive revivals, view irony ironically, or camp up camp. There won't be anything of the seventies to revive. From this distance, the sixties—or, at least, the latter part of them—seem to represent the last period when fashion spoke with a kind of common voice. Women of different ages, social backgrounds, political opinions, and nationalities very often chose a single distinctive silhouette—namely, skirts above or well above the knees. It need hardly be said that the sixties also opened a lot of flood-gates. After that, everything came pouring down: wide skirts, slim skirts, short ones and long; jeans and running shoes one day, teetering heels the next; trousers in every imaginable shape and length; women moving schizophrenically from buttoned-up boardroom suits to near-naked evening silk. Everything and everyone moved back and forth in a single tapestry that constantly unraveled and re-formed. Everything was in style and yet nothing was. Here was freedom or chaos, depending on your point of view. People had by no means abandoned the hope of finding the spark of fashion, but they were convinced that it was somewhere other than where they were. If it wasn't always on the professional runway, could it be in the streets of SoHo, in the latest discothèque, or in punk, perhaps? The American fashion industry kept hoping the new ideas were in Paris, while young people in Paris thought maybe style was lurking on the American campus or in American sporting goods stores. And did fashion automatically reside with young and rebellious extremists, or could quieter, established citizens get in on the act?

The most dispiriting aspect of nostalgia (which means, literally, homesickness) is that the successive waves of it have come from precisely the group that society depends on to push its culture blindly forward—the young and avant-garde. Older and more conservative designers have for some time been keeping pace with their juniors a season and a decade or so behind. In 1979, some young Paris designers were obsessed by points and spikes drawn from the crests of dinosaurs, while others turned to ancient Egypt. Mary McFadden, in New York, claimed to be inspired by the buried civilization of Pompeii and Herculaneum. It's discouraging to see modern sensibilities flirting like this with the romantic idea of extinction, but staring into the far-distant past of design is a phenomenon of long enough standing in the history of fashion, after all. It seems more ominous to see some young designers choosing to revive sixties fantasies, miniskirts, and short white boots.

If even the symbolic costume of rebellious energy is not just a revival but a revival of a revival, the rebellion looks anemic indeed. If teen-agers—female ones, that is—are now dancing away in their miniskirts, they may be too young to have seen the look before but they know and somehow accept that their gesture is an exercise in style. It has all been done more tumultuously, more authentically, by people who are barely their seniors in the life span, let alone in history. One French fashion magazine recently published a photograph of two ordinary young Parisiennes in the street, with the implicit suggestion that such girls were trendsetters to be watched. They were wearing ponytails, black leather blousons, and drainpipe pants, and they puffed away on cigarettes in an anti-establishment kind of way. How did fashion wander through the looking glass? Surely such a costume has been the symbol of rebellion for at least thirty years, from the postwar Greenwich Village beats to the British punks of—what, is it already a whole half decade ago? At its birth, punk at least had some weirdly real vitality—enough to give a few original twists to the classically rebellious garb. I'm brought to a halt at the brink of the same old vacuum—on the point of regarding the distant, once spontaneous eccentricity of bright green hair and safety-pinned noses with a feeling akin to nostalgia.

A Woman's Age

Anumber of designers have been showing very short skirts alongside very long ones. It's interesting to see extremes of length resurfacing. We are given the chance to compare our present attitudes toward fashion with those of the late sixties and early seventies, when lengths were still controversial, and when fashion was intimately and sometimes painfully bound up with the question of a woman's age. The miniskirt symbolized youth and various new freedoms; the midiskirt, arriving too soon and in the wrong shape, was seen by most women as aging, and they traumatized the fashion industry by flatly rejecting it. After that last era of long and short skirts, things were never the same. To some observers, the reappearance of extremes seems an admirable sign of fashion's current variety and freedom. To others—particularly those who remember the previous commercial debacle and are now trying to sell clothes in hard times—the idea seems lamentably confusing. In truth, all fashion now is both free and confused, like the women who wear it. It is groping (with constant backward looks to see how far it has come or perhaps to regret lost certainties) toward some sort of visual definition of what it may now mean to be a grown woman. And that, of course, is a far from straightforward question.

In retrospect, the fashion picture of a decade ago looks astonishingly simple. In the days of the mini, there was a lot of pompous talk about whether it was suitable or flattering for grown women to reveal their upper legs and—what was somehow considered even more misguided—their knees. There must have been a real concept of suitability and flattery, still, for some to be so indignant about its violation and others to defy it so enthusiastically. Skirts, albeit vestigial ones by then, continued to be the only real theme of women's fashion, as they had been for centuries. And when, at last, women seemed ready to lower their hemlines, some seasons after the aborted midi, the industry launched into ponderous pseudo-educational theses about customers' getting exactly "the right proportion" in their completed effect, as though fashion design were a classical art—subject, like Palladian architecture, to strict geometric rules. All those holdovers and illusions have gone, by now. Every rule and guideline, every last certainty has been systematically toppled in the last few years. No shapes or styles are perceived as being any more flattering, suitable, or desirable than any others. The persistent recycling of fashion design might almost be an admission on the industry's part that the clothes of twenty, ten, or five years back—even those of last year, a radically uncommercial thought—are just as valid as intrinsically similar clothes designed today.

After the last fling of significant skirt lengths, in the early seventies, there came the present age, when fashion images began flickering past our eyeballs in a faster- and faster-spinning procession of ironies, disguises, evasions, fragmented meanings and nonmeanings, chaos—and possibly some genuine forms of self-expression. In a time of psychological self-absorption, fashion became a matter of feelings quite as much as of appearances. If women felt good in whatever they happened to put on, they looked more attractive than women who were by old standards exquisitely dressed but looked somehow lost. The only real fashion faux pas these days is to lack self-confidence. To look too carefully put together in all the latest fashions is self-defeating, because it looks unfashionably unself-confident. (Only in these times could *Women's Wear Daily*, which depends on keeping alive the idea of fashionable dress, coin the ugly term "fashion victims," for women who look *too* fashionably dressed.) For some time, the question of what women wear has been firmly controlled by women themselves, even if it did take quite a while for this to sink in. Like prisoners rattling the bars of their cage out of habit, not realizing that the door has been unlocked, women went on muttering about the "dictatorial" ways of designers long after these had ceased even to guide. In dress, at least, women must stand on their own two feet. They can take credit for their own successes, and they must take responsibility for their own mistakes. If a woman of forty wants to wear a thigh-high skirt or shorts, she'll have to make her own choice; there's no one out there who is going to tell her what people of her age should or should not do.

Everything seems to be in the mind these days—especially people's age. More people than ever are grown up, now that the population is getting older. "Grown up" is the term that people use of themselves, as well. It's childish, whimsical, detached—nice and modern—and it suits the difficulty that people have in considering themselves adult and in defining what adulthood means. They don't feel the way they imagine their parents did at the same age, their marriages and careers are far less settled, and they don't have a middle-aged shape. It's not so much that people deny being adults, though. They are secretly quite proud of having survived their experiences; they simply want the right to be adult in a new kind of way. Youth, if it means innocence and physical immaturity, ends early; old age, if it means rocking-chair retirement and physical decline, tends to start late. In the long, elastic time between, people of very different ages are free to go on doing what they have done for decades—playing strenuous sports and games, for instance—or to do new things, like beginning new marriages and families, or learning to roller-skate. Fashion has reflected the changing, if not declining, significance of age. Styles now vary not so much according to generation, the way they did a decade ago, as according to taste, class, philosophy, and the wearer's interest or lack of interest in keeping up with fads. And, of course, according to body. The gymnasium, the tennis court, the jogging path are all considerable levelers. In clothes, at least, a fit body looks much the same at forty as at twenty, at sixty as at thirty.

The eroding of preconceptions about roles and ages makes it easier for some to live and more complicated for others. Many "older women" in this country have had a trying time of things. While a Frenchman might consider a woman in her forties, fifties, or sixties not only seductive but an absolute mainstay of civilized life, the notion has not yet gained acceptance here in any big way. (When a waiter in France is uncertain of a woman's age or marital status and doesn't want to insult her, he calls her "Madame." His American counterpart plays safe with "Miss.") In part, it was America's puritanism that for so long prevented the thought that anyone but the very young could be interested in sex—as though it were all right if you were officially considered irresponsible and incapable of quite understanding what you were doing. The works of Henry James point up an ambivalent American attitude toward all worldliness and experience—particularly in women—which is still in evidence to some extent today. And while advertisers everywhere in the world sell all sorts of products by promoting the correlation of youth and sexiness, the influence of advertising—a world of standardized young bodies and blank faces for audiences to project their fantasies onto—is nowhere more pervasive than here. As if all this were not hard enough, women who are now in their middle age have seen all the rules of womanhood, marriage, and child rearing changed dramatically in the midstream of their lives. Before the days of divorce, cohabitation, self-expression, careerism, and sexual experiment, an older woman could depend on an ordered society to give her security and respect. She was even specifically represented in the pages of *Vogue* by the character of Mrs. Exeter, whose style depended on the rewards of maturity. Younger women, seeing her, had every reason to suppose that when their turn came they would have earned the right to her elegance and her serenity.

Up until the nineteen-sixties (during which Mrs. Exeter quietly faded from view), it was still entirely thinkable that a woman's style of dress should define both her age and her marital status, just as it did in the nineteenth century. Only a year or so before the arrival of the mini, which was so outrageous and so unstoppable that it wiped out such fine distinctions forever, there were still styles and colors that young girls could not wear without seeming "fast." It is hard for people to let go of the idea that skirt lengths are significant, perhaps because of a tribal memory of days when girls too young for courtship wore their skirts above the ankle and their hair down, and young girls signaling their readiness for a husband put up their hair and let down their skirts. Even now, there are residual feelings about what women ought to do with their hair after a certain age. I overheard two women at the movies condemning the inappropriateness of Meryl Streep's Alice in Wonderland mane.

It remains to be seen whether women now in their twenties and thirties will turn fifty and sixty with more or less tranquillity than those who are that age now. Perhaps there will be less anxiety about the loss of youthful good looks than there was in times when capturing a husband and bearing and rearing children were the principal choices for a woman's life. Some of our culture's ideas about aging women—a "fading beauty" being a more tragic reminder of mortality than an aging man or an aging horse—may have depended on seeing a woman's function in society as being done when she had raised her children to maturity. Time will tell how much of women's traditional distaste for their wrinkles will really disappear, and to what extent the old anxieties will be augmented by the new. Women are no longer obliged to dress to show financial dependence on men—parading evidence of a husband's or father's money-making skill—but they do not, for the most part, choose to look unattractive to men. In a time of flexible or unstable relations between men and women, anyone may be shopping for a new partner at any time, so window dressing is more important than ever. And the competitive career world sets great store by attractiveness, a look of youth and vigor. Far from seeing women free themselves from the promises of the cosmetics industry, we are seeing male Senators having hair transplants and male executives getting face-lifts. Much of what both men and women accepted as their lot in the stuffy, sometimes wise old world has no place in the brave and "ageless" new one.

Modesty

Viewing the toplessness, scantiness, or outright jettison-ing of women's bathing suits these days—partic-ularly on the Mediterranean beaches—one wonders whether all idea of modesty has vanished. Definitions of pro-priety in hot-weather dress here in town are certainly laxer than ever. Women go bare-legged, bare-backed, and braless to the office and to restaurants, and after working hours they sometimes career around on roller skates in handkerchief-size shorts. If women are ever really men's social equals, will modesty survive in any way? Much of past modesty has been imposed by the code of menfolk who saw women as personal assets to be protected from corruption by outsiders. Women who are proud of their fitness and slimness do not *seem* to be particularly interested in modesty at the moment. That quality is most often found in people, of either sex, who are embar-rassed by what they think is their own imperfect body com-pared to our culture's endless images of ideal nudity or semi-nudity. In mixed company and with lovers, it is men who are probably more inclined to cover themselves. Colette, in telling of a young bride who took only too exuberantly to honeymoon life without clothes, referred with reason to the "shadowy, delicate modesty of the male." And one version of the Adam and Eve story has it that when the pair adopted fig leaves he used his for the proper purpose while his flightier companion used hers to make herself a charming hat.

The beaches of the South of France, in particular, seem to bear witness to a womankind brave, free, and pagan, which, after centuries of confinement by masculine rules, has finally thrown off the shackles of the brassiere. It is not just the dazzling young blondes on the decks of white yachts who go topless, either. So do the conservative middle-aged matrons who sit composedly under beach parasols, knitting and holding court for grandchildren and sons-in-law. Fashion has moved far and fast since the bikinis of the Brigitte Bardot era, twenty-odd years ago. To eyes accustomed to the string bikini, the early prototypes seem almost prim period pieces. Constructed in the armored-corsetry tradition of the fifties, they depend for titillation on the sight of the navel set in a comparatively narrow band of flesh. When Rudi Gernreich promoted his "monokini" in 1964, it was banned in France. Most of Gernreich's bare-breasted designs seem antiquated now but still quite indecent—especially a demure black bathing suit with built-up straps which just happens to be scooped to the waist in front. In 1967, Yves Saint Laurent introduced the braless look to the haute couture, and his gauzy, spangled semi-toplessness was briefly taken up by night-club habituées. But—like "hot pants," which were initially quite respectable, and which have emerged a decade later with the healthier name shorts—such toplessness was always toying with vulgarity and rapidly became part of the uniform of society's real underworld. (Ironically, this was all at a time when high fashion was reaching down to that underworld to reproduce the "hooker look" or some camp notion of it.)

The definition of what part of woman is too erotic to be decently revealed has shifted around quite a bit. Traditional Arab mores decree that everything should be hidden from public view except the eyes. In the Middle Ages, it was the hair that was seen as a dangerous snare, something to be hidden away under coifs and plucked away from the brow. The ladies of ancient Crete, seventeenth-century Venice, and the Paris of the Directoire bared their breasts but had skirts or draperies, however flimsy, round their legs. And the patriar-

chial Victorians, taking the concept of modesty to unprecedented lengths, covered up the legs of pianos, referred to
men's pants as "nether garments," and considered it unthinkable that upper- and middle-class women should be seen to
have two legs. (Women working on farms and in factories,
being beyond the social pale and the decree of modesty, could
hitch up their skirts in order to work better.) Respectable
women moved smoothly along in bell-like skirts as though on
wheels. Shoulders, necks, and bosoms meanwhile rose white,
soft, and vulnerable from above the rigidly corseted torso. Man
was prevented from getting too close to this tempting display
of upper flesh by the huge crinoline skirt, which kept him a
flirtatious arm's length away.

The history of modesty and that of flirtation are hopelessly
intermingled. Imagination has traditionally played a great part
in seduction, and the tantalizing glimpse of the unseen but
guessed-at feature has often proved more enticing than the
totally revealed. I noticed in France that only when women
don their bikini tops, wrap a *pareo* round their hips, and sit
down to lunch does it become safe for the atmosphere of flirtation between men and women to set in. While sun-bathing,
the new Amazons are wrapped not only in suntans that are
like a copper-colored body stocking but also in an invisible
aura of untouchable innocence, childlike self-absorption, and
defiant lack of sexuality. The current wave of nudity follows
the general interest in sporty naturalness and health. It is in
most cases studiously unprovocative. But, clearly, there is a
narrow line between fashions that are simply healthy, spontaneous, and feminist rejection of unnecessary garments and
those fashions which seem to play on the taste for striptease.
The minimal style of dress calls for just the same social instincts as any other style, the same fine distinctions. In an age
of sexual emancipation, standards of modesty may be eroded.
But women are still expected to have an understanding of
what can only be called propriety. In the topless world of the
Côte d'Azur, quite subtle rules have evolved about when it
would strike a false note to take off a bikini top and when it

would be almost impolite to leave it on. "Comfort" and "naturalness" remain small considerations in the fashion scene compared to the rules of society, questions of taste, and the sense of appropriate place and time. And people will never be induced to wear any sort of fashion if they see it being worn by people with whom they prefer not to be identified. Among other reasons, some people's perception that the "wrong" people are in exiguous two-piece suits may account for the current popularity—at least in this country—of the one-piece maillot.

Several factors have combined to make skimpy clothing more visually and socially acceptable than it was in the past. The passion for boyish slenderness has made for fewer distinctively feminine, hourglass figures. But the current fashion in the female shape may not be the last. *Vogue* recently moved to redress the balance of androgynous, if not anorectic, youth with the image of classical womanliness. It published a photograph of a naked girl of what it called "appealing plumpness," and pointed out that for some bodies this was healthy and attractive. The popularity of suntans, which have also made it easier for our eye to accept the sight of near-nakedness, may not be indefinite, either. Limbs are transformed by a tan, made to look more plastic and more hygienic. The color evens things out—eliminates knobs, imperfections, and textures. But, like smoking, which was also chic in its day, deep tanning can be aging and dangerous, and may decline in favor. For the moment, though, tans go on getting darker and bathing suits get smaller. At the same time, sunglasses have been getting darker and growing in size. If there is no longer any modesty of the flesh, there is still the modesty of the eye. At present, sunglasses are modesty's last frontier, the masks behind which people protect their thoughts—a more intimate matter than sexual encounters. It's not our bodies we're interested in keeping hidden so much as our reactions to others, or our lack of reactions. Sunglasses are the perfect accessory for that part of the modern sensibility which prides itself on being "cool." Sunglasses are worn over the modern eye—an organ that functions best in solitude and under cover of the dark. It's the eye for movie going and television watching and for going to the beach. If ever women are plump and white again and people all take off their sunglasses, there's a fair chance that old-style modesty will be revived.

1981

Electronic
Shopping

I
t seems that the spread of the new technology will before long lead to changes in our shopping habits. Electronic shopping—by means of two-way cable-television systems that permit customers to touch buttons on home-computer terminals and summon information to the screen, then to make purchases and charge them to a credit card—is already a reality, although in limited use. And it seems likely that when there are enough video-disc machines in existence, the catalogue of an L. L. Bean or a Bergdorf Goodman will come in the form of a video disc, with images of hunting boots or lingerie flowing past our receptive gaze as we sit in our armchairs at home. The technology for new ways of shopping, which overlaps the technology for new ways of entertaining, promoting, educating, and informing, is basically ready. What remains to be seen is how it fits into our lives and what kind of messages and programs it conveys to us—the not always predictable human element.

The buying, selling, and presentation of fashion have their own quite distinct relation to that human element—one that makes them different from the buying and selling of things like dishwashers or bicycles, which are what existing electronic shopping systems tend to emphasize. Yet any claim that fashion is a purely personal business is only partly true. The fact is that the fashion industry involves a peculiar tug-of-war between the impersonal and the personal. In laying in stocks and styles, a store can have considerable confidence in a certain robotlike behavior on the part of customers, in their sense of themselves as cogs in the social machine. Usually, they vindicate the store's calculations and buy what they are supposed to buy—whatever is billed as the latest thing, or else whatever other people with the same sort of job, income, spare-time pursuits, and shape are wearing. But more than once balance sheets have been imperiled by another factor—the individualistic and sometimes openly rebellious side of human nature. From time to time, shoppers simply balk before goods, by all the rules, they might have been expected to want to buy. The constant threat of this anarchistic spark of self makes retailers cling all the tighter to what they think they can be sure of. Paradoxically, the fashion industry, whose lifeblood is change and the constant process of assimilating new ways to look, is in many ways a cautious and hidebound business.

What can safely be counted on by all concerned, in any event, is fashion's unstoppable motion. It's one conveyor belt of our life and times, moving either fast or slow, where we can tinker with our common image and make unending visual modifications in the definition of society and its individual members. It must be said that fashion is creeping sluggishly at the moment, or even moving in reverse. The times are not conducive to innovative design. We have the perplexing and depressing sight of two disparate groups—some prominent participants in a conservative Administration and some ardent young new-wave fashion followers—finding common ground in a loyalty to the looks of the early nineteen-sixties. And Robert Sakowitz, the president of the Houston department store that bears his family name, predicted in a recent speech that the nineteen-eighties would see the introduction of fewer products and fashions than the seventies, and ascribed the slowing down to the natural conservatism of a population that is growing older. "The customers of the seventies were young and physical," he said—and, he might have added, narcissistic. "In the eighties, they'll be middle-aged and mental."

The promotion of products by means of designers' names, which was probably the quintessential merchandising method of the seventies, is the fashion industry's skillful manipulation of people's urge to think that they are buying things for personal reasons. The designer empires thrived in a time when the stores were full of bewildering and proliferating choices. The designer was like a familiar personality standing as a benevolent intermediary between customers and the chaotic wealth of choices, which might cause the unwary to make mistakes and lose both time and money. Consciously, shoppers may have recognized that the belief that the designer was their personal guide was an illusion, but the idea made them feel more comfortable just the same. What was at stake was far more than just confidence in a particular brand name. Anyone flipping through our magazines for the first time and coming face to face with huge, idealized images of Diane Von Furstenberg and Calvin Klein might fail to see that they were advertising makeup, clothes, or perfumes, and simply take the pictures as portraits of film stars. The product came to seem a vulgar detail, to be passed over as lightly as could be, or not even mentioned; the personality was all. Purchasers would get the feeling that they were acquiring not mere things, like sheets or blue jeans, but a little piece of the person whose signature those things bore—a few essential drops of that person's life, looks, wealth, success, and fame.

As business people and advertising agencies kept fine-tuning the coolly calculated machinery of merchandising and hype, they sought to offset that machinery's potentially chilling effect by pumping up the human element of the process and making the designers' personalities larger than life. And so the ever more sophisticated industry of manipulating consumers through images spawned a spinoff—the industry of personality, of specially manufactured charisma or trustworthiness. Just as agrarian societies had their coopers and wheelwrights and industrial ones their engineers, our post-industrial technological world has been creating many new professions, among them that of official "trust me" person and full-time endorser. Television abounds with practitioners, from Robert Young and Joe DiMaggio to Alistair Cooke and Walter Cronkite—the last of whom until recently gave a masterly impression of endorsing the news of world events. Ronald Reagan, whose career actually included years as a professional endorser, may have attracted votes by coming across convincingly in that same role—as a sort of trustworthy anchorperson for the United States. We all seem to feel perfectly secure when we are alone with a book or are looking at the pictures in a magazine. But apparently images and events on the television screen have the power to make us feel a little vulnerable. We can assume that if television shopping gets off the ground in a real way goods will be presented by armies of endorsers, talking to us very, very soothingly.

Here in New York, a woman named Emily Cho has been thinking about women's private thoughts on fashion and how to join them to the possibilities of the new technology. She has set up a mail-order fashion-guidance service that employs a specially programmed computer. Clients fill out a multiple-choice questionnaire about the image they seek to project ("authoritative and formal" at work, perhaps, and "exotic and dramatic" in the evening) and modifications they would make in their characters (if they feel "too aggressive," for instance, or "too meek"). The computer matches these goals with information about clients' sizes and shapes to come up with suggestions of how they might build or improve their wardrobe. The greatest number of clients, it seems, are working women who want speedy help in finding clothes that will look correct or, better yet, help the wearer get ahead.

Miss Cho told me recently that it had been a laborious matter to program the computer to her satisfaction after she had isolated the specific message projected in our society by a woman wearing, say, a ruffled blouse or a hand-knit vest.

Then, when she set the service in motion, her first instinct had been to draw clients' attention away from the idea that their private hopes and dreams were being fed into a coldhearted computer. But it was soon brought home to her that the idea of the computer was precisely what appealed to the women. They welcomed the involvement of technology, because they could believe that the clothing suggestions were particularly accurate and scientific. To some extent, they liked the endorsement of the machine. What they demanded was a clear-cut formula for dressing well, rather than capricious ideas springing from another woman's brain. At the same time, Miss Cho found, they needed to believe that that other woman—Miss Cho herself—was somewhere around, to supervise, and reassure them that they had not turned over the serious, delicate question of their image to a distant, possibly runaway machine. She concluded that what clients wanted was not the obtrusive presence of an actual person in the whole business of guidance—dealing with a real person requires just the sort of time and effort they wanted to save—but the *ethics* of that person, somehow lingering in the technology like a perfume after its wearer has left the room. "And with a computerized service like this you've almost got to be more ethical than if you were giving the same service in person," she said. "You've got to start out with more care and effort, more sincerity, or the end result will be hopelessly diminished. You have to begin with more, because value keeps seeping away in the process—that must be some natural technological rule."

It's logical that such a computerized fashion guide might in future be linked with video discs or perhaps with a little television magazine discussing and showing the season's fashion changes. Then, too, such a service might dispense not just guidance but the clothes themselves, from a store or a warehouse, whose inventory, inevitably, would be computerized. Many people continue to find it unthinkable that they would buy an article of clothing by remote control; they claim that they have to touch fabrics, see colors, and try clothes on in the store. But enough people see things otherwise for clothing to have played an important part in the great mail-order-shopping boom of the past decade. It is estimated that the mail-order retail business has increased tenfold in that period, with stores all over the country and the world sending out their catalogues not simply to local charge-account customers but to nationwide credit-card holders and to people on lists of what is assumed to be a compulsive species, the established mail-order customer—who, having once ordered something from a firm in New Hampshire, starts receiving catalogues from people in Texas and California as well. It's not just basic, necessary items that change hands, either; unusual, luxurious goods also play their part in the mail-order process. Customers save time, gas, and even—if they order over the telephone and use a credit-card number—the effort of writing a check and mailing an order. Merchants try to create the idea that it's all fun— a way of capturing a customer's imagination—and not just practicality. Great care and expense go into the production of catalogues that are more and more like magazines, with top photographers presenting top models on ambitiously designed pages. Bloomingdale's has set some dramatic examples in the catalogue genre: a notoriously provocative lingerie booklet, photographed by Guy Bourdin; the issue for its China extravaganza, with fashions looking decadent indeed in photographs showing them in paddy fields next to bent-backed peasants; and the current offering, which has several of the highly publicized young Lolitas of the model world photographed by Francesco Scavullo.

Gradually, our attitude toward shopping is being transformed, and, with it, our expectation of what we hope to find when we leave home to visit a store. The large, impersonal department store with a wide choice of basic goods and a large staff of salespeople appears to be an institution that is on the wane. Its origins were in the nineteenth century, embodying two by now somewhat outmoded nineteenth-century notions: stores as great celebratory hymns exalting the glories of mass production and expanding markets; and institutions whose sales counters would always be manned by an infinite force of courteous, humble workers. The department store's function as a supplier of goods is more efficiently performed by an impersonal warehouse and a personal-seeming catalogue—currently a printed booklet but in time, presumably, in video form. For many years now, it has been inadvisable to seek courtesy, or even attention, from salespeople in department stores. Service is more likely to be found in boutiques and specialty stores, and shoppers who depend on it will seek out such places.

For all the women who are out at work all day, shopping trips involving quiet afternoons of meandering indecisively through department stores are a thing of the past. But there are still times when women, men, and families can and will go to department stores—not just because they need to buy but in search of stimulation and entertainment, as if they were off to the movies. The department stores that will survive into the future seem likely to be not necessarily those with the biggest or best choice of goods but those with the most ingenious displays, the most dramatic décor, and a way of convincing shoppers that they are places to see and be seen. Although department stores must continue to make sales, that activity appears to be subsidiary to their broader social function as a form of theatre, with the customers as the cast. Settings designed to make shoppers feel that their workaday selves have been transformed range from the Disneyland-cute, adult-scale "streets of shops" at Bendel's and Macy's to the alarming, aggressive, mood-altering blackness of Bloomingdale's main floor. Through such settings, people wander—scrutinizing each other as they float up and down on escalators, and catching sight of their image in miles of reflecting glass and chrome, in stores that are the mirror of our time.

Fashion
on the Move

Although the clothes we see and wear in life are constantly in motion, it is rare to find convincing images of fashion on film or videotape. Fashion, as such, has never really worked on television—for a number of reasons, including the respect that the eye continues to give to still photography of fashion and to the authority of generations of talented practitioners. Making fashions look good involves considerable sleight of hand and a disciplined craft, both of which continue to be best understood by people working with the static images of print. We are more inclined to believe in a picture in a magazine, which we can look at privately and at our own pace, with only our imagination on the move. Presumably, this will change in time, as it becomes commercially feasible for film- and video-makers to use the sort of effort, good equipment, and careful editing which goes to create the controlled illusion of the best fashion photography. Up to now, there has been little opportunity even for the advertising of fashions on the television screen. Costs would be prohibitive for most products apart from those with mass appeal, such as cosmetics, perfumes, and, of course, blue jeans, which have brought on the plague of commercials specifically aimed at an ever younger and apparently more moronic audience of teen-agers and children.

A new market for images of fashion in video form appears

to be developing, ironically, at a time of declining interest in the way women's fashions look, per se. There is every sign that some of the proposed new cable-television programs for women will treat fashion—if they approach it at all—not as a question of decoration and aesthetics but as a tool and a weapon in women's thrust to get ahead. (ABC and Hearst have announced plans for the formation of a new channel for "the working woman," with information about "careers, finances, and fashion"—in that order.) The print magazines that were formerly fashion magazines long ago adopted the self-help approach, with instruction not just in how to put on makeup and take off weight but also in how to succeed simultaneously in the corporate and the sensual life. The standard lyrical photographs of earlier fashion days have been replaced by practical treatises interspersed with photographs of young women in provocative poses and pretentious rags who stare unhappily at the photographer's lens.

For women's-fashion design, this is a time of redefinition, if not of actual disarray. Economic uncertainty and the current mood of women have brought great anxiety to the business of selling and publicizing new styles. Prettiness and femininity, the traditional base of women's fashion, have become somehow too politically loaded, too painful to contemplate. Men's fashions, by contrast, are at a simpler stage of evolution. The last real fashion magazine in this country is probably *Gentlemen's Quarterly,* to which one may safely turn for a nice, old-fashioned enthusiasm about the look of style and for photographs in which both clothes and models are treated with tender respect. For women, fashion can no longer be something they blithely and beautifully put on their backs. It's nothing quite as simple as Mrs. Reagan in her Galanos gown. That kind of elegance seems a curious period piece, a reminder of a different fashion age—something one may regard with interest because of its social context and because, like the couture of prewar Hollywood movies, it's right there on our television screens.

. . .

Whether in spite of or because of the disintegrating, decadent stage that women's fashion may have reached, there is tremendous interest in the subject at the moment. Fashion has floated off the women's pages and into the more gossipy sections of news magazines and television schedules. The general public is astonished or titillated by the beautiful young women and huge sums of money involved in the fashion world. Readers and viewers learn of very young teen-agers earning thousands of dollars a session for being photographed wearing grown-up clothes in sexy-looking ways. Something called "the model wars" has angry beauties battling for cash and casual observers thinking vaguely of female gladiators or mud wrestlers. The luxurious, show-biz ways of life of the successful designers bring Calvin Klein a quarter-million-dollar swimming pool and Oscar de la Renta a dinner table packed with powerful people.

Sometimes this salacious new public interest in the fashion world spills into fictionalized television, too, with prime-time dramas and miniseries. Stories drawn from novels written specially for the television audience often show hard-faced women characters using sex to further ruthless ambitions and wearing expensive wardrobes that seem almost more important than the characters themselves. Sometimes the fashion industry, which has seen its fair share of monstrous, financially triumphant businesswomen, itself provides the setting and the opportunity to depict as the central character a female tycoon. Fashion and the fashion industry have always had their worldly side, to put it mildly. Judith Krantz is scarcely the first to know how social doors will open to a clever, pretty woman in the right clothes. The cast of characters in the fashion arena—tough entrepreneurs, homosexual designers, jaded editors and photographers, and an endlessly replenished supply of fresh young beauties modelling styles to be bought by rich old women—has appealed to novelists before Harold Robbins. Fashion has always been a tussle between ugliness and commerce, on the one hand, and youth, dreams, and beauty, on the other. On television, at least, and probably in the real fashion world as well just at the moment, cynicism seems to be gaining ground. Viewers in search of romantic visions on television should turn firmly away from well-dressed women and switch to the graceful athletes, both male and female, on the sports programs.

Except on the networks, where fashionable clothes are seen mainly as symbolic trappings of money, sex, and power, the public is exposed to few moving images of fashion. The video-taping of fashion as though it were a minor art form is at a limited and early stage and is a radical enough idea to appear in downtown rock clubs, where it can often rely on the good will of a like-minded audience to overlook some fairly gauche techniques. There are also various forms of video fashion which are more functional and commercial, being commissioned by the fashion trade to educate salespeople and customers about such things as designers' collections. Stores have in recent years taken to setting up television screens in various departments—Better Sportswear, say—where videotapes play repeatedly and voice-overs rattle on regardless of whether shoppers choose to pause and watch or not. I have always found these displays a rather depressing little gesture of up-to-dateness, like an electric stove inside a thatched hut that has no power supply. The tapes themselves all too often underscore the aspects of fashion and video which do not as yet overlap; for instance, fashion models who are good at wearing clothes but are accustomed to taking up different poses for still photography look jerky in their movements on tape, like clockwork toys.

Sometimes the store video screens give a record of a designer's fashion show, but this, too, is often unsatisfactory. It may be—a heretical thought in our visually documented age, when some guests at parties see fit to circulate in silence taking photographs of guests who are struggling to make conversation—that some occasions really are ephemeral and ought not to be recorded. However skillfully a fashion show is taped, it is clearly a strange little hybrid event, whose success depends largely on the audience's getting excited about being in the right company at the right time. Fashion has the most delicate relation to timing and form, and depends greatly on immediacy. Something might strike the naked eye as being wonderfully new and fashionable. But when it is viewed minutes later on videotape its effect might well seem diminished, banal, already passé. Fashion is a capriciously timed perception of worth mysteriously linked to living, breathing life. This is why costume history in books or museums can seem sometimes so intimate and often so barren. The constant play of caprice on real life is also what makes fashion perennially disturbing and seductive.

For many reasons, the television screen brings us little of the particular shape and detail of women's fashions. But if shape, detail, and women were the sole origin of fashion these days, Seventh Avenue would be far more desperate than it is. Instead, fashion keeps rolling along as a much more generalized form of awareness, an expression of people's feelings about being alive in a particular time and culture. And television, as the deep, dark loam of popular culture—rich in half-buried old movies, junky bits of nineteen-fifties plastic, and weird amalgams of war, famine, false teeth, and soap—has an incalculable influence both on feelings and on fashion.

It is often said that people who have grown up with television (two and a half generations of them is a common count) are unprecedentedly aware of images and skilled at interpreting visual codes—including the exact social meaning of what other people choose to wear. There has lately been some horn-tooting about the emergence of a new breed of intelligentsia which is visual rather than verbal. Certainly New York has a very large community of visual people, working with various degrees of success in film, photography, architecture, television, art, and design of all kinds, including fashion. The worlds of theatre and music, and even of restaurants, also place great emphasis on the way things look. Because we have so many cameras to record the world these days, there exists a simple faith that we are the first people really to have turned responsive eyes on it. (In reality, eighteenth-century London, for instance, was a very visual society—quite as full of fashion-mad social climbers and famous faces as New York today.)

Anyone might doubt whether the television generations see any more clearly or intelligently than their parents or their ancestors. But being visual probably does combine with the post-Freudian sense of self to produce a special, modern kind of visual self-consciousness. People live as both the watcher and the watched, the person moving through the world and the observer of the world. The video screens in rock clubs, to show dancers to themselves while they are dancing, are one product of this sensibility. As we walk down the street, we are conscious of our mirror image in shop windows and the sides of buildings; as we enter fashionable restaurants, we surround ourselves with imaginary cameras, directed on us from interesting angles. In this whole process, fashion becomes the habit of using one-self to project a visual idea in a way that is related to the dance or to performance art. The most artistically pretentious and fashion-conscious of the visual people actually see themselves and their clothing as a sculptural mass filling a given space—in a loft in SoHo or Tribeca, no doubt—and choose the whole as thoughtfully as if that mass were a fancy lamp, or an avant-garde coffee table from Art et Industrie.

Part of the new visual self-consciousness stems from seeing movies, photography, or art. But many of its characteristics stem from sitting in front of the television screen. The half-watchful, semi-interested eye will alight arbitrarily (perversely, some might say) on the program itself or on some infuriating and therefore mesmerizing commercial for a vegetable-slicing gadget or a pair of blue jeans. Strangely unaffectionate visual affections get going—oddly impersonal definitions of what is interesting. Fashion has learned to pretend that someone's style is somehow quite detached from what he or she really is, and television schools us in dislocation from the real world and defuses questions of morality or aesthetic value. In the purely visual world of the screen, political questions about Mrs. Reagan's costly wardrobe or moral questions about pubescent fashion models seem absurdly sententious and quite irrelevant.

What matters is only that the parties involved have the right look for now—in the case of both the First Lady and the models, a chic combination of toughness and vulnerability. Beneath the cool, post-modern surface of a lot of fashionable people these days, there's a steely ambition, a knowingness, and a determination to exclude people who are not useful or who have the wrong look. It can be no coincidence that the resolutely advanced school of fashion design which once took to punk is now absorbed by two new themes—the Regency Dandy and the Buccaneer. Make way for stylish emotional detachment combined with stylish aggression. The visual generations want the look, all right. But they want the look that wins.

Fortuny

Mariano Fortuny's clothing and textile designs, a selection of which is being exhibited at the Fashion Institute of Technology, have the same power to fascinate today that they did in the first decades of the century, when most of them were created. Fortuny's pleated-silk gowns, colored like jewels or hothouse fruits and shaped like Greek chitons, and his fluid wraps of extraordinarily textured and patterned velvet have a legendary place in the history of twentieth-century fashion. Unlike other significant chapters of costume history, though, that on Fortuny has never been closed. He stood aloof from fashion in his day and, as a result, has never entirely gone out of fashion. Rivals and would-be imitators have come and gone, but his styles remain as moving and as wearable now as they were when they were created. Women who have collected, inherited, or, in some few cases, retained original Fortunys still wear them with affection and a kind of reverence—although on increasingly rare occasions, since the garments are now worth many thousands of dollars on the investment market. Even on inanimate mannequins in the basement galleries at F.I.T., these clothes have a prodigious, palpable vitality.

Mariano Fortuny was a man of great personal style. He was born in Spain (in 1871), but he is totally associated with Venice, to which he moved in his youth, and where he lived until his death, in 1949. He turned his attention to women's clothing design in his late thirties, after decades of artistic work in a remarkably wide variety of forms, from painting, engraving, and sculpture to photography, set design, and a novel system of stage lighting. He brought to dress an artist's concern for matching the medium to the vision and a painterly eye for color and the effect of light. He also brought to the subject a sensibility with an intuitive philosophical and spiritual comprehension of time. His work is steeped in the spirit of Venice—the history of its art, its heritage of trade with the East, and a beauty based on a splendor that has declined but not decayed. Fortuny was creating at a period when modern art movements were fermenting all around him, but he resolutely ignored them, studying instead the art and artifacts of the past—among them those of ancient Greece, the Renaissance, and a whole range of ancient non-Western cultures, particularly Arabic, that had not yet been affected by twentieth-century notions of perpetual, restless change.

The notion that everything in life passes and yet nothing really changes is anathema to fashion as a rule. One might say that fashion's whole mandate is to kick over yesterday's traces and to provide immunity to the potentially unhappy idea of tomorrow. It gives the illusion that none of us will ever be any less beautiful than we are today, let alone grow old or die: fashion anchors us all in the here and now. Fortuny's kind of fashion, on the other hand, somehow accepts the implications of mortality, and gains depth by it. He was often referred to by contemporaries as an alchemist, because of the secrecy with which he labored in the workshops of his dramatic head-quarters and home—the enormous Palazzo Orfei, overlooking the Grand Canal—and attained magical effects through tech-niques unfathomable to outsiders. He deserved the title, too, for what he did with past time: dipping his gowns in history to give them a life that outlives the beauties who first wore them. It is small wonder that Fortuny's designs were appre-ciated to the full, from their first appearance in the fashionable world, by that other alchemist Marcel Proust. Proust, who was a poetic and also a closely analytical observer of fashion, left in his novel a glittering series of descriptions of Fortuny gowns which would, if every last garment had been lost or destroyed, have been sufficient to insure their immortality.

In the constantly seesawing visual debate between the natural and the unnatural, exaggerated, and distorted silhouette which is the history of women's fashions, Fortuny stands with the natural school, for all his refined and educated eye. He was not the first to conclude that the stylized version of woman he saw around him—belling skirts, hourglass waists, pouter-pigeon bodices, and mounds of hair and millinery—was in-artistic and unworthy of her. Some who proposed a more liberated style had practical or hygienic motives, but Fortuny's were purely aesthetic. He preferred, for instance, to see the hems of his famous, shimmering, columnar silk-sheath gowns splay languidly out around the wearer's feet—hardly facilitating sprightliness but making her look like a mermaid or a beautiful vase by Emile Gallé. These gowns, which he called the Delphos gowns, hang straight from the shoulders and cling to the natural figure in a way that must have been striking indeed in Fortuny's conventionally corseted era. Sometimes the Delphos has sleeves, sometimes not. Some examples have hip-length overblouses whose hems hang in jesters' deep points weighted down by little glass beads, like the old-fashioned cheesecloth covers for the tops of milk jugs. The length of the silk is marked by many narrow, irregular pleats, permanently set in the cloth by a process that is one of Fortuny's many patents and secrets. For storage, the gowns become narrow tubes of contracted pleats, coiled into serpentine figure eights. On the female form, the light catches the silk in different ways and is refracted not only off the vertical pleats but also off the horizontal undulations that sometimes interrupt them, looking like the crimps in a length of unbraided hair. The colors that Fortuny created are still rare and luscious after the passage of decades: blushing peach and apricot, purple grape and candlelit claret, blue of fountains and of peacocks' tails.

Fortuny's virtuosity with textiles had even freer rein with all the loosely structured garments—tunics, chasubles, capes, scarves, and kimonolike wraps—that were worn over the Delphos gowns, for reasons of warmth and modesty as well as artistic effect. These were very often made of velvet, which Fortuny regarded as the aristocrat of stuffs, as the Renaissance world that so often inspired him had. His large collection of antique textiles and ecclesiastical vestments included many velvets from that period, and he studied them closely, reproducing even their patina of wear and age. (Fortuny was an omnivorous collector of all kinds of art and *objets*—as had been his father, a famous, widely travelled Spanish painter, who died young, leaving his son his collections and his taste for eclectic acquisition. The Palazzo Orfei was as much of a legend in Fortuny's day as his work and his strikingly dressed person. Cavernous salons were filled with his own art and his father's; ancient statues and suits of armor stood guard over divans strewn with cushions, in the Moorish way; draperies and panels of Fortuny's textiles hung from the ceilings like banners in the naves of Gothic churches.) In the workshops and studios, velvets and other fabrics were patterned with Fortuny's great repertory of historical ages and civilizations, by hand methods ranging from painting and stencilling to printing and engraving. The velvets were also treated with a special technique of multilayered dyeing, which sends the base color floating up mysteriously through pile that has a different tint and catches the light in different ways according to the nap and the drape. This dreamlike haze of color is sometimes compounded by fine metallic frostings—designs in gold or silver that seem to swim and hover across an ever-changing field.

If Fortuny's designs were the art of the past transformed into modern fashion—"faithfully antique yet markedly original," as Proust called them—they were also, very often, the styles and patterns of ceremonial grandeur crystallized into garments of great tenderness and intimacy. Fortuny's sense of form and color was joined to an intense feeling for women, as ideal romantic visions but also as creatures of flesh and blood.

Artistic technique alone might have made the clothes interesting to historians after all these years, but it is Fortuny's respect and empathy for women that make the clothes still wearable and so peculiarly touching. An informative book, *Mariano Fortuny: His Life and Work*, written and compiled by Guillermo de Osma (Rizzoli), includes many photographs of women wearing their Fortunys—from the young Mrs. Condé Nast, in 1919, to the young Mrs. Tina Chow, the fashionable wife of an international restaurateur, in 1977. In a way, though, the clothes are less compelling on the pretty fashion plates of various decades than on women with an air of leading real lives, of a complexity that complements the clothes. There is, for instance, a 1907 color portrait by Alfred Stieglitz of his sister, Mrs. Selma Schubert, that is quite striking. A stern, almost grumpy-looking woman in early middle age, she sits on a park bench among a scattering of autumn leaves, with a blowsy bunch of flowers in her belt and a very well-worn woolly cardigan pulled over her gold silk Delphos. Then, there is a symbolic pair of portraits of the art collector Peggy Guggenheim, Fortuny's neighbor in Venice, wearing what might be the same Delphos in both—first as a young woman, then as an old one. In the first, she stands statuesquely on some sunlit terrace by the Grand Canal, toying with the flowers on a rosebush and aiming a happy, hoydenish smile at the photographer. In the second, she sits forlornly in the gloom indoors, on the edge of a big bed, with her gown slipping off one withered shoulder and her gaze turned blankly to one side—the picture of tragic old womanhood. The Fortuny gowns seem to occupy a special place in such women's lives. Where other designers' garb might trivialize experience, these clothes add a poignant kind of dignity.

Essentially, Fortuny went on producing the same styles for forty years or so, while dramatic shifts of mood and shape were taking place around him. In his lifetime and after, a succession of different kinds of enthusiasm were brought to his work. At the beginning, before the First World War, Fortuny was known to an élite—the women of the Faubourg, whom Proust observed in the gowns, but only in the privacy of their homes, and a few more daring women in the arts, such as Eleonora Duse, Isadora Duncan, and Ruth St. Denis, who began to wear them for public soirées and for their performances. Fortuny reached his largest and most obviously fashion-following audience in the nineteen-twenties and thirties, and it was in this period that he became widely known in America. The same clothes were worn for different reasons. Before the Great War, they seemed to carry on a tradition of idealistic and artistic female dress begun with the nineteenth-century Pre-Raphaelites and Aesthetes. After the war, they seemed liberated, even slightly naughty, and totally modern attire for wear to cocktail parties in the Jazz Age. The years leading to the Second World War saw a gradual decline in the designer's popularity in Europe, although he was still quite popular in America, thanks to the efforts of a businesswoman named Elsie McNeill. In the fifties, Fortuny's garments were largely relegated to closets and attics, and the Delphos pleats lay coiled in their special little boxes. But the end of the nineteen-sixties saw them sinuously out in the world again, rediscovered by a new audience—of young women with fashion tastes that ran to nostalgia for the quality of past creations. The seventies saw full-scale rehabilitation for Fortuny, with serious exhibitions and escalating prices at Sotheby's and Christie's. The designer's devotees are given to saying that he is beyond fashion, that his artistry is too serious to be covered by a term associated with the frivolous and the temporary. In truth, Fortuny's garments *are* fashion, but of a rare kind that is beautiful, durable, and very passionately felt. Even in his own time, Fortuny was a model of what fashion might have been.

Façades

What do women writers wear? Biographies, letters, diaries, and autobiographical writings of women from the past leave us with many snapshot glimpses, and sometimes with homely details. The sketchiest descriptions of how literary women looked and chose to dress can have the perennial immediacy, the mysteriously compelling life, of these women's voices in their books. Here's a wasp-waisted Colette wearing a dashing black fur toque as she steps out with her little bulldog in the Bois. Virginia Woolf, in a comfortable old cardigan and stockings she mended last evening by the fireside, is writing away in the potting shed. Dorothy Richardson's autobiographical heroine is venturing forth from her boarding house after performing yet another miracle on her shabby old evening dress by means of a cheap piece of lace. George Sand, when she encounters Robert Browning, is wearing rather too fine and fashionable a gown —a shade too *"endimanchée,"* he relates (along with copyable details) to his wife. George Eliot, yearning to be loved, leaves off her translation of Spinoza to experiment with a modish Parisian hairstyle, supposed to soften her powerful features. Edith Wharton, having been dressed with intimidating elegance for dining out, may be seen in bed the next morning, with her writing board on her knees, wearing a funny, old-fashioned silk cap.

Fresh in our minds, thanks to the new biography by Victoria Glendinning (*Edith Sitwell: A Unicorn Among Lions,* published by Knopf), we have the quite amazing clothes style of Dame Edith Sitwell. Edith Sitwell's life, like that of many another writer, was a process of defining, perhaps even re-inventing, herself—of giving birth to herself in her own image. Like many another woman, she used clothes to further that process—albeit in her case in an utterly fanciful and un-conventional way. Her girlhood was awkward and painful, and her nose, hands, limbs, and body were so freakishly long and thin by prevailing Edwardian standards as virtually to ex-clude her from a normal life of matrimony. On the foundation of her original self and circumstances and out of instinctive self-defense, she built up the Gothic edifice of a highly visible and highly eccentric public persona. Her style evolved, by means of ever more intricate historical allusions and accretions of glitter that blinded or dazzled, into a walking version of some madness that could have been commissioned by King Ludwig of Bavaria. With her weird, sculptural hats, which played on the commonly noted resemblance between her pro-file and that of an effigy on a Plantagenet tomb; her massive rings, made of chunks of semi-precious stone and designed to draw attention to hands about which she was supremely vain; and her strange, shapeles robes and cloaks made from Liberty brocades or upholstery fabrics, she must certainly have merited Elizabeth Bowen's description of her as "a high altar on the move." "If one is a greyhound, why try to look like a Pekingese?" her biographer quotes Dame Edith as saying. "I am as stylized as it is possible to be—as stylized as the music of Debussy or Ravel." Not for the title of her best-known work alone is the poet's name indelibly associated with the word "façade."

It would clearly be foolish to draw general conclusions about women writers' dress from the example of Edith Sitwell, whose style in both verse and clothes was so energetically sui generis. In fact, any such generalizations would depend on the viewing of literary women, past and present, as a group, whereas, of course, they encompass an enormous range of types, with retiring, introverted scholars at one end of the spectrum and formidable *grandes dames* and show-biz figures at the other. Perhaps there really are women writers who are wholeheartedly devoted to content rather than form in their work and who are also completely oblivious of the way they look out in the world. Women writers dress differently according to their temperament, way of life, income, and—perceiving themselves and being perceived as either plain or beautiful —what they choose to make of their natural looks.

Perhaps if one *were* to imagine women writers as a group, and pose them hypothetically beside a group of women actors or bank executives, they might look less fashionably dressed. But since fashion is largely to do with being part of a group— going along with the swim of people like oneself—whereas being a writer is largely to do with being an individual, one might not be surprised to find women writers holding more complicated views on fashion than women who are not writers. Being able or unable to keep in fashion forms the basis of a delicately oscillating self-scrutiny by Miriam Henderson, the alter ego of the novelist Dorothy Richardson, in the autobiographical series called *Pilgrimage*. She finds a certain humiliation but also a pride in the poverty that keeps her making do—scheming up ingenious and sometimes startling new ways of trimming the same old hat. In time, necessity forms the basis of a whole philosophy of eccentricity and originality in dress. Like her poverty, it is a badge of honor and a part of the hard-won independence that has permitted her to think of becoming a writer.

In conversation with a friend who is a working woman like her (but more content to define herself as such), Miriam tells her friend that she is more fashionable, or "smart." Miriam says, "It may be quite right, perhaps you are more sociable than I am."

Her friend replies, "One is so conspicuous if one is not dressed more or less like other people."

Miriam says, "That's what I hate; dressing like other people. If I could afford it I should be stylish—not smart. Perfect coats and suits and a few good evening dresses. But you must be awfully well off for that. If I can't be stylish I'd rather be dowdy and in a way I like dowdiness even better than stylishness."

This almost coveted costly stylishness involves, in Miriam's mind, I suspect, tailoring of rather masculine sobriety of color and strictness of line. Many women writers have adopted this authoritative severity, this no-nonsense, dark-suited approach to their public life over the years, as if in recognition of the androgyny that is supposed to characterize the artistic mind. Some women writers—notably George Sand and Colette—dressed on various occasions and at different stages of their lives both in men's suits and in intensely feminine fashions. As for Edith Sitwell's style, so rooted in art history and childhood dressing-up fantasy, it doesn't seem exactly masculine or exactly feminine. On the whole, however, the loose Pre-Raphaelite dresses, the hats and furs and mandarin-length fingernails seem female, although of some exotic variety of femaleness which is safely shut away like a natural-history specimen beneath the glass dome of a bell jar. Unlike Miriam, she would not have openly endorsed the philosophy of dowdiness—even though the majestic garments she trailed around in for years eventually acquired a venerable and aristocratic air of tattiness. But she, too, once declared roundly that she "wouldn't dream of following fashion."

What Edith Sitwell's life and style did have in common with those of other women writers was the divide between her appearances in public and her hours spent practicing the solitary business of putting words down on paper. This divide was, like everything else about her, an exaggerated one. She was not unique, certainly by today's standards, in both being a writer and performing in public the role of writer. But in her case the performance went far beyond the present-day custom of appearance on a talk show or two upon the publication of a new book. In their heyday in the nineteen-twenties, especially, the private social life of Edith and her brothers, Osbert and Sacheverell, was so feverishly public that it brought the great critic Dr. F. R. Leavis to his famous summing up: "The Sitwells belong to the history of publicity rather than of poetry." Edith Sitwell knew "everyone." The writers all wrote descriptions of her appearance in letters and memoirs; artists and photographers, fascinated, made scores of portraits of her; gossip writers put her in their columns. And in addition to the highly visible amateur performance of her social life there were Edith Sitwell's actual performances, on the stage and the lecture platform, reciting her own work. But, as Mrs. Glendinning observes at one point in her story, these performances, private and public, posed a danger for the poet: "Being a star and an icon was no substitute for writing."

Dame Edith's garb, which she saw as a spontaneous expression of herself, might also be taken as a form of self-parody, and even of disguise. Like many writers, she seems to have been of a shy, secretive, hypersensitive nature, at once unworldly and ambitious. Onlookers who do not share such a temperament—or those who, sharing it, cope with it in an entirely different way—are sometimes astonished that its possessors might cultivate flamboyance and seek out the stares of the vulgar crowd. But in some way the tender and retiring tenant of a gaudy self-made carapace of style regards herself as perfectly safe and as if magically unseen. The impulse and the will to carry through an unorthodox style are no casual matter. The way Edith Sitwell dressed her person was an intense, ritualized art form, which she practiced alongside, and sometimes instead of, her writing. In the last decade of her life, she gave a regal interview to *Harper's Bazaar* under the title "My Clothes and I." In spite of its humor ("I couldn't possibly wear tweeds. . . . People would follow me on bicycles") and its oddly disingenuous disclaimers ("I am entirely unselfconscious, always"), this was not idle fashion magazine chatter. Her revelations—about being supplied by Miss Pery, the millinery buyer at Whiteley's; about the aquamarine that Osbert found in China and the necklace that Millicent Rogers made for her in the pre-Columbian style; about going to Peggy Sage for her manicures—seem a reverent, poetic incantation, as if she were reciting a rosary. In common with many other women writers, past and present, Edith Sitwell wrote in bed.

The *Harper's Bazaar* interview did not omit a seemingly intimate but finally guarded view of Dame Edith "working in bed." At the last moment, when the audience has been led right up to the bedside of the writer, caught in the act of functioning as a writer, a gauzy scrim of discretion is thrown up and we are permitted only to see the writer *almost* writing. "I do all my writing in bed," Dame Edith asserts, but she goes on, in the same breath, "I sit there reading and knitting bed jackets to wear while I'm writing. They are white with intricate work down the front. I found the pattern before the First World War and know it by heart by now." The picture-within-a-picture-within-a-picture conceit of knitting bed jackets to wear while knitting bed jackets and so on down the years forever is pure Edith Sitwell. There is something more generally feminine and literary, though, to the tone—protective, affectionate, ironic, slightly detached, and far from unself-conscious—of this sketched outline of her clothed portrait. It is as if by describing the elements of her appearance she were writing her autobiography.

That many women writers work in bed—in a bed jacket or some sturdier woolly to keep their shoulders warm in winter—we know from acquaintances. This habit has less to do with any quality of women's writing—lolling and imagining among the pillows or dreaming away on divans while more businesslike men writers put in their purposeful hours behind huge desks—than with the tricky problem faced by women who work at home and also run the household without help. As long as she stays in bed, the woman writer is insulated from the prosaic saucepans and dirty kitchen floors —as safely cut off from "reality" as if she were cast adrift on her own little ship. The French fashion magazine *Jardin des Modes* ran a picture story earlier this year on the way women writers dress for work at home, and based it on the assumption that they wore some comfortable sort of second skin, if not actually a kind of dishabille. The story, called "Belles de Lettres," is one of many that this fashion magazine alone could pull off with dignity. And, for a hundred cultural reasons, the magazine itself could only exist—with its endearingly feminine and feminist attitude, its witty artwork, and its frequent quotations from Mallarmé and Balzac—in Paris. These photographs, of some half-dozen well-established French women authors who are seen first in their idealized fantasy of their writing clothes (silk pajamas and lace-encrusted peignoirs) and then in some outfit corresponding more closely to reality (men's flannel pajamas, several layers of old sweaters, and ski socks), do more than avoid tastelessness; they are charming and quite moving.

Each of the writers is also invited to say something about the part that clothes play in her life. One of them expresses a vague desire for some single uniform she could put on in the morning, as her lover puts on his business suit, and so be satisfactorily defined for the course of the day. In the end, though, this strikes her as too rigid, and she is committed to pursuing the fluid definition of herself through her writing. She is disturbed by gifts of clothing, even from people who love her, because they impose on her a definition of self, a wholeness that is not her own. She is so solicitous about this whole self, and so protective of it, that she doesn't take the risk of owning a mirror large enough to show more than bits of her person at a time. Women get accustomed to chopped-up images—eyes, nose, and mouth in a powder compact; the back of the head in the hand mirror; the feet and ankles in the sloping glass at the shoe store—but it seems particularly writerlike for the women in the *Jardin des Modes* story to do such head scratching about whether or not to make a philosophically and psychologically connected shape from the random jigsaw bits of mirror.

How women look, and how their looks change in the course of their lives, is not a frivolous question. It is a part of their experience, perhaps a crucial one, and, as such, a valid target for the curiosity of writers. Women writers have been known to study their own looks as well as those of other women. They have even been known to seek the confirmation of their existence in the mirror as well as in the works they write. Once, in a movie about Devil's Island, two solitary-confinement prisoners were permitted to swivel their heads through the bars and, after years without a mirror, to scrutinize each other. "How do I look? How do I look?" they asked each other anxiously. When the woman writer stands looking at her reflection in the glass—dressed up in some stylish façade for going out in the world, or in her work gear of baggy-kneed pajamas and out-at-elbows sweater—there is no more of vanity in her than in those prisoners. "How do I look?" she asks as her eyes meet the eyes in the mirror. She listens carefully for an answer, because it might prove quite illuminating.

1982

Architectural Fashion

O ver the past year or so, fashion has undergone a significant change: it has been in the process of becoming "modern" and "visual." To label this a change may seem puzzling, since fashion is always new by definition, and since it has always been inescapably before our eyes each day. But it is a change just the same, and one that has broader implications than the fashion details of each new season's collection. For until quite recently fashion was a despised stepchild in the design world, an irrational, feminine form of fetishism, additionally damned by virtue of being at the mercy of commerce at its most corrupt. And now this view is being eroded by a growing group of people who see fashion as a perfectly respectable part of the whole mosaic of contemporary visual expression. There seems finally to be a new and genuine attempt to look at fashion in terms of painting, photography, dance, performance, sculpture, architecture, and the like: as a question of shape, form, mass, structure; of moving through space or simply taking up space in particular ways; or of the play of color, light, and shade.

This emphasis on the way fashion looks, on form rather than content, represents a radical shift from the social and humanistic concerns that seemed to dominate fashion in the past decade. That whole long era of self-expression, with fashion meandering along in the hands of amateurs encouraged to "put together their own look," appears to be petering out. We are witnessing a return of fashion that has been carefully designed by real designers, willing to impose coherent-seeming formal visions. On occasion, the designers make those visions bear burdens of theory, and so their realization has sometimes been dubbed "intellectual" or "conceptual" fashion. But any ideas involved turn inward on the worlds of art and design rather than outward to explore social and political ideas, such as women's ideas about their lives. (In an elevator, going to a Seventh Avenue show last week, I overheard two professional fashion women discussing the season's color schemes of black-and-white and off-black in terms of the paintings of Franz Kline and Ad Reinhardt.) Fashion's old preoccupation with social meanings and messages, with emotional signs and signals, and even with physical fitness is giving way. What matters now is appearance for its own sake. Though the style goes out into the world on real women, it is not about society or about the body but about the eye. Of course, there are meanings to be discovered even in a style that seems to deflect curious observers on purpose, and perhaps what we are seeing is fashion in a deeply felt flight from feeling. For this is style that deliberately removes itself from the chaotic context of relations (particularly those which involve new definitions of women and the effect of the revised definitions on men) and sets up camp in a cooler, purer sort of visual country, where satisfying images fill a flat screen— images that no one should waste energy trying to pierce. This is fashion for the stylized self living out a ritualized experience. Its aim is the old Dandy ideal of detachment—an ideal reinforced by the modern habit of passively watching a second world (more real and less so than the one we know directly) continuously rearrange itself in moving pictures on a screen. It has been said of the fashionable performance artist Laurie Anderson, with her mysterious utterances and gestures, that she somehow gives her audience a provocative experience by withholding that experience, as if at the last minute she vanished or jumped behind a curtain. There is that quality of enigma and tension in the new fashion as well. It seems to draw the observer irresistibly toward it, only to withdraw, chilly and inviolate, behind a bafflingly invisible barrier—a

resilient, transparent sheath, like the chitin encasing the body
of a dragonfly.

The most progressive fashion designers are much concerned
at present with paring away clutter and permitting shape and
line to speak clearly for themselves. This goal is not, of course,
a completely original one in the history of design, or even in
the relatively inarticulate and undocumented history of fashion
design. In many ways, it all simply looks like the latest expression of the old familiar modernist, sometimes utopian ideal.
Several designers were stirred by last year's exhibition in
New York of the art of the Russian Constructivists, which
included boldly geometric and abstract clothing designs intended to bring revolution, art, and enlightenment to dress
at a time (the nineteen-twenties) when artists could be wholeheartedly optimistic about the revolutionary state. (For the
most part, though, the progressive designers of today have as
little interest in mass production or the sacrifice of élitist
standards of materials and workmanship as their most conservative colleagues.) There are also echoes, in this new
modernism, of an even more recent flurry of futurist enthusiasm—the Space Age fantasies explored in the early sixties
by Cardin (who studied architecture at one point), Courrèges,
and Gernreich. These are reborn in modified form in today's
New Wave. But reference to modernist moments in the past
does not cancel the genuinely modernist impulse of the most
compelling current of today's fashion design. In its turn, even
if it is only the latest member of a long-established company
of idealists and iconoclasts, this design is essentially anti-
nostalgic and anti-historicist. It is also anti-pastoral, anti-
romantic, anti-pretty, and almost certainly anti-feminine as
well. But then, it emerges at a moment when all the gorgeous
"old-fashioned" garden-party lace and linen and ruffled taffeta
that have plagued us so long are playing themselves out in
something like absurdly reactionary self-parody. After the
visual orgy of costume dramas on television in recent years,
there was more than a whiff of perfumed decay about that

whole silk-cushioned fashion world of women in frills and wafting fancies. Women dressed in such a style can easily slide into a look that is dazzling but somehow strange, as though they were really transvestite stars.

I have referred to the new mood of fashion as modernist, but fashion, in spite of its new sense of worth as a branch of design, would still not quite have the temerity to use such a grandiose term. What it took to calling itself instead was either linear or architectural. As feminine fashion began to be self-conscious and to search for a language capable of expressing more serious thoughts than where to buy what, it looked with awe and envy to its big brother architecture. Here was a domain that simply swirled with theories, that had a tradition of debate leading back to Socrates and Plato, and that was confident enough to mantle itself in big words like "modern," and even "post-modern." Little fashion pressed its nose to the windowpane and saw architects moving freely in a bright and privileged world—long-established, powerful, public, and masculine (to the point of being, especially with skyscrapers, notoriously phallic). And then, in recent times, architecture has been generating publicity and excitement, which spilled over into fashion—as most excitement must, in one way or another. To fashion designers, architecture gave the appealing impression (probably illusory for the most part) that creative theories could influence the course of style, and that designers could be actively in control. Architects could sit up at night talking about what a house should be, what makes a city work, and so forth; fashion, on the other hand, apparently just sort of *happened*. Fashion drew near to architecture for all these reasons, and also because architecture provided the look that it was after—a look that would match up with what it sensed as a kind of psychic need, a feeling in the air. What fashion found was a certain impassive, hard-edged, sharply outlined quality, traditionally associated not with female forms clothed in fabric but with edifices clothed in steel, concrete, glass, stone, or marble. What fashion took up, in short, was precisely the kind of "modernism" from which post-modern architecture was vociferously in flight.

It is foolhardy to try to determine which particular branch of design first gives shape to any particular trend. Even within the same field, seemingly opposite tendencies have a way of running parallel or being intertwined. I do not claim here that "architectural" fashion has clearly supplanted nostalgic femininity, or even is on the point of triumphing. In the recently shown spring collections, contradictions often coexisted, as witness Perry Ellis's conventional corseted waists above more experimental geometric, "box-pocketed" pants. In the whole tapestry of contemporary design, threads run along the surface, go underneath for a while, then re-emerge, sometimes in unexpected places. Still, it is one of the ironies of this process that just at the moment when architecture seems to have taken on some of the traditional properties of feminine fashion —a taste for relatively rapid change, apparently for its own sake; for ornamental detail; and for publicity and promotion that seem almost more important than the finished product— progressive clothing design has been seeking out the very austerity and visual purity that architecture is rejecting as sterile and inhuman. It is even tempting to see Philip Johnson's A.T.&T. Building, with its neo-Chippendale twiddly bits, as some kind of giant late flowering of the historicism that the fashion world knows as "thrift-shop chic," and which it seems to be trying to leave behind. Domestic architecture— as well as public building—has been self-consciously accepting the need to incorporate the past, in the form of memory-laden bric-a-brac (often thought of as "feminine"). In further gestures toward the idea that buildings should *feel* human as well as *look* impressive, there has been a general softening of rectangles into roundness and plumpness, and a great interest in indigenous structures that people built spontaneously, without calling upon architects or theories at all. The post-modernist architects have, for instance, looked at the ugly flowerpots and monstrous aluminum awnings with which, over the years, the inhabitants of Le Corbusier's rational-looking workers' housing had made themselves feel at home, and deemed these accretions aesthetically acceptable, and cozy, too. But the sort of fashion that feels newest at the moment is marching firmly in the opposite direction. After years of permitting women to individualize their outfits with cute memorabilia and touches of often self-deprecating whimsey, fashion is talking about the austerely linear, and some designers are even working out schemes on graph paper according to the rational and mathematical principles of the Cartesian grid. This new fashion is anything but—to use the current architectural buzz word, the explanation for the benign eye turned on those flowerpots and awnings—"consolatory." In fact, it may prove a little frightening to its wearers.

Earlier this year, there was an exhibition of fashion in the Hayden Gallery at the Massachusetts Institute of Technology. The show, which was organized with great sensitivity by the curator, Susan Sidlauskas, and was entitled "Intimate Architecture: Contemporary Clothing Design," was relatively modest in scale, but its reverberations were complex and fascinating. How stimulating fashion can be, displayed in this controlled and edited way, plucked out of its habitual environment of commercial hype, and separated from the sometimes distorting personalities, figures, and social lives of wearers far removed from the designer's vision! We have lately become more accustomed in this country to shows of fashion dating from the past—the eighteenth century, the Belle Epoque, or (once he was safely dead, and not simply living half-forgotten in the half-world of the Chelsea Hotel) the work of the designer Charles James. But a group show of contemporary fashion designers is rarely seen, because of designers' clashes of ego and their unwillingness to concede that their best and most illuminating work is not invariably the latest collection they want to promote. (Excellence may well have been achieved a couple of seasons back, even if, because *Women's Wear Daily* panned it, it didn't sell.) The designers chosen by Miss Sidlauskas as representative of the intimately architectural style were the Italians Giorgio Armani, Mariuccia Mandelli (of the firm of Krizia), and Gianfranco

Ferrè (who is actually an architect by training); Claude Montana, a French designer working in Paris; Issey Miyake, a Japanese who has lived in Paris and New York and now works in Tokyo; and three who live and work in Manhattan— Ronaldus Shamask (a Dutchman by upbringing), Yeohlee Teng (who grew up in Malaysia), and Stephen Manniello (a native New Yorker). Since "architectural fashion" is something of a vague term, covering many variations on an assertive approach to design, Miss Sidlauskas was free to choose contributors to her show according to her taste. Arguments could clearly be made for including, for instance, some of Norma Kamali's distinctive, often broad-shouldered silhouettes; the cool rationalities of Catherine Hipp; something by the Frenchman Thierry Mugler; or the innovative, often oversize clothing by a number of the newly prominent Japanese, such as Yohji Yamamoto. And tribute could well have been paid to the New York designer Linda Hopp, who, unlike most of the others I have mentioned, is certainly not internationally known but secured a special little place in the history of architectural fashion in New York with her store on West Broadway; the combination of her idealistic design and the purposeful gray-toned interior designed by her brother, an architect, had a symbolic life that survived the store's closing, just as buildings that have been torn down, or perhaps never even built, can have a lasting effect on the imaginations of succeeding generations of architects.

In characterizing "Intimate Architecture" and the style it demonstrated, Miss Sidlauskas said in an article for *Vogue*: "The recurring characteristics of this 'architectural' vision are: a clarity of line, sharp edges, discrete shapes, and the impression that the garment possesses its own architectonic structure and could stand on its own without the necessity of a human wearer." That is a statement with startling implications in the history of contemporary fashion. It is not only that shape and structure, per se, seemed insignificant for a couple of decades or so but that it was impossible to consider them without trepidation or alarm. Of course, shape had gone right on changing anyway. In fact, silhouettes had undergone some extreme transformations in that period. What mattered, however, was not those changes but what those changes meant—the mini standing for youth and sexual freedom, the anti–midi pants revolt for some sort of cockeyed fashion independence, and so forth. It was always important in those years for women to believe that particular fashion changes were brought into being because women willed them. In that earlier period, the very idea of "discrete shapes" would have been abhorrent to the "human wearer." It would have raised the old spectre of shapes being somehow imposed on sleepwalking fashion followers by an international cabal of homosexual (still in the closet at that time) fashion designers bent on making women look weird. The last era of unquestioned homage to shape was the nineteen-fifties, when the great Balenciaga was designing at full sculptural tilt and Christian Dior was coming up with lines based on the alphabet—the H-line, the Y-line, and the A-line. In a recent book about Dior (*Dior in Vogue*, by Brigid Keenan, published by Harmony), we hear of an irate husband writing to the designer, "With your so-called genius you have succeeded in disfiguring my wife." This protest—made man to man, so to speak, over the dizzy little head of the victim—now strikes us as unthinkably proprietary. If at this point women adopt shapes that exaggerate, disguise, or distort their natural contours, they must take responsibility themselves.

The catalogue of "Intimate Architecture" (mostly photographed by the fashionable Robert Mapplethorpe on the fashionable body builder Lisa Lyons) was at pains to point out that the show's designers were linked by "their reliance on forms that are deliberately distinguished from the organic curves of human anatomy." What is involved here, then, is not the exaggerations of the female figure—wasp waists, extra-rounded hips, puffed-out sleeves, emphatic bosoms—that appear throughout fashion history (and, in fact, are appearing right now) and somehow, even at their most lunatic, seem profoundly conservative. There is certainly some distance maintained between the new style and the human body, but it would be less than accurate to claim that all the design shapes concerned are abstract and geometric. Some of the designs depend on curves abstracted from those to be found in the natural world, if not necessarily in the female form. Mariuccia Mandelli's contributions to the M.I.T. show were more often rounded in outline than rectangular. There was, for one example, her astounding crinkle-pleated black silk top and pants whose winging arms and legs were reminiscent of a pair of sycamore seeds in flight, or perhaps a mythological griffin. Issey Miyake, true to his Japanese heritage and to his professed admiration for the environmental artist Christo, often engages in a design dialogue with the natural world. And although the examples of the work of Ronaldus Shamask seen here were primarily Japanese or architectural in inspiration (he also studied architecture for a time, and his now-famous "one-seam coat" spirals round like the famous unbuilt helter-skelter tower designed by the avant-garde Russian artist Vladimir Tatlin as a monument to the Third International), the designer sometimes works with more organic lines, as in his rounded "cello" sleeve or in a striking red dress from a recent collection which looked suspiciously like a female praying mantis.

For all its organic reference, "Intimate Architecture" was probably more concerned with the modernist notion of quasi-geometric or mathematical abstraction that would somehow free the imagination from the banality of bodies, their feet planted firmly on the ground. The catalogue quotes from a turn-of-the-century art historian named Wilhelm Worringer, who noted the geometric ornament of African, Greek, and Eastern cultures with some satisfaction, calling them a "refuge from appearance"—a way for the eye and the mind to re-organize the universe more satisfyingly—and characterizing them as "life-denying, crystalline, and inorganic." One of the appeals of architectural fashion is that it seems a reassuring visual system, bringing order to a confusing world. It seems a haven of clarity, a balance between many irreconcilables, such as women's sense of vulnerability and their new perception of the need to act aggressively—between the instinct for self-protection and the projection of a sense of power. Here, perhaps, is a form of "feminine" fashion for a world in which femininity is in great crisis. The traditional attribute of yielding softness and the whole rich yet private and domestic mesh of inherited female skills and sensitivities are under fire at the moment, not least from women themselves. Architectural fashion may look bold or tough. It may even look life-denying, crystalline, and inorganic. But it never looks dependent or subservient.

Again and again in the M.I.T. show, the idea of armor cropped up—in a highly stylized way, to be sure. It was often filtered through the fascination with all things Japanese and then expressed in the refined silken code of high fashion. The Japanese filter in this case was the traditional costume of the samurai warrior, which had a particularly powerful effect on designers who were influenced by Akira Kurosawa's film *Kagemusha*. Among the spawn of the samurai fever were Armani's blue satin tunic and tubular quilted legs squared off like kitchen-match boxes, and Issey Miyake's rattan-and-bamboo corselet top—an astonishing sculptural structure with airy black ribs and extended shoulders, seeming at once to cage the torso and to endow it with the magic power of dragonfly wings. This piece—one of only a handful made by an artisan who normally makes implements for the tea ceremony —attained still greater symbolic significance by appearing on the cover of a mystifying issue of *Artforum* apparently devoted to the admittedly elusive question of fashionability in the arts and in life. Not that all Japanese design reference was militarist. Besides Shamask's kimono sleeves and obis, his fanlike pleating and origamilike folded effects, there were Krizia's funny crinkled-silk Spanish-guard bloomers, which looked like those globular Japanese paper lanterns.

The idea of stylized combat was also carried through in the Western tradition, with Yeohlee Teng contributing a strikingly angular suit of black and white wool that paid tribute to the traditional fencing tunic. (The thrust-and-parry of fencing is also a favorite visual theme with other fashion people at present. I saw a fashion photograph the other day where the

model wore as accessories roller skates and a fencing mask.)
And in addition to the fencing tunic, with its padded protection, there were several garments providing the idea of armor
or disguise for the breasts. Armani's strapless white silk top
ironed out those irrational bulges with a cardboard-stiffened
front panel, creating a sculptural whole not unlike some
modernist Italian lamp but with an elegance that had an
element of menace. Krizia showed funny-colored brassieres of
rigid molded plastic (for wear with those crinkled paper-
lampshade bloomers), and Issey Miyake took the idea a stage
further with a bustier, or corselet, encasing the wearer in a
hardened, iridescent mimicry of her own flesh, complete with
stylized nipples and navel—like a very modern, very female
version of those idealized metal pectorals and rippling stomach
muscles on the breastplates of Roman centurions.

Although seen in the catalogue on a woman with a powerful body, the clothes were mounted for the show itself in a
manner that reintroduced the ideas of delicacy and vulnerability to often aggressively powerful shapes, and this seemed
a wise decision. The eye and the mind have come far and fast
in accepting new definitions of women, but most people are
still not ready for the combination of powerful envelopes of
clothing on powerful female shapes. For the *Artforum* cover,
Miyake's black rattan-and-bamboo corselet (together with a
long, mermaidlike black imitation-leather skirt) was photographed on an androgynous-looking model, staring into the
camera lens for an effect of aggression, not to say sadism. The
effect, as was no doubt the intention, was shocking. But the
brutality of the corselet outfit was considerably mitigated
when it was seen in the show on a feminine-looking plaster
mannequin shell that hung suspended airily above the floor
from invisible wires. This shell, identical to all the others on
view, had been created around a superannuated window
mannequin dug out of a store basement. The body language
of the forms had that faded, almost forgotten fragility of the
idealized feminine posture of the nineteen-fifties and sixties.
So above the armored corselets of the new architectural fashion
ghostly white shoulders emerged in the old defenseless way—

hunched forward, collarbones standing out, delicate and brittle as the stems of clay pipes. Between the new style's football-hero shoulders, women's necks craned forward long and white, like those of anxious swans. These plaster bodies seemed at once to cower and to draw attention to the bosom—bending in on themselves as if both dreading violation and inviting it. (How remote, in our age of Jane Fonda-like bodies fiercely "centered" on rock-hard abdominals, seems the classic Marilyn Monroe stance, with one kneecap swivelled in front of the other, bottom stuck out, head jutting forward to kiss or pout!) To bring the vulnerable-looking female body out of mothballs and press it into the service of the consciously in-vulnerable-looking architectural fashion was a sound idea. So was the curator's notion of slicing off the heads of this floating female company of plaster ghosts at around the level of their earlobes. It was visually effective, and, this way, there were no brains to be taxed with a fashion that turned their persons into a sort of architectural structure, and perhaps a fortified one.

To find the perfect symbol of the most progressive fashion style today, we need look no farther than the Statue of Liberty. She has that strong, ceremonial, larger-than-life quality. She is at once an icon at the center of a cult and, in her own remote and self-sufficient way, a part of the downtown scene. With her weight lifter's arm portentously upraised and showing off the sculptural lines of her robe, she could have stepped from a performance piece or from the sort of fashion show that is in-fluenced by performance art. Or she might have stepped down out of one of the strange, stylized window displays in today's fashion stores. She was created to be looked at and has been recorded ad infinitum on film—so often that when we see her in her hammered-copper "flesh" we have to make a real effort to remember that we are human ourselves, standing there on the ferry with the sea-smelling breeze on our faces, and that our eyes are not simply augmenting the millions of cameras that have set down her image in the past. Like much of the most interesting fashion at the moment, she couldn't be called feminine, exactly. She is female as a source of visual power, female as pure form. (Of course, while fashion only aims at creating certain sculptural and architectural effects these days, she actually *is* a statue and an edifice.) She's very much of America, but even more of the particular urban crossroads that is New York. And, like much of modern fashion, she represents the response of a complex international sensibility (she was made, appropriately, in Paris, and reassembled here) to the idea and setting of a cosmopolitan new world.

Intentionally, appearances—"visual values," if you will— take precedence in fashion now over what clothing feels like or means. It is as if fashion were deliberately abdicating its function of serving as the most intimate form of self-expression, the first barrier (other than psychological ones) between a person and the outside world. More than that, fashion is deliberately denying its sensuous connection with the body. The new fashions often have a shape and a structure that not only fail to match the shape and movement of the body but are actually at odds with it. Clothing grows to unnatural size, with figures walking inside as if in a swaying tent; or it irons out natural bulges and replaces them with sharp rectilinear protuberances where before there were none. (I was mesmerized, in a show I saw in someone's loft one day, by a satin dress that had built into it a sort of neo-bottom, with sharp corners, like a grocery bag's.) In fashion now, the most dramatic distortions, laying of false clues, and hiding behind all kinds of screens and masks are the means toward the end of pleasing the eye. All else is subsidiary to that goal. The worlds of art and architecture—whose theories fashion has lately turned to with increasing frequency, as visual categories have broken down and fashion has sought a way of expressing itself other than by spontaneous eruption—have long taken heed of the dangers of pleasing the eye at the expense of all else. The visual image, at once so seductive and so formal, can blind us to the lack of qualities as elevated as spiritual meaning, as homely as feeling good to the touch. Architects, unlike dress designers, are obliged to live with permanent monuments to the folly of being carried away by grandiose visual ideas that fail to take account of human feeling. (Lincoln Center is an oft-cited example.) But fashion is apparently unwilling to learn about the risks of visual hubris at second hand. It is not possible, either, to dismiss what is happening merely as fashion —an isolated and junior branch of the artistic and visual hierarchy—making its own mistakes. In other fields—in the theatre or the movies, for instance, where lighting changes and camera angles often seem more important than plot—the emphasis on form over content holds just as true as in dress.

Because of the emphasis on form, the new fashion is often tremendously exciting and yet somehow alienating at the same time. It's as though these strong shapes, impressive structures, elaborate plays of light and shadow (the clothing is often in black-and-white or in some solid color such as red, in conformity with the stylistic principles of the Bauhaus) were all existing in a world separated from our world by an invisible screen. The fashions on display in "Intimate Architecture: Contemporary Clothing Design" had a tone and a silhouette that projected great power. But this was inextricably entangled with a second impression—that of withdrawal into a dispassionate detachment. Although the designers represented often referred in their work to the idea of armor (whether of the East or of the West), this armored shell turned out to convey the idea of inward-turning self-protection quite as much as outward-facing aggresion. The clothing represented less a fighting machine for the wearer than a mobile sculptural carapace. This is clothing as deterrent, for those who seek only to be left in peace in their own world, like the ambling armadillo, the accordion folds of whose protective shell one designer borrowed for a sleeve pattern in the show.

But references to aggression and self-protective withdrawal convey the visual style of "Intimate Architecture" too actively. It might be more accurate to say that what these clothes were "about" (if one has the temerity to say they are about anything other than their image, their arrangement of forms and contours) was the still point, the balancing point between the tensions of projecting power and of hiding out. For all its strength, here was modernist style calmly taking the lotus position in the bottom of a vortex, distinctly allying itself with quasi-religious pacifism and quietist meditation. And, overarching all the contradictions, there was the contemporary taste—the *hunger*—for ceremony and ritual. The triumph of the eye allows these to be severed from the encumbrance of meaning, dogma, content. The more mysterious, systematic, and even irrational the ritual, the better, as long as it looks good. Here is the explanation for the packed houses during a run of the Grand Kabuki at the Met; the emotions stirred worldwide by the sight of gold-braided uniforms and royal events; the way a whole subculture in New York won't simply attend the opera or the ballet in the old social and cultural way but go night after night, like junkies for a fix, as if in an attempt to live out life in an ornamental code.

In the M.I.T. show, the way the prevailing taste for ceremony led designers as readily to the habits of religious orders as to the uniforms of warriors showed clearly how style took precedence over philosophical content. What fascinated these visual sensibilities in the case of the samurai was not so much his warlike calling but the ordered system of style by which he acted in all things, whether performing the tea ceremony or killing. And it is the *look* of religion that appeals, more than its dogma. The new visualists are not the first in this fancy. After all, worldly people have been coolly admiring for ages the traditional robes worn by those who have deliberately chosen an unworldly path. Decadence is less inventive than it would sometimes pretend, and generations of fashionable Dandies in the mold of Oscar Wilde and Ronald Firbank have raised languid, bloodshot eyes to the medieval monastic or ecclesiastical style and declared it in the end the *only* thing with any claim to chic. Ronaldus Shamask—the inclusion of his work in the "Intimate Architecture" show was particularly appropriate—has been known for staging highly ritualized fashion shows that have often reminded observers of processions of black-robed friars moving slowly through Gothic naves. On one occasion, the show was accompanied by Gregorian chant, and there has invariably been some form of repetitious musical or spoken accompaniment. Models with facial expressions as wooden as masks have paced at snail speed, often unfurling their arms to show off monkish sleeve styles, Japanese-kimono undersleeve rectangles, or dangling appendages like semaphore flags. So frequent and dramatic have been these revelations under the extended arm, for most of the designer's career, that one might have been tempted— were it not for the tone of high seriousness that prevails on these occasions—to think of those surreal popgun barrels that suddenly release little banners reading "Bang!" Shamask has played a singular role in the history of that self-consciously structural and modernist fashion that came to be called architectural. He introduced a unique hybrid of civil-engineering terms and lyricism to the genre of fashion-show program notes, describing his clothes as featuring "torsion sleeves," "prism pants," "trestle dresses," and "winged jackets." And his shows were certainly an unusual combination of fashion and performance and ritual, never quite repeated elsewhere. I say "were" because his shows came to be staged before wider audiences than they were a year or so ago, when they were probably at their most interesting and most extreme. These wider audiences included a greater proportion of impatient buyers. Busy Seventh Avenue professionals are not generally receptive to an event that has much in common with sitting on a Tibetan mountain watching devout Buddhist pilgrims take days to circle the monastery on hands and knees. And so, as if consciously bypassing the average onlooker and the unfocussed naked eye, Shamask declared that the latest of his shows—his spring 1983 collection, shown in the Ed Sullivan television studio—was not a show at all, in the old sense, but a "photo opportunity" that was "structured primarily for the convenience of photographers." By eliminating seats within range of the runway and discouraging passive spectators, Shamask was taking to its furthest conclusion the gradual transformation of all fashion shows in recent years by the presence of an ever-increasing and mobile corps of inter-national fashion photographers.

The new style of fashion is neither verbal nor gregarious in intent. It seems to have stepped out of the visual world into our own only briefly—just long enough for the click of the photographic eye—and to have its bags packed ready to re-turn. If you seek to conjure up some hypothetical example of the style, the image that springs to mind will probably depend heavily on photography—probably on the slickest of con-temporary visual clichés, with the wearer in sharply focussed silhouette, the light behind her, her shadow unrolling at a crisp diagonal from her feet, and her face in darkness, its ex-pression being irrelevant. We are all the children of photog-raphy as surely as we are living in the age of Freud, even if we have never picked up a camera or given a second's thought to the hidden places of the mind. Our eye is almost inseparable from the camera's eye. We find beautiful in person those men and women we know the camera will favor—the people with prominent cheekbones and skinny shapes. We can look at a woman's face, with Apache-like cheek markings of terra-cotta rouge, and see right through the artifice as though it were invisible. The naked eye jumps so readily to the photograph that the act of shooting and printing becomes almost re-dundant. If this is true for people who are innocent of photo-graphic technicalities, how much more of an influence must photographic values exert on the ever-growing number of citizens who are technically skilled and self-conscious—the generation for whom family photographs are not snaps of incompetent human muddle (Grandma's hand or the dog's tail in the foreground by mistake) but ambitiously composed, carefully spontaneous portraits mounted on the wall in gallery frames.

The new, strongly shaped fashion style is very much a product of self-conscious visual and photographic values. It's as if it were created by designers who, light meter in hand, looked through the viewfinder for an effect—always one composed for a context (visual, not social, of course) and for some sort of frame. This is fashion that feeds on and is in turn fed by new visual forms, such as gallerylike displays in stores and the sort of museum context provided at M.I.T. This is fashion for a society in which gatherings are important chiefly for their visual effect—for those interestingly bare living rooms with white-painted floors and walls, or for those exquisitely stark restaurants whose big windows are like video screens set up on garbage-filled streets, affording passersby a scene of diners making entrances as stately as any Kabuki *onnagata*, then being led to ceremonial tables to scrutinize each other through invisible lorgnettes. And then, this fashion is very much a style that has stepped straight out of the frequently bizarre world of contemporary store-window design. I remember a window I saw in Bergdorf Goodman not long ago: The clothes were displayed on mannequins whose heads had been removed and replaced by large white lampshades of the shiny, conical type. The feet were connected to a snaky coil of snow-white wire plugged in to a socket in the wall behind. Was this electric stylization of the female person a gesture of *son et lumière* homage or electrocuting fury on the part of the window designers? Or was it somehow a combination of both? The word "androgyny"—so often bandied about these days—has been dragged in again in discussions of the strongly shaped new fashion style. I don't think it's a question of androgyny so much as of exaggerating the idea of the powerful female presence, just as the guardsman's busby was meant to terrify his enemy by making him seem twice as tall. It's not always a happy thing for heterosexual relations, of course, when women become "fabulous," monumental creatures—exaggerated versions of themselves. When women become illuminated lanterns, photographic shapes, or studies in pure form, this can only add to the already baffling complications faced by men and women living the modern urban life.

After all, modernist, visual, and architectural fashion is an essentially urban style. It's not just that it is worn in the city (so are Ralph Lauren's prairie-style flounces and Laura Ashley's vicarage-pastoral prints) but that it seems a direct attempt to express the urban sensibility, to devise a visual style to match the feeling of living in the setting of the big city. The feeling this style expresses, once again, is visual more than social: what a person with such-and-such a shape or shadow looks like—or feels as though he or she looked like—in relation to the greater shapes and shadows of the city, the frame formed by its buildings and its streets. This visual sense of the urban self is international. The designers represented in the M.I.T. show speak many different languages and work in Milan, Paris, and Tokyo as well as New York. But it is tempting to see the strongly architectural fashion style as one that was custom-made for the appallingly sordid, fantastically romantic stage set that is Manhattan.

Perhaps it is true that the unyielding environment of Manhattan, which deprives inhabitants of the most banal human pleasures (breathing fresh air, for instance), compensates by developing the eye. If we know the skills of passing within a hairbreadth of our fellows without touching, there is no taboo against looking, even with our headphones on. New Yorkers exercise their eyes continually in dramatic ways: looking out and down from high up in huge office towers; looking into the highly charged light-into-dark of the subway entrance; looking through the dust-filled shafts of sunlight in the scaffolded sidewalk tunnels around unceasing demolition and construction; looking up at the old Empire State Building steaming with colored light, like ectoplasm, on a winter night; looking over at the Citicorp wedge on summer evenings, shining away like an angular silver moon. Luxury in Manhattan means seeing in an expansive way—living on a high enough floor to see the skyline (the *idea* of the city) and to be exposed to the sight of the sky and the changing light. And in some Manhattan circles at the moment the ideal seems to be for people who are ever more successful in their careers but ever more solitary and self-sufficient in their personal lives to reside in ever larger, more minimally furnished spaces with ever more spectacular views.

It is one of the paradoxes of architectural fashion that it is both solitary and urban. When one pictures its sharply outlined silhouette in that quintessential photographic setting I have referred to, it is easy to imagine the style playing out its exercise in shape, light, and shadow against the backdrop of the bigger architectural shapes of the city, with their stronger light-and-shadow effects: the windswept cat's cradle of the Brooklyn Bridge, perhaps; the no man's land around the base of the World Trade towers; or some cast-iron façade in SoHo, on a totally deserted street. If these hypothetical settings for architectural fashion seem like touristic clichés, that is in some way the point. They are the modern, visual, urban contribution to ceremony and ritual—a sort of iconographic mantra, whose repetition is designed to set observers free. The peculiarly circumscribed code of New Wave visual imagery, to which the new fashion is closely allied, and which is now filtering down to the broadest level of popular culture through television commercials, involves more than the continual appearance of those narrow, wraparound James Dean–era sunglasses. That code centers in an obsessive way upon people with almost ludicrously photogenic bone structure, often photographed from such a strange angle that they seem to veer off into the sky—more like skyscrapers or like spaceships on the launch pad than like people. They are often magisterially alone or, at most, with one or two Olympian others, and they are almost always surrounded by some sort of empty space. The empty spaces that lie in strange perspective around these looming figures—deserts, deserted highways, unrippled swimming pools, or the trafficless streets of an otherwise sleeping Manhattan, seen by the people who go out dancing in clubs in the middle of the night—are not *dead* spaces, exactly, but rather intensely felt psychic frames shimmering and reverberating with mystery and menace.

The new, strong, sharply focussed fashions stand right at the center of this sometimes eerie camera-created world, as if it were sealed off by images. The often difficult and demanding new style can easily seem hermetic, the exclusive fiefdom of an international, visually sophisticated élite. Out of what would have been, before the common visual world of the electronic media, a number of disparate cultures, this élite has created a new language of imagery, semi-private yet international, with a remarkably systematic code of reference to cultish influences and stars. This new organization of what was previously multi-layered cultural chaos is undertaken quite naturally now, without the old sense of irony, parody, and quotation marks. The times are too serious for whimsey or for consulting a Mickey Mouse watch. *Of course* there is a pattern linking Brian Eno and Kabuki, Captain Marvel and the Carmelites, the Statue of Liberty and Milanese design. What else would a modern consciousness expect? It is no coincidence, either, that architectural fashion comes along at the same time as a revival of the myth of a tiny, self-contained colony of human beings hurtling through inhospitable outer space. They may have left the earth behind them, but they are cushioned by dazzlingly beautiful special effects, and look as though they were surviving with tremendous style.

KENNEDY FRASER

grew up in England and was
graduated from Oxford University. She
came to the United States in 1968 and since
then has been staff writer and fashion
critic for *The New Yorker*. This
is her first book.

A NOTE ON THE TYPE

The text of this book was set on the Linotype
in Fairfield, a typeface designed by the
distinguished American artist and engraver
Rudolph Ruzicka. This type displays the sober
and sane qualities of a master craftsman whose
talent has long been dedicated to clarity.
Rudolph Ruzicka was born in Bohemia in 1883
and came to America in 1894. He designed
and illustrated many books and created a
considerable list of individual prints in a variety
of techniques.

This book was composed by the
Maryland Linotype Composition Company,
Baltimore, Maryland. It was printed and bound
by Haddon Craftsmen, Scranton,
Pennsylvania.

Book design by Judith Henry